BERKS, BUCKS BUSES AND BEYOND

BUS OPERATORS IN BERKSHIRE AND BUCKINGHAMSHIRE 1986–2010

MATT COOPER

AMBERLEY

First published 2023

Amberley Publishing
The Hill, Stroud
Gloucestershire, GL5 4EP

www.amberley-books.com

ISBN 978 1 3981 0786 1 (print)
ISBN 978 1 3981 0787 8 (ebook)

British Library Cataloguing in Publication Data.
A catalogue record for this book is available from the British Library.

Origination by Amberley Publishing.
Printed in the UK.

Introduction

The counties of Berkshire and Buckinghamshire lie to the west of London, separated from the suburbs of the metropolis by the M25 motorway. A National Bus Company subsidiary, officially bearing the name of both counties, was created on 25 January 1987 to operate the northern part of Alder Valley, which had been split prior to privatisation. Following sale on 16 December 1987 the company (the fifty-forth of seventy being sold) would market itself as The Bee Line with a bold, yellow livery. We will journey through both counties, roughly over the area covered by its network, seeing many other operators, big and small, over the period of three decades between 1986 and 2010. This was the era between the end of nationalisation and the corporate standardisation of today's PLCs.

Starting in the royal county of Berkshire, split by the M4 motorway and Great Western Railway, in 1998 the six boroughs making up the county became unitary authorities. To the east of the county a more urban bus operation was found and to the west that of a very rural nature. Numerous established trunk routes ran between the major centres. A tough operating territory for bus operators, these were and still are affluent areas where car ownership is very high, coupled in more recent years with improvements to the railway network, which also provided strong competition. Staff were as hard to find as potential passengers, with higher pay rates in the London and Heathrow areas together with numerous coach and HGV operators vying for drivers. Our journey will sample relevant operations at Heathrow along with a look at coaching routes into London that once played a significant role. We will then head to the neighbouring county of Buckinghamshire, across the Chiltern Hills and its northern extremities at Milton Keynes. The Bee Line's 'Bucks' operations were based at High Wycombe depot, which ran interurban and express routes, as well as local services, some co-ordinated with London Country's North West division. Both counties produced impressive public transport publicity with bus stop-specific timetables featuring in Buckinghamshire. It was 50p pocket money well spent getting the latest *Connections* timetable book for yours and other areas! In the post-privatisation era, many operators were seeking brand image in a similar fashion to high street stores or supermarkets. The Bee Line's bright yellow livery was certainly distinctive; so too was the publicity. Maps and timetables featured a bee, accompanied by suitable puns to match, and in the beginning there was even a radio advertising campaign. Luton & District had its own printing and publishing department with equally good marketing and publicity.

Each of The Bee Line's depots served the county town of Reading, the home of Reading Transport. Now known as Reading Buses, it remains one of very few local authority-owned bus companies in the UK and has acquired several other operators, thus expanding its network to such places as Newbury, Bracknell and Maidenhead. Today's appearance is very different to that of the earlier period of this book with bold colour-coding, distinctive branding and on-board features today's passengers have come to expect. The only thing you may have wanted to plug in years ago was the top of a hot water bottle for a winter's journey aboard a cold vehicle! The municipal operator used the area around the railway station as its terminus, with out-of-town services using the former Thames Valley bus station just off Station Hill. This is one of many bus stations we will visit on our journey, most of which have either been demolished, relocated or refurbished. The upper floor of this brutalist structure was once the Top Rank Club and while great bands of the day played up above, great buses of the day arrived and departed below. It was later used as a bingo hall, the bus station closing on 16 May 1993 with services being relocated to stops around the railway station. Remaining in situ, its swansong was in 2010 when it was used by bus services one last time during the Reading station remodelling. The whole area has since been redeveloped.

In Newbury, operations of a rural nature were more common and even featured Postbus services. The location of the town's bus station has moved back and forth between The Wharf and Market Street and a wide range of vehicle types have featured in the area. The sprawling Bracknell bus station will be our next stop. Courtney Coaches was established as a taxi firm in 1973 and entered the private hire coach market in the 1980s. The company then went on to build up a bus network, and by July 2015 it had acquired First Group's Bee Line Bracknell operation. Reading Buses purchased Courtney in 2019, giving that organisation three of the five original Bee Line depots.

Coach services from Berkshire and Buckinghamshire towns to London were once extensive and we take a quick detour to look at these. Beginning as early as 1923, two express routes were shown on the 1935 Thames Valley map, joining Berkshire towns with London. By 1974 service B ran from Reading to London Victoria hourly with a total journey time of 2 hours 10 minutes, with Bracknell offering two-hourly route 310 via Heathrow and taking 2 hours 22 minutes. Demand increased significantly and we will see service branding for Londonlink and Goldline in use on a range of vehicles, the easily accessible M4 motorway shortening journey times. With services not subjected to the volumes of traffic experienced nowadays the Bracknell service sped up to reach the capital in an hour and a half. Railway services during the 1980s were not at the levels they are today, which allowed the coach industry to have something of a renaissance during this period. Green Line was improving its image and independent operators such as Armchair also offered journeys to the capital, with season tickets and fares significantly cheaper than rail. In some cases, local bus stops could be used to access these services. Victoria Coach Station was at capacity and a new terminal at Bullied Way was opened, many operators taking advantage of this facility. There was even a proposal at this time to convert the railway terminus at Marylebone into a coach station. Height-gauging tests were carried out using ECW-bodied Leyland Olympian double-deck coaches, as used by several Home Counties operators, for potential suitability in the tunnels approaching the station. In 1990 off-peak rail departures from High Wycombe to Marylebone were hourly, with the quickest journey time being 40 minutes, and were formed of 1960s diesel stock, but by the end of our chapter the situation had reversed. British Rail's Network South East operation saw significant investment in infrastructure with a large quantity of new rolling stock delivered by the mid-1990s. Ever-increasing traffic congestion would also cause the many coach services once on offer to diminish or even cease.

Tourist attractions in Berkshire allowed for an all-day timetable to and from London. A coach could depart with a healthy load for Legoland Windsor at the same time as those from most other areas were being parked up awaiting the evening peak journey home. In the past, other work was sought to utilise such vehicles and Alder Valley even ran its coaches on sightseeing services to keep the wheels turning. Heathrow had provided funding and initiatives to improve public transport and, with operations on its doorstep, this included a number of The Bee Line's services. There was already an association with the airport via the Railair coach service from Reading, which started in 1963, and, for a short while in 1986, a wheelchair-accessible service marketed as 'Careline'. Alder Valley and later The Bee Line were very proactive in their approach to introducing accessible services. The Leyland Nationals deployed on the service also worked a route around central London stations, which was later marketed as Stationlink. Although hard to imagine at the time, within ten years fully low-floor accessible vehicles would begin to see widespread use in the area.

London Transport's iron roads serve Buckinghamshire as far as Chesham but in Berkshire we only see a solitary 'Red bus' route. Or do we? London Buslines, established by Len Wright's Q-Drive Group, won London Regional Transport route 81 in the first ever tender round in July 1985. Red buses became yellow and the company expanded quickly across north-west London. Today the buses are red once more and Transport for London's Elizabeth Line (Crossrail) runs through Berkshire reaching as far as Reading.

Brunel lent his name to Slough's bus station but certainly had no part in the design of this brutalist edifice. But, as with other similar structures, we will see they were designed with access, space and suitability in mind rather than to be pleasing on the eye. As part of First Group, Bee Line came under the London division and was later joined to First Hampshire and Dorset. Today Slough is the only depot remaining of The Bee Line's operations.

We meet the activities of London Country in south Buckinghamshire and east Berkshire. With co-ordinated services developed under the National Bus Company's Market Analysis Project (MAP), many of the routes established at the beginning of the 1980s would remain post-privatisation. What became London Country North West inherited routes and garages across the western Home Counties, with Green Line coach and London Regional Transport tendered services also being operated. The publicity material again was quite impressive, the timetables keeping to an LT style. Returning to bus garages, the former London Country depot in High Wycombe (coded HE) and that of Thames Valley at Wycombe Marsh both remain but as an office stationery outlet and tyre and exhaust centre respectively. Larger depots at Amersham and Windsor are now sadly demolished, having been located on valued 'real estate'. Newlands bus station was used for garaging buses by Alder Valley and its subsequent owners. The operation ran in full public view – great for enthusiasts.

Significant service changes occurred from 23 July 1995 and involved a number of Buckinghamshire operators. Several small batches of second-hand vehicles, mainly minibuses, arrived for use at Wycombe around this time, replacing older conventional types. Most bizarre was a batch of nine Mercedes Benz L608Ds from Brighton & Hove and Go-Ahead Northern, arriving in late 1994. Their manual gearboxes prevented most staff from driving them and, despite being repainted, they stood in the bus station for seven months until being sold, unused! Subsequent acquisitions, mostly of London origin, were more suitable. After a decade of ownership by City of Oxford, forty-six-vehicle Wycombe Bus was sold to Arriva on 13 December 2000. New opportunities to integrate routes, staff and buses arose and would be achieved over a period of time. This included a new combined depot and eventually the gloomy High Wycombe bus station closed on 12 August 2006. Go-Ahead Group would again run in the town from 2012 with the acquisition of Carousel Buses, which had an operation of similar size to that of The Bee Line acquired twenty-two years earlier.

Deregulation gave smaller operators the opportunity to have a go at bus work either commercially or on tendered routes and networks. In both counties, operators such as Motts Travel established stage carriage services. The company's Yellow Bus division had daily services running to and from Slough, Oxford and Milton Keynes with some interesting positioning journeys registered for the public. Established operators reviewed their services/networks accordingly. Several new operators were formed during this period, each building up different types of work. Reading Mainline gave a traditional Routemaster feel and Carousel Buses offered a quality competing service around High Wycombe. Woottens Coaches established a coach business and commenced bus operation as late as 2008. Their 'Tiger Line' routes sought to complement existing operators' services and although they had the commercial flexibility to adapt quickly, the services ceased in 2011.

Luton & District was formed in 1986 from the split of United Counties. It was ready for privatisation, a process we have seen before. Operations expanded soon after, with significant local acquisitions strengthening its position. These included South Midland's Aylesbury operations, Red Rover, Motts Travel Yellow Bus, Buffalo Travel, part of Sovereign Bus & Coach and London Country North West. LCNW was the largest acquisition, and their established green and grey livery inspired a red and cream version applied to vehicles at L&D's 'traditional' garages, although all drivers wore the red uniform. Rebranding as 'The Shires' in 1994, under British Bus Group ownership, one common livery and fleet numbering system was introduced, seeing the end of the London Country-influenced class codes for vehicles. Eventually renamed Arriva the Shires at the end of 1997, further expansion would see Wycombe Bus Company and MK Metro join the organisation.

At the northernmost part of our journey we find ourselves at the self-proclaimed 'new city' of Milton Keynes (since granted official city status). Established in 1967, the area has evolved ever since, with some grand plans for public transport initially drawn up that even included a monorail. In the end the city would favour the motor car and bus operations would struggle in this challenging territory. United Counties operated in the area and would develop a network around the new city, which was initially based on the main grid road system. Upon privatisation a radical change saw all but a handful of conventional vehicles replaced overnight with ninety-two Mercedes minibuses. These would better serve the housing areas, but their image wasn't too appealing. A multitude of operators would become involved in running buses in the city, mainly on tendered routes, with most offering journeys to and from the surrounding area. In May 1982 a central railway station opened and on 27 May 1983 a central bus station and new depot. All three were over a mile away from the shopping centre, which for many was the ultimate destination of their visit. With 350 daily departures planned when new, by 1997 the bus station was only in use as a parking area and crew-change point. Now a Grade II listed building and displaying a sign stating 'The old bus station', its new status of community hub has allowed a tidy up to take place and means that the resident skateboarders have finally outlived the buses! The purpose-built Winterhill depot would also close. However, things weren't all bad. National Bus Company had established the Citybus brand name and off-bus ticket sales achieved an impressive 60 per cent of revenue in the mid-1980s, partly due to the introduction of roadside ticket machines. A wide range of tickets was always available, more recently on plastic reusable cards. A successful dial-a-bus operation also ran in the early days of the city. Under MK Metro ownership considerable investment saw the image improve and the operation is now integrated into the Arriva the Shires network.

I have tried to include as many operators and vehicle types as possible but sadly couldn't cover them all. There may be a bias towards High Wycombe and Milton Keynes as I spent my childhood years at the former and worked in the bus industry at the latter. I hope this snapshot of the bus and coach operators in the two counties evokes memories and shows the development leading up to what exists today. A lot has changed in a relatively short space of time and today's scene is very different to that portrayed by this book.

My grateful thanks are due for the photographic assistance of John Law, Raymond Bedford, Colin Lloyd, Rob Edworthy, Stewart J. Brown, Brian Botley, Hugh Jones, Ian Pringle and Kevin Lane. There are many other unattributed shots that I've chosen from my collection. Thanks also to Bob Jackson for the proofreading and advice, and to Connor Stait and the staff at Amberley Publishing for taking on the project. Most importantly, I am indebted to my wife and family for their support, help, understanding and patience throughout this book's creation.

Let's begin our 'buzz-about' across Berks and Bucks!

Reading

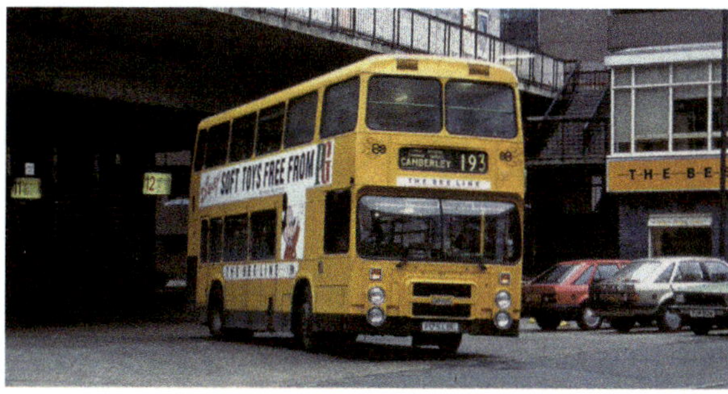

We begin our journey in Reading at the bus station built for Thames Valley and opened in 1967. A travel office was located at the Station Hill end with administrative offices and canteen at the Garrard Street end. Originally traffic flowed in the opposite direction with bays suited to rear-loading vehicles. The Plaxton Expressliner-bodied Volvo B10M of PMT bound for Liverpool loads at the row of bays now more suited to Continental coaches. The main focus of the picture is smart Northern Counties-bodied Leyland Olympian 604 (F175 LBL), one of five used by The Bee Line (Berks, Bucks Bus Co.) and frequently found on the 19x trunk routes. Working the 193 to Camberley, the bus would be around a year old in this autumn 1989 view. (John Law/author's collection)

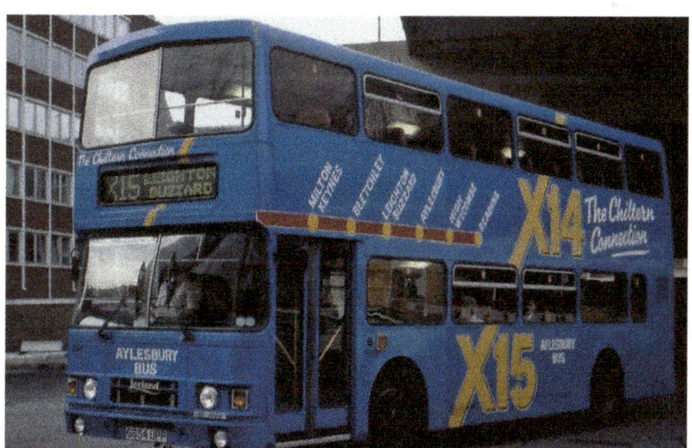

Another frequent Leyland Olympian visitor to Reading, this time with Alexander RL bodywork, was Luton & District's 654 (G654 UPP). Six out of thirteen of the 1989 batch were allocated to Aylesbury depot, with this example being coach seated and branded for the 'X14/X15 Chiltern Connection' upon which it worked for many years. This journey of some 57 miles was worked jointly with The Bee Line (later Wycombe Bus) and during the National Bus Company era continued northwards to Northampton. Departing on the 17.44 journey to Leighton Buzzard in 1991, this destination would be reached nearly two hours later. Spending its whole life at Aylesbury, the vehicle was initially preserved when withdrawn from service. (Author's collection)

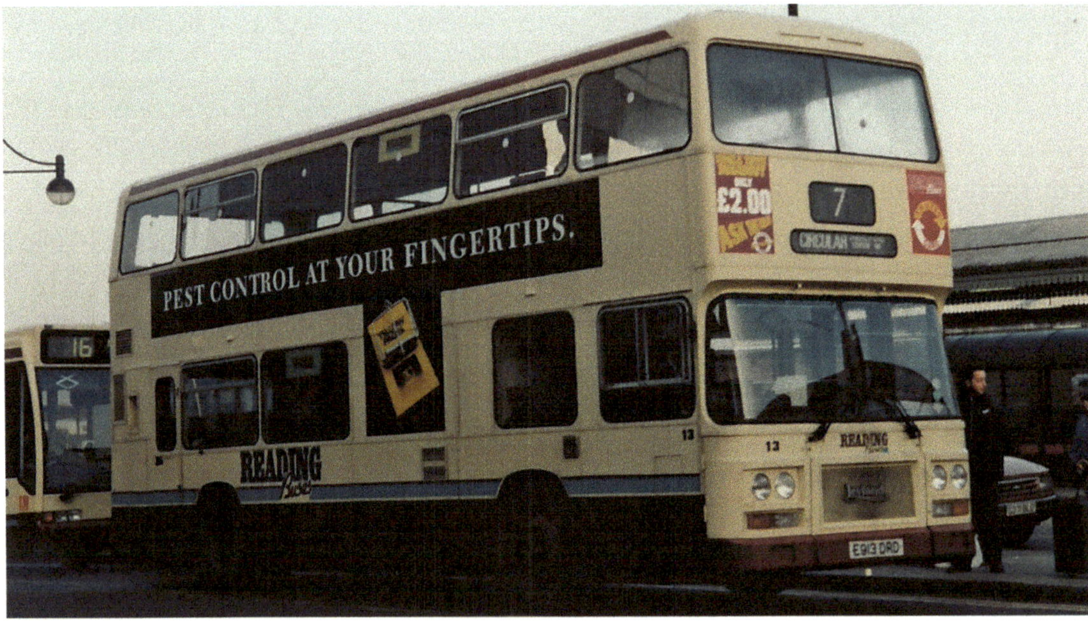

Reading Transport (later known as Reading Buses) utilised the streets surrounding the railway station as a terminus. At Station Hill on 18 October 1997 Optare-bodied Leyland Olympian 13 (E913 DRD) is operating a circular route to Whitley Wood. The body styling was almost identical to that of ECW for which Optare bought the rights when that company closed. Reading would go on to become big customers for the Leeds-based bodybuilder.

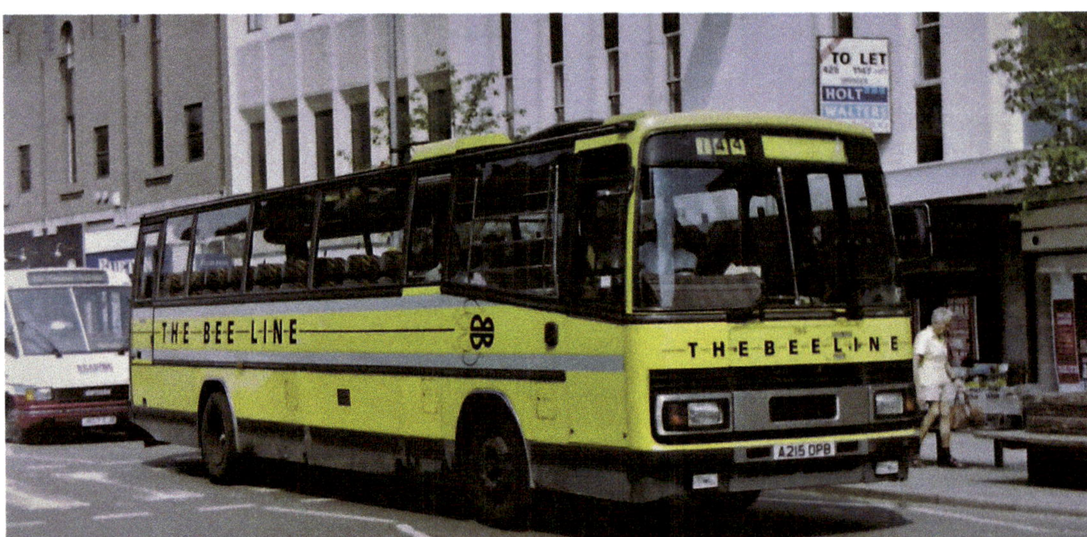

The Bee Line's Plaxton Paramount 3200-bodied Leyland Tiger 765 (A215 DPB) has been demoted from Londonlink duties to bus work and is returning from Wokingham and Arborfield in this view on Broad Street in June 1992. In July of the same year parts of this main thoroughfare would become pedestrianised. One of a trio based at Bracknell, coach work would again beckon for 765, which, along with its sisters, was used on the company's Green Line associated services. (Author's collection)

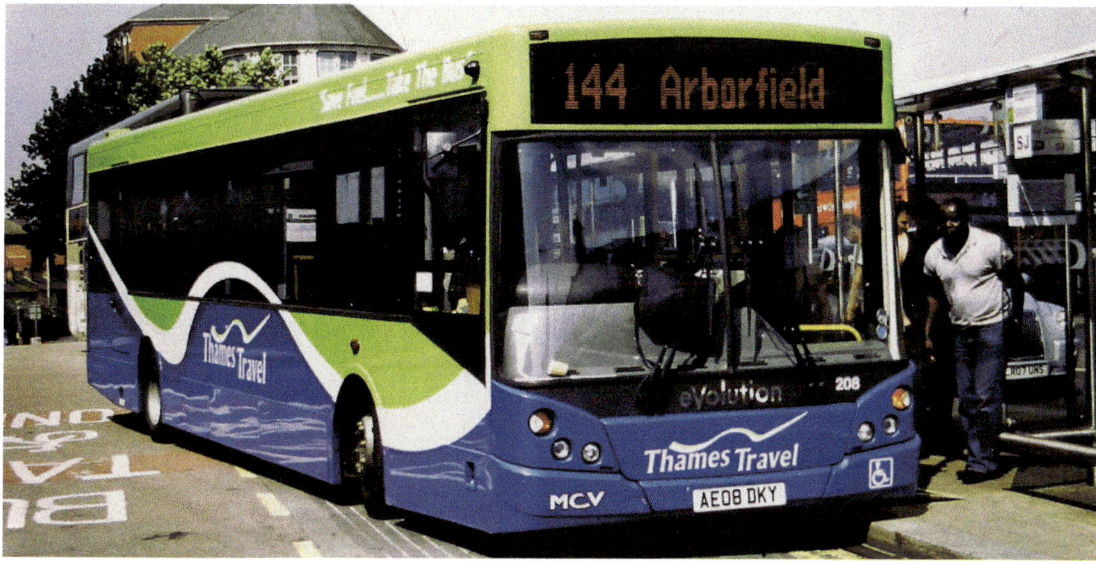

By 2008 route 144 was being worked by Wallingford-based Thames Travel. Founded in 1998, this operator expanded in both Oxfordshire and Berkshire mainly on tendered work, some of which was awarded following the closure of Tillingbourne and Chiltern Queens. In contrast to the previous picture, MCV Evolution-bodied MAN 208 (AE08 DKY) offers a low-floor step-free entrance to those boarding at the station. Thames Travel became part of the Go-Ahead Group in 2011. The bus, along with several others in the fleet, was sold via Ensign Bus to a dealer in New Zealand in 2012. (Author's collection)

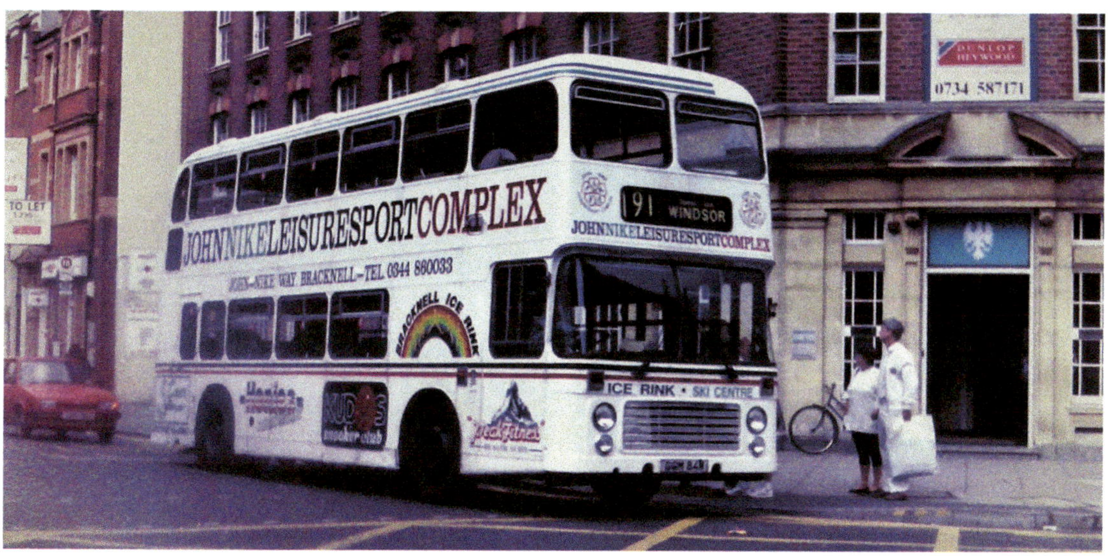

Joining The Bee Line from fellow Q-Drive Company Alder Valley in 1992 was a pair of ECW-bodied Bristol VRs. Both new to Alder Valley, former 614 (GGM 84W) became 559 and was allocated to Bracknell. John Nike Leisure Complex, located in that town, had overall adverts applied to various vehicles over several years (see photo on page 45). This bus would go on to have fame at the end of its life with three of the type appearing in episodes of BBC's *Doctor Who* series, after which parts from this vehicle were sold at auction. (Author's collection)

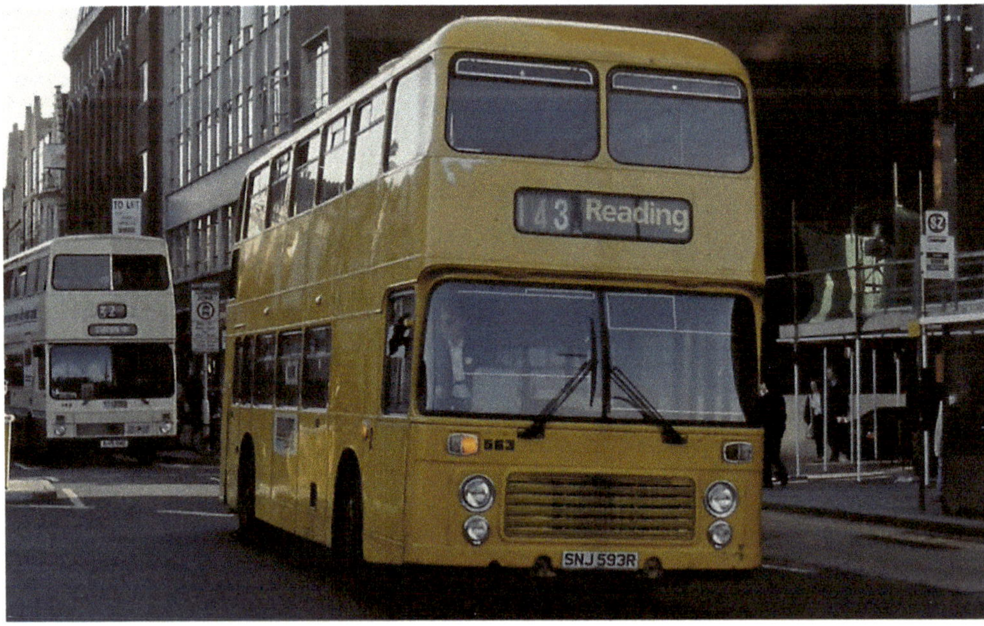

Not quite what it first appears! When Reading Buses bought The Bee Line's Reading and Newbury depots in 1992 vehicles ran for some time in the yellow livery. Eventually new or cascaded vehicles from the main fleet would take over but there were some interim acquisitions for both towns. Numbered 563, SNJ 593R came from Brighton & Hove in 1993 already painted yellow having been used by B&H on routes competing with Haven Coaches. Arriving at Reading station from Tadley, the vehicle is now preserved. (Author's collection)

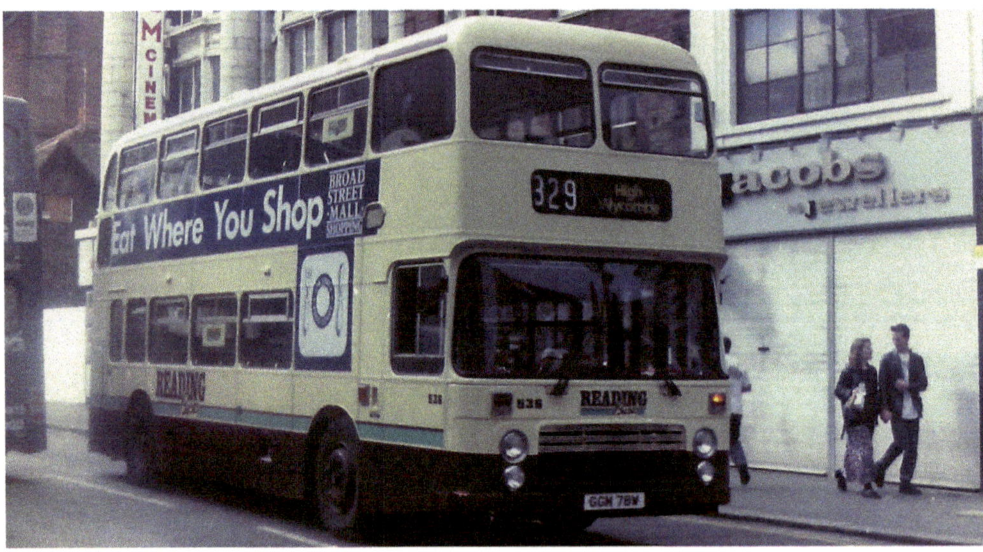

A handful of Bristol VRs inherited from The Bee Line acquired standard Reading Buses livery, which suited the type very well. Routes 328 and 329 along the Thames Valley to High Wycombe were jointly worked with Wycombe Bus Company at the time. About to turn onto Station Road from Friar Street, 536 (GGM 78W) is running from the depot to take up a turn on the 329. The MGM cinema has since been demolished and the site redeveloped. (Author's collection)

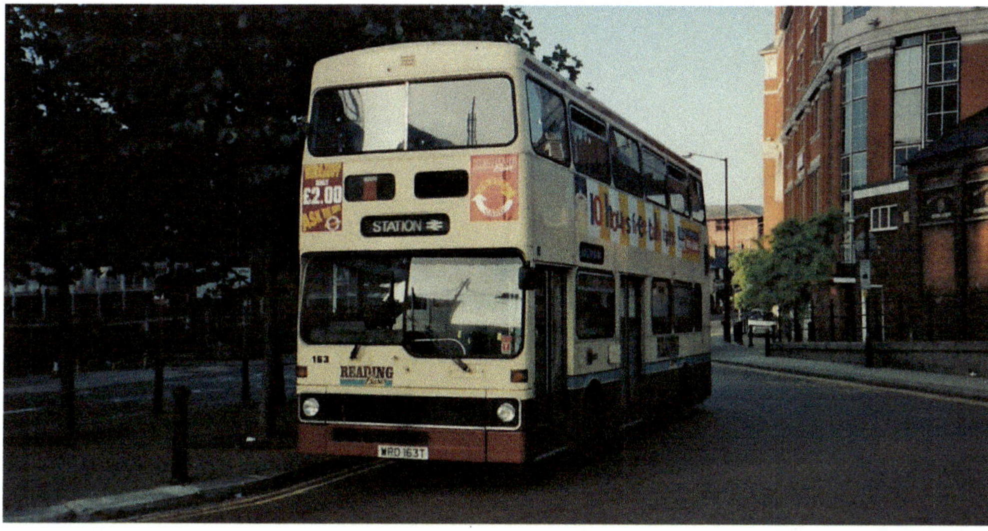

Originally buses showed the destination 'Stations' for those terminating there, which harked back to the days when the Great Western and South East & Chatham Railways had separate stations at this site. Now just in the singular, MCW Metrobus 163 (WRD 163T) lays over at the western end of the bus stops opposite the old Thames Valley bus station on 18 October 1997. Reading Transport's double-deck deliveries in the 1970s and early 1980s resembled that of London Transport, and dual-door layout was also specified.

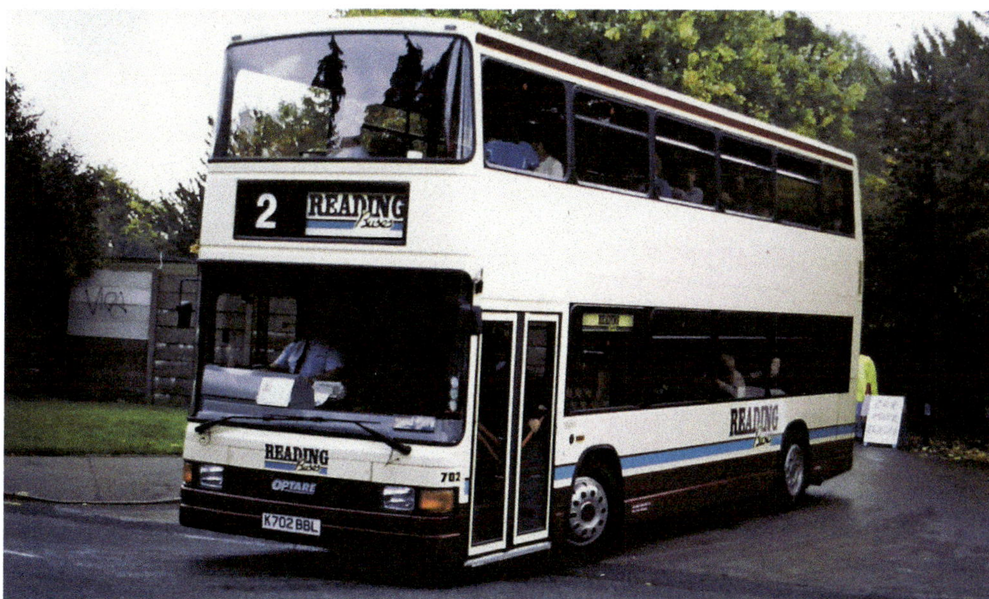

In late 1991 Optare launched the double-deck Spectra, another stylish and modern product from this bodybuilder. With a DAF DB250 chassis, the design was largely inspired by the MCW Metrobus combination with which Optare became involved when Metro-Cammell decided to concentrate on building rail vehicles. Reading Buses received the first to be built, which is happily now preserved. The second was 702 (K702 BBL), spotted attending a bus rally when new. Optare Spectra production ran until late 2006. (Author's collection)

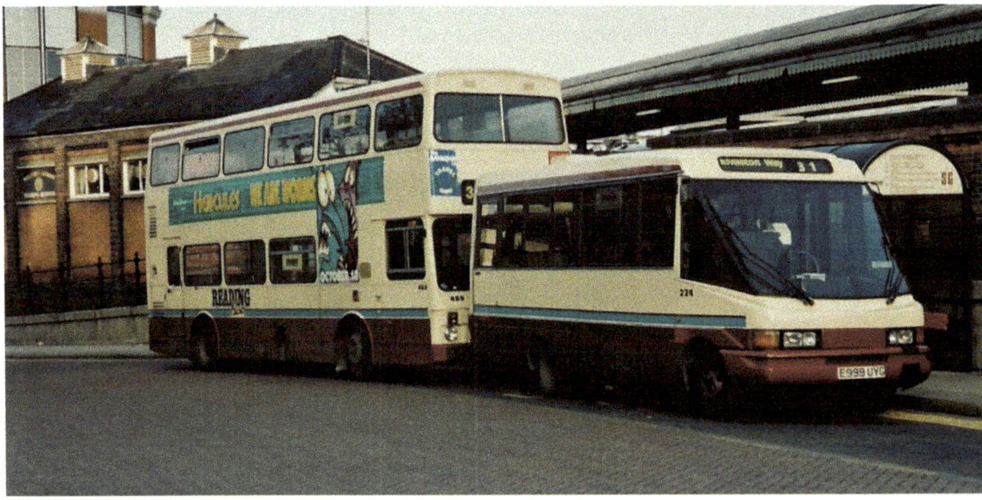

Launched in 1985, Optare's City Pacer, based on a VW LT55 chassis, broke the mould in minibus design at a time when most similar products available were van conversions. Reading Buses acquired nine second-hand examples between 1992 and 1997. New in 1988 to Welwyn Hatfield Line was 224 (E999 UYG), at Reading station on 18 October 1997. It is in the company of 465 (E465 SON), one of fifteen Metrobuses acquired from London Buses in 1991, which had used it on the Harrow Buses network. Route 31 to St Michael's was introduced to compete with Reading Mainline.

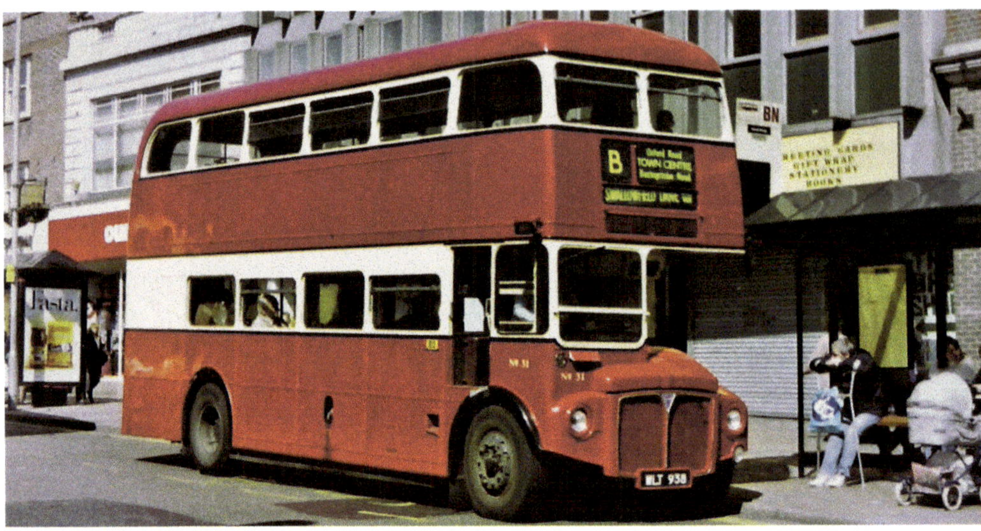

The Routemaster found itself a post-privatisation tool across the UK, marketed with faster boarding times, customer-friendly conductors and the notion that Brits love the older buses. A comparative latecomer in 1994 was Reading Mainline, which established a fleet of forty-five RMs to compete directly with Reading Buses. Routes were lettered and vehicles wore this smart red and cream livery as exemplified by No. 31 (WLT 938) operating route B on Broad Street in 1997. The bus, on loan from a preservationist, had also seen use with the Stagecoach Group. Reading Buses bought Mainline in 1998 and ran it as a separate unit until 2000. Many of the RM vehicles then returned to the Metropolis to assist with Mayor Ken Livingstone's extension of Routemaster operation for a further five years. (Author's collection)

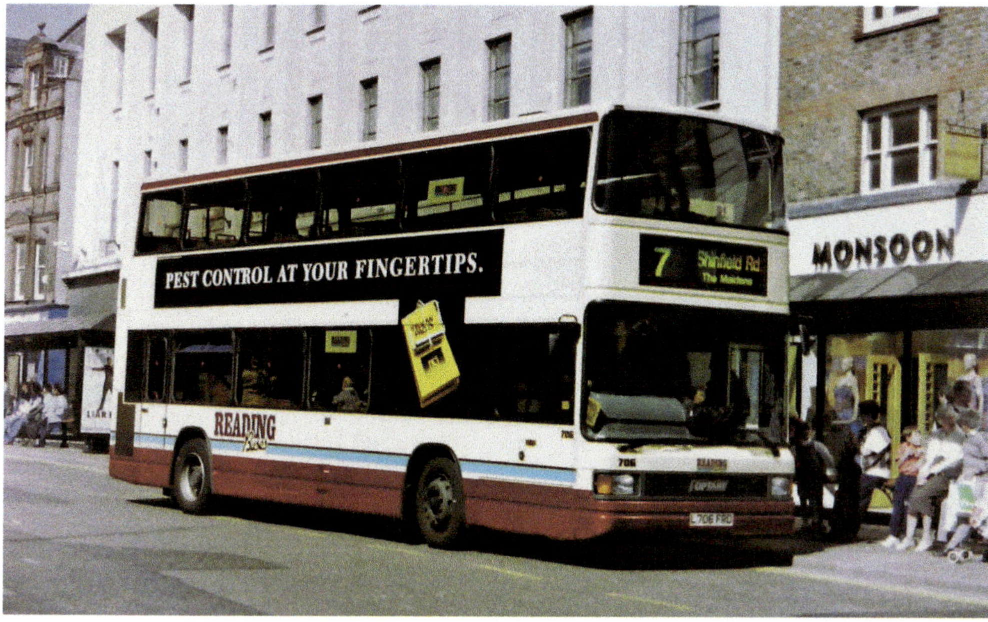

Reading Buses was something of a working showroom for Optare, operating examples of all of their models by the end of the 1990s. A trio of DAF DB250s with Optare Spectra bodywork entered service in 1994, with 706 (L706 FRD) being numerically piggy-in-the-middle. Loading on Broad Street in the summer of 1997, it would be another four years before Reading Buses operated the low-floor version of this type. (Author's collection)

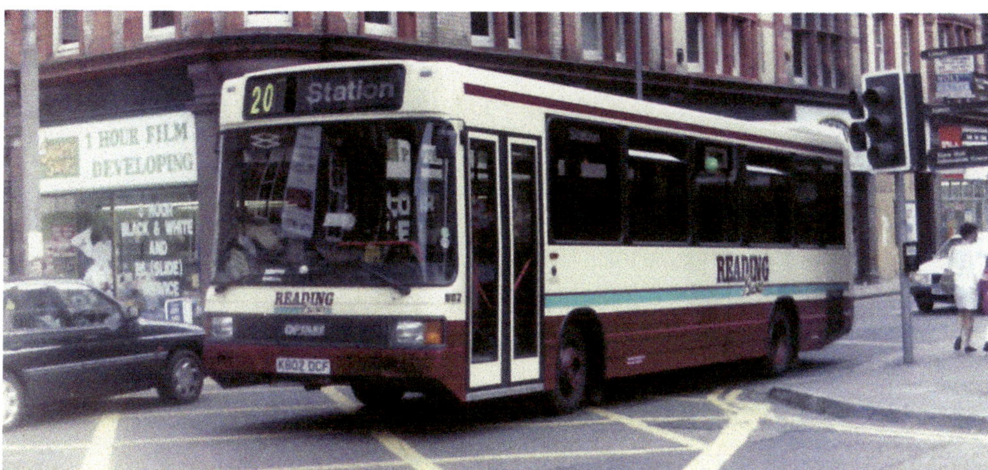

Optare built 130 Vectas based on MAN 11.190 chassis, Reading taking fourteen split between the home town and Newbury where they were used to upgrade the acquired fleet. Frequently used on services to High Wycombe, they also performed the marathon Sunday route 325 to Milton Keynes. Heading along Queen Victoria Street towards the station is 802 (K802 DCF) on its journey from Lower Earley. This street is now pedestrianised and you can still use Snappy Snaps. The whole batch of Vectas was allocated to Newbury before withdrawal, with 802 being bought by Hertfordshire County Council in 2004 and converted into a mobile exhibition unit. (Author's collection)

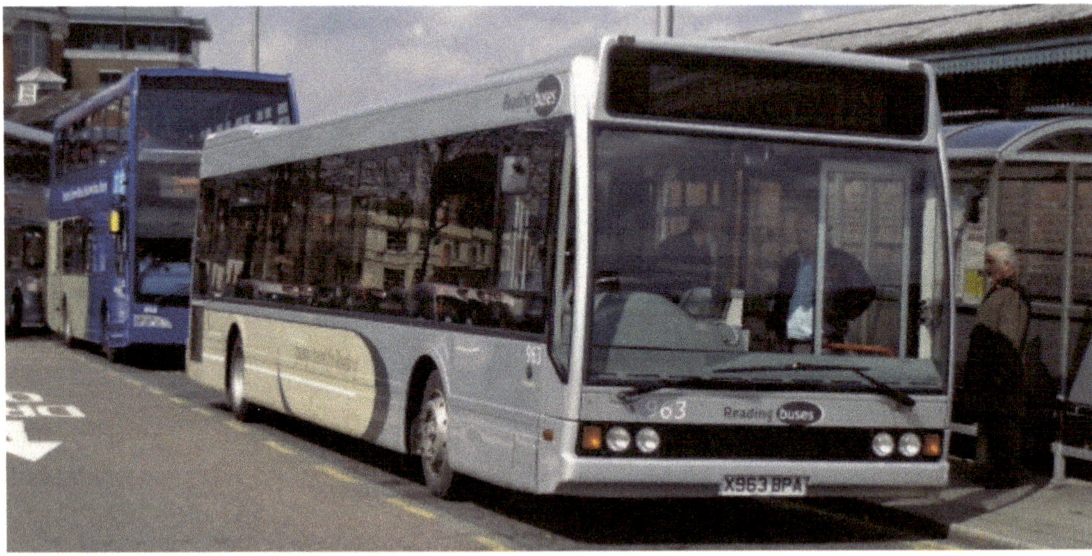

Wearing Reading Buses generic livery at the station on 16 April 2008 is Optare Excel 963 (X963 BPA), new in 2000. Sixty-four of the all-Optare product would be used by Reading. 'Low-Rider' branding was applied when new and after service in Reading some were shipped to New Zealand for further use.

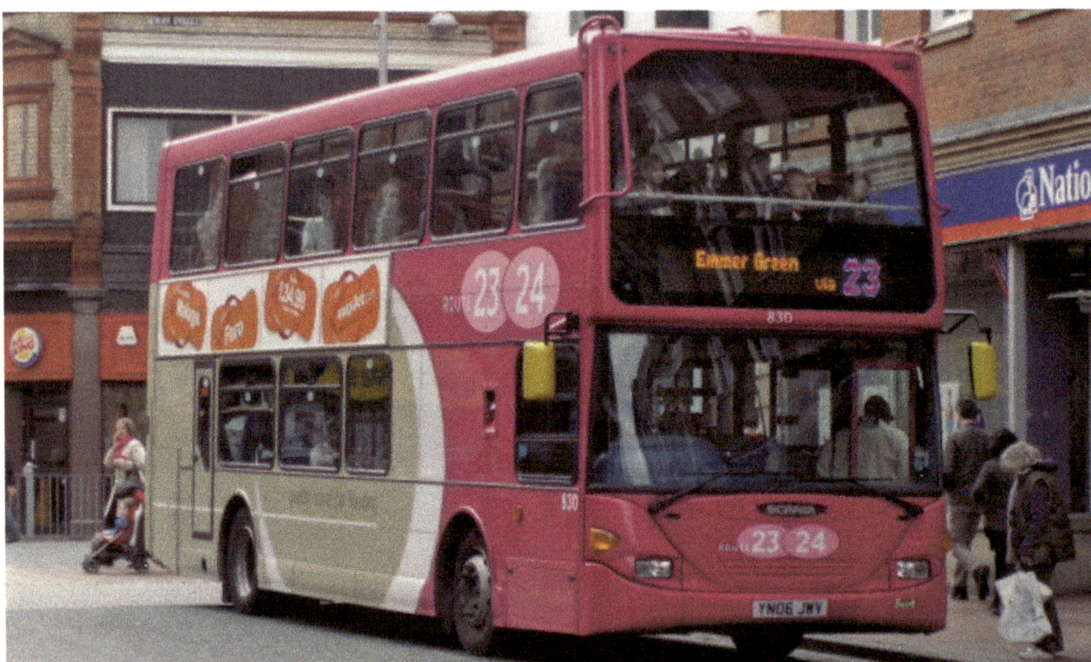

Strong colour-coded route branding was in use by the company from 2003 and vehicle purchasing policy had switched to favour Scania. Excellent visibility for the driver and passengers was a feature of the East Lancs-bodied Scania Omnidekka and 830 (YN06 JWV), on Station Road heading towards the station on 16 April 2008, was one of sixteen delivered in 2006. The use of colour LEDs for the destination equipment was a new feature.

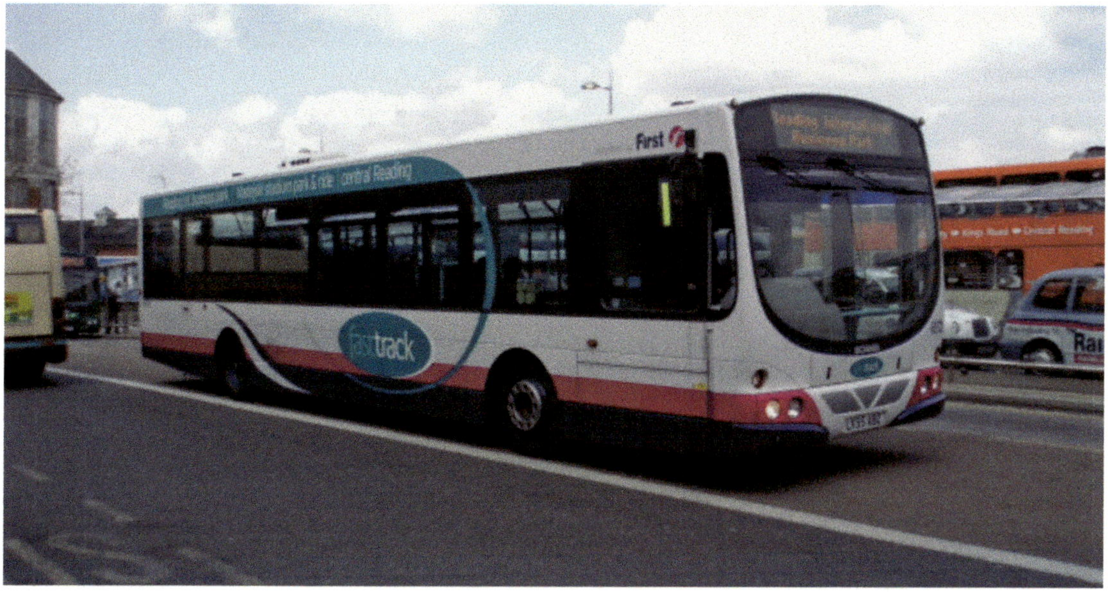

As well as retaining the lucrative Rail Air operation in Reading The Bee Line also won Park & Ride work and ran from an outstation at Reading Buses depot. One of a trio of Wright Solar-bodied Scania L94UBs, 65724 (LK55 ABZ) works a Fasttrack service towards Reading International Business Park on 16 April 2008. Now owned by First Group, this was their standard low-floor livery at the time and simple branding has been applied. Note the Rail Air advert on the taxi waiting on the rank.

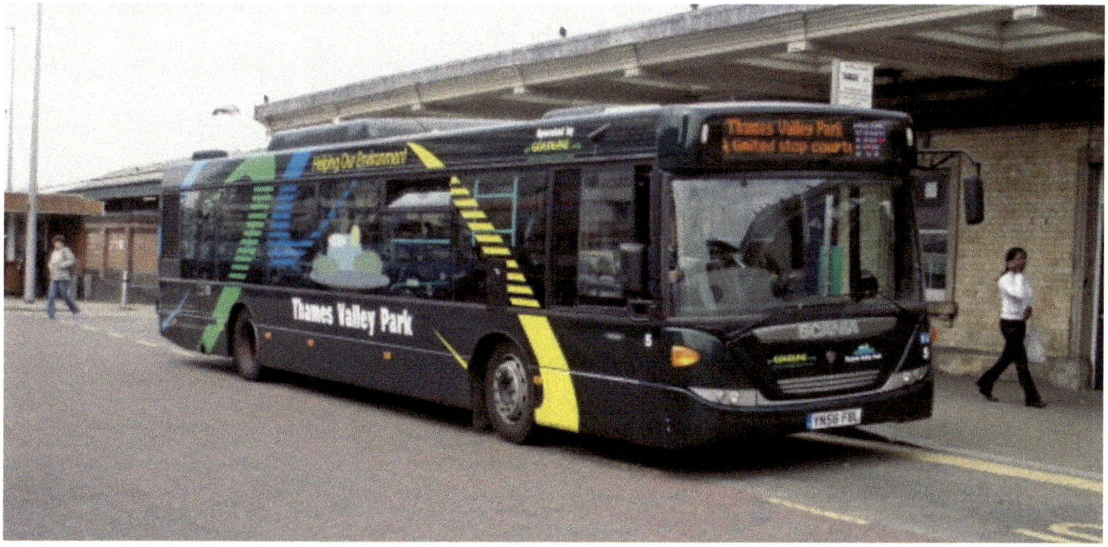

Another shuttle service linking the town centre with Thames Valley Business Park was operated under contract to Reading Buses' Goldline division. This high frequency route operated Monday to Friday between 6 a.m. and 8 p.m. and was aimed at workers employed at the business park. The five Scania OmniCity single-deckers normally used featured leather seats and Wi-Fi. Number 5 (YN56 FBL), at the station on 16 April 2008, shows off the livery, branding and a registration that under the previous system would denote a Reading vehicle.

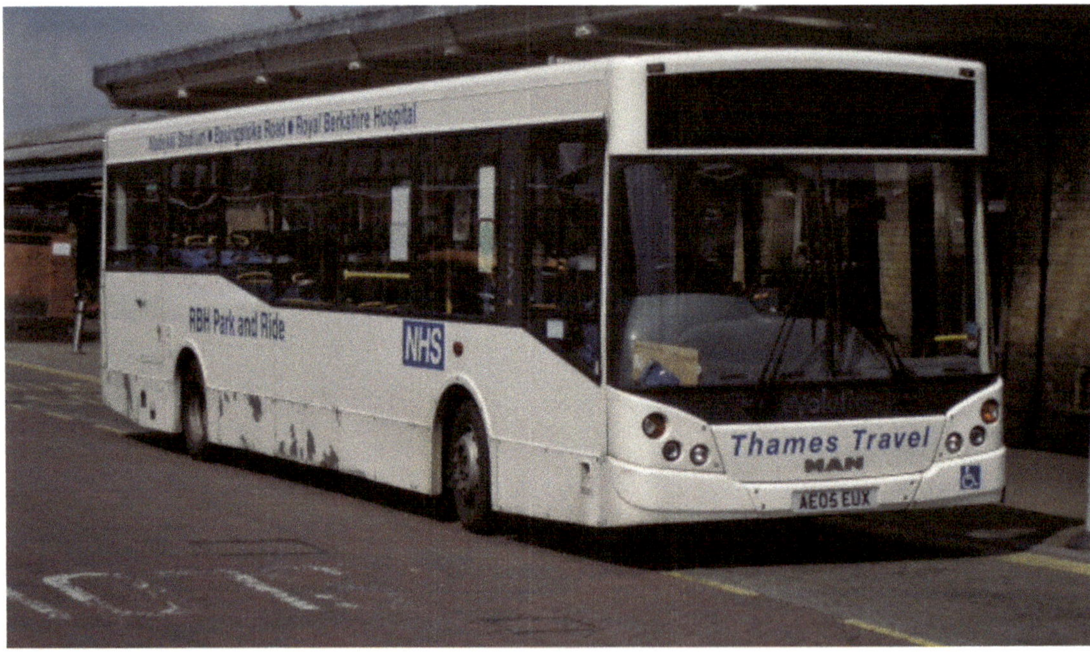

Contracted to Thames Travel was the NHS Park & Ride service for which MCV Evolution-bodied MAN 105 (AE05 EUX) was branded. It could also be found working other routes, as here when captured at Reading station on 16 April 2008. The bus later received standard fleet livery. Following sale, it went on to work for Faresaver in Chippenham.

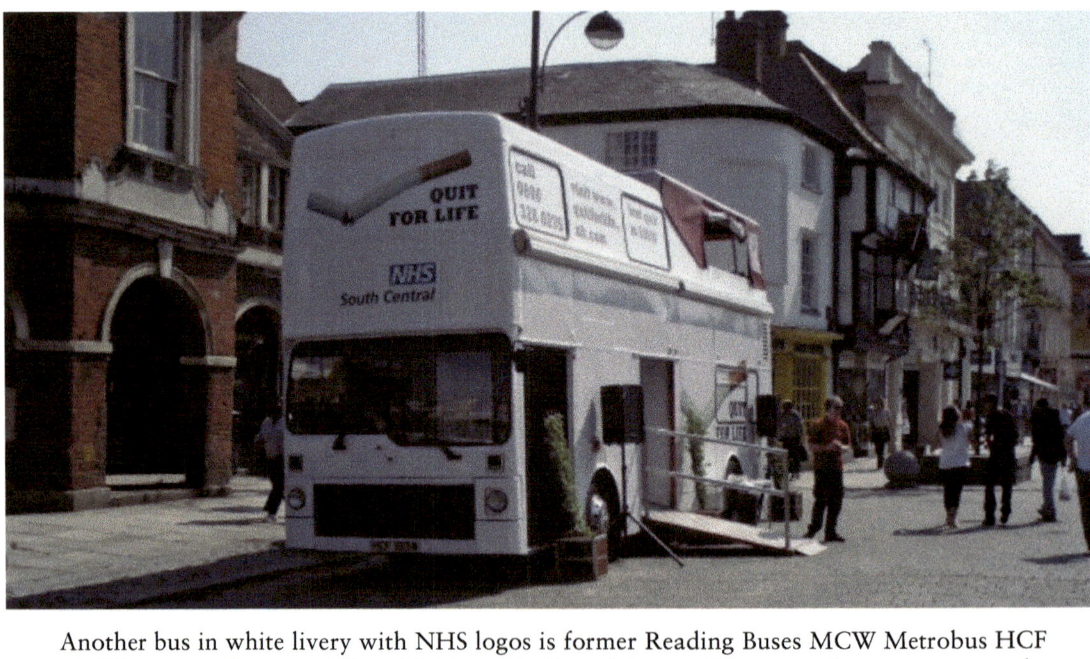

Another bus in white livery with NHS logos is former Reading Buses MCW Metrobus HCF 183W, converted to a mobile exhibition unit. On 7 May 2008 it was trying to encourage the people of High Wycombe to quit smoking. The location is the pedestrianised High Street in front of the historic corn market.

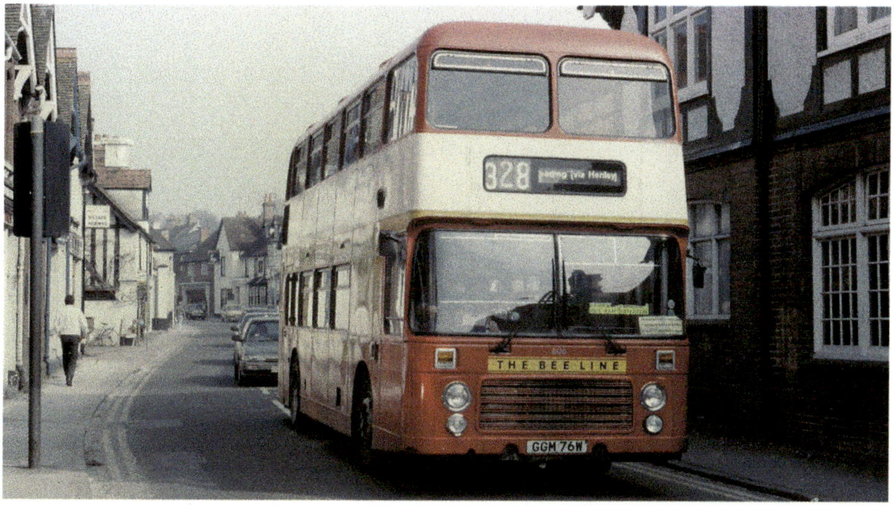

The main routes linking Reading to High Wycombe were the 328 and 329, worked jointly by The Bee Line's depots of both towns. Representing HW is ECW-bodied Bristol VR 606 (GGM 76W), later renumbered 534. Carrying 'The Bee Line' fleet names, the livery resembles some of the experimental schemes tried before yellow and grey was chosen. It was, however, a wrap-around advert for Morrells Brewery. Passing through Wargrave in 1987 is this 328 variant, with the 329 running via Shiplake. Both routes closely followed the River Thames from Marlow to Reading and good views could be obtained from the top deck. Becoming part of Wycombe Bus Company in 1990, the vehicle was sold two years later to Walls of Manchester. (John Law/ author's collection)

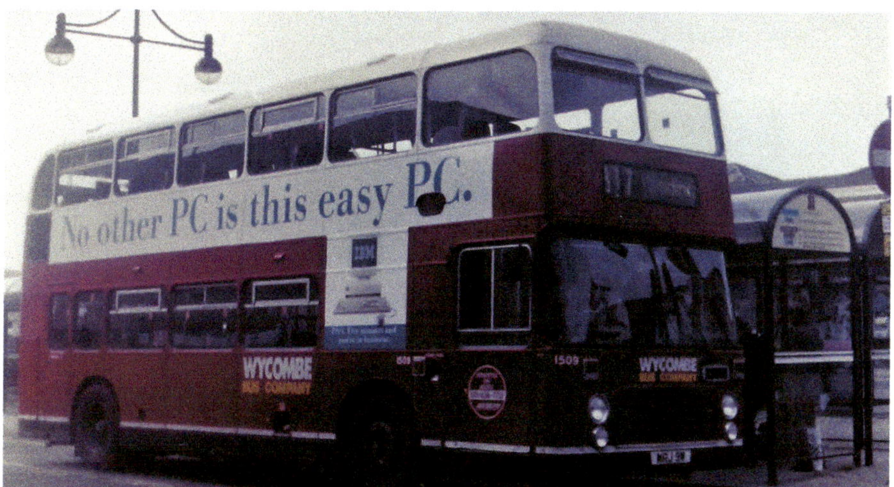

Taking a longer route between the two towns was the 317 (previously numbered 315/6). This was a projection from Maidenhead with an end-to-end journey time just short of two hours. When this 1993 view was taken Reading bus station had closed and Oxford Bus Co. had owned High Wycombe depot for some three years. New to Mayne of Manchester as its No. 9, MRJ 9W became 1509 and was one of a pair of DP-seated ECW-bodied Bristol VRs received in exchange for a Wadham Stringer-bodied Dennis Falcon (pictured on page 35). In October 1994 the 317 would be curtailed at Maidenhead. (Author's collection)

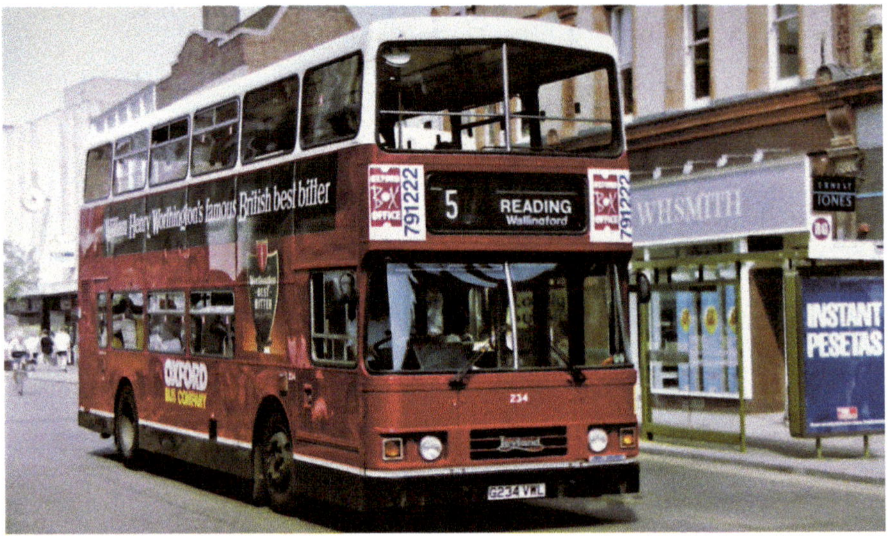

Oxford Bus Company ran to Reading on route 5, the number historically being part of the Thames Valley numbering system. Operated jointly with The Bee Line (later Reading Buses) on an hourly frequency, it would take nearly two hours to reach the university city. In 1990 six dual-door Alexander RL-bodied Leyland Olympians were received and were frequently used on the service. With the Timtronic ticket machine in view the driver is about to make a left turn from Broad Street into Queen Victoria Street. This was June 1992 and 234 (G234 VWL) would still be able to terminate at the bus station. If the clock above Union Street to the top left of the picture was correct the bus would have left Oxford at 08.55. In March 1996 the bus was transferred to High Wycombe and converted to single-door. (Author's collection)

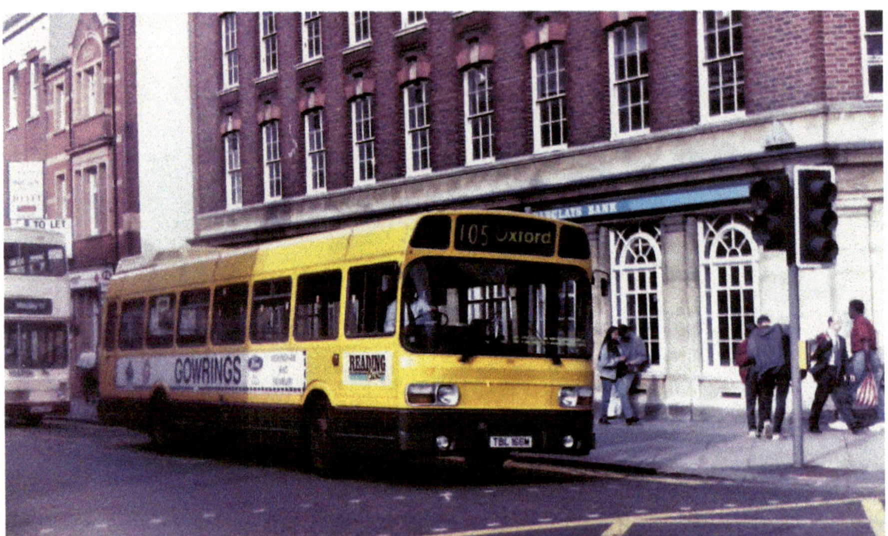

By November 1992 the route had become the 105, as Reading Buses already used the number 5. With Broad Street pedestrianised in stages from July 1992 the routes and stops altered accordingly. Turning from Station Road into Friar Street is elderly Leyland National 322 (TBL 166M) devoid of The Bee Line's roofline fleet names and now carrying those of Reading Buses. (Author's collection)

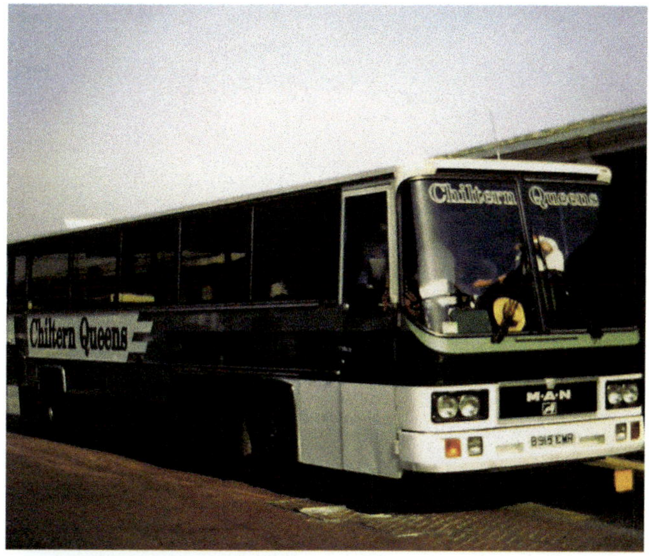

Chiltern Queens was an established coach and bus operator based in Woodcote, Oxfordshire. Three main bus routes were operated in Reading along with rural services in Berkshire and Oxfordshire. Buses wore a red and cream livery while coaches carried this two-tone green and white livery. A little unusual was this MAN SR280 integral, B915 CMR, new in 1984 to Lee & Black of Caversham and acquired in 1991. The fifty-three seater is loading for an excursion at Reading station on 29 July 1992, passengers getting a help up from the courtesy step provided by the driver and once quite a common sight. (Author's collection)

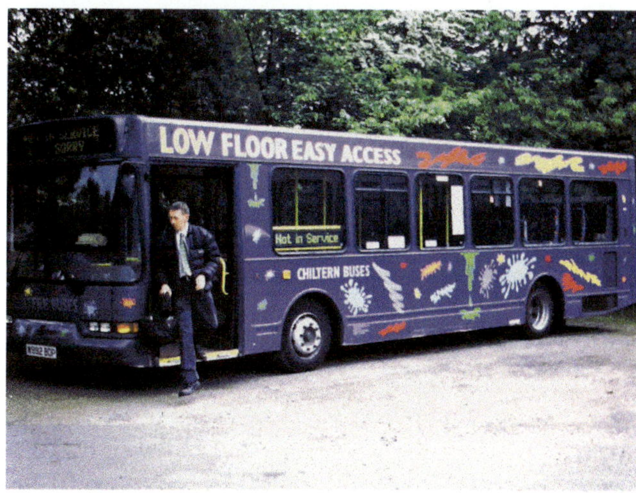

The bus side of the business was latterly known as Chiltern Buses. Returning to Woodcote depot the driver shouldn't have any problem locating his bus after his break, although he might be unaware if it had been subjected to graffiti. This interesting livery was worn on the three East Lancs Spryte-bodied Volvo B6LEs bought new in 2000/1, as exemplified by W992 BDP. Horseman Coaches took over the operation in 2002 and this vehicle went on to work with Go-Whippet in Cambridgeshire. (Author's collection)

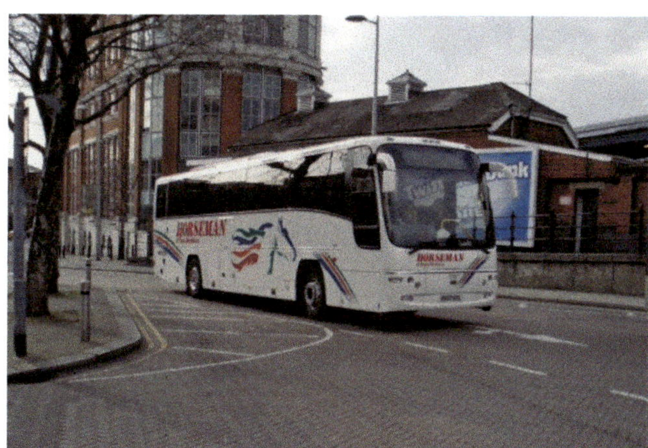

Established in 1977, Horseman Coaches has run a very modern fleet from their depot in Whitley Wood, Reading. Plaxton Panther-bodied Volvo B12B RX57 GXL is seen at Reading station on 16 April 2008 when only a few months old. Behind the coach is an impressive-looking building standing on a plot previously occupied by a drab, square-looking office block. Station Hill and the railway station itself have now been completely transformed.

Newbury

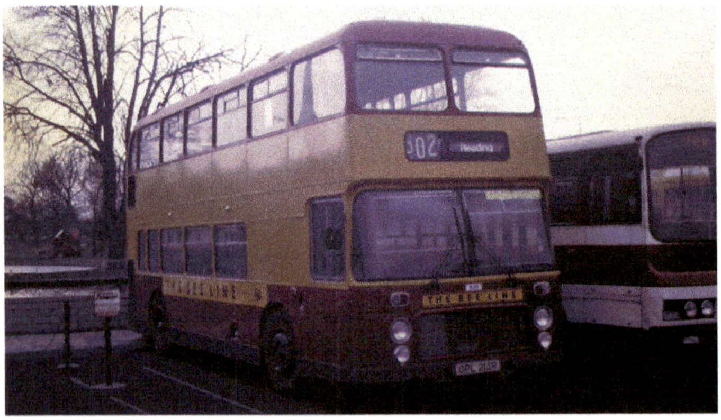

As mentioned earlier The Bee Line experimented with some livery variations in its early days. Retention of the red associated with Alder Valley would be dropped in favour of all-over yellow with a grey skirt. Renumbering of the fleet had yet to take place when Bristol VR 939 (later 516) OPL 215R was caught in March 1987 resting at the town's temporary bus station at The Wharf. (Author's collection)

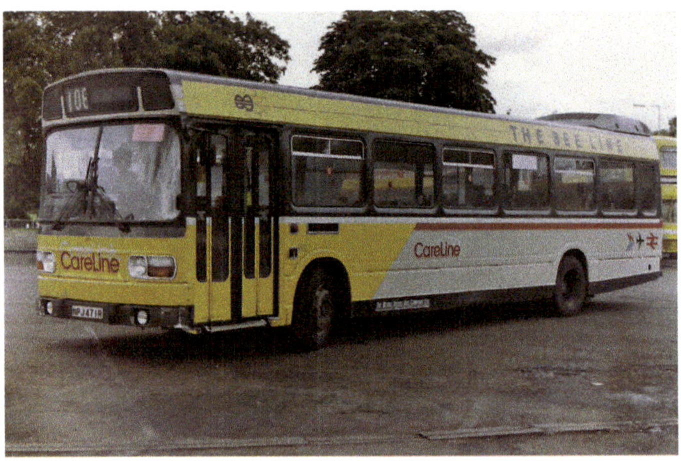

Between July 1986 and February 1987 Alder Valley North ran an accessible service linking London station terminals to Heathrow. Seven dual-purpose Leyland Nationals had wheelchair lifts and anchoring points fitted for this role and were branded 'Careline'. London Regional Transport would take over this operation becoming Stationlink in central London and Airbus on routes to Heathrow, both wheelchair accessible. One of the Careline vehicles was 377 (NPJ 471R), seen at Newbury reversing off the stand. Fresnel screens were commonly fitted to the rear windows for assistance. (Author's collection)

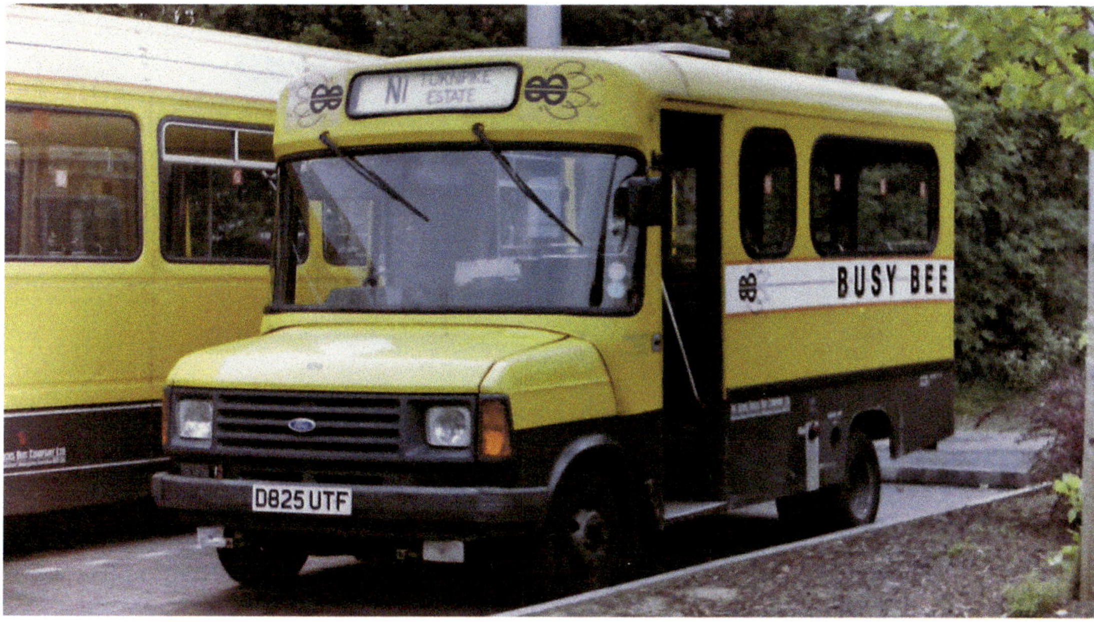

Eleven Ford Transits with Carlyle bodywork were inherited upon the split from Alder Valley. These would use the new Busy Bee fleet name for minibuses and were allocated to various depots. Taking the next registration mark to the coach Olympians, 104 (D825 UTF) was new as Alder Valley 325. Laying over at Market Street bus station in May 1992, the Wayfarer ticket machine looks precariously placed above such a low driving position. (Author's collection)

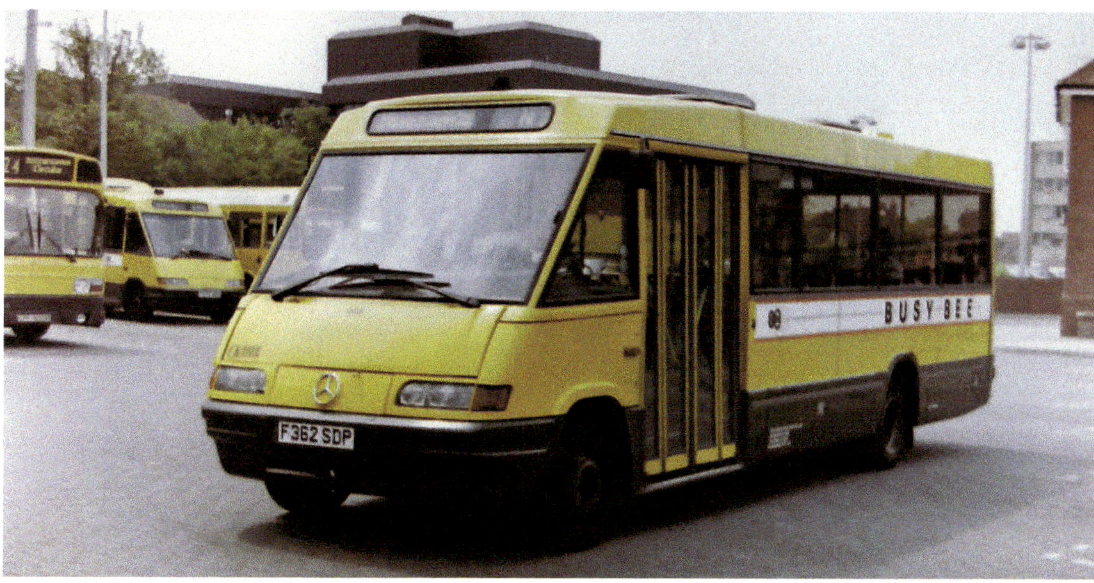

By contrast in 1988 The Bee Line received ten Mercedes-Benz 811Ds with handsome Optare StarRider bodywork for duties at Newbury. These twenty-six-seaters provided almost big-bus comfort compared to the Transits, and a lively ride. In May 1992 208 (F362 SDP) heads towards Thatcham. The Bee Line had no standard vehicle type but instead bought several small batches of buses specifically suited to the location or type of work. (Author's collection)

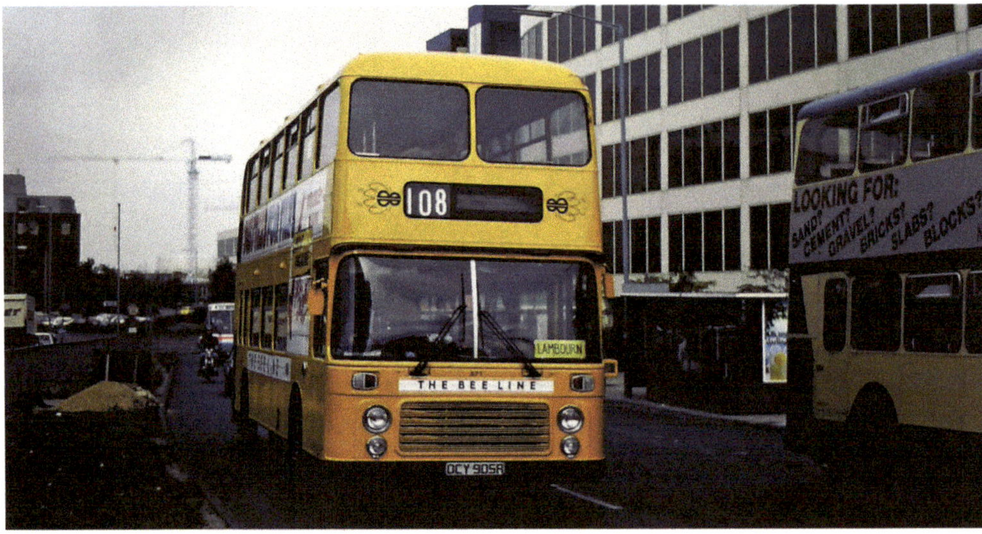

At the western border we cross into Wiltshire to serve the town of Swindon. On Mondays to Fridays, route 108 only ran within Berkshire between Newbury and Lambourn; a change could be made here onto Thamesdown Transport route 47 to Swindon, although through fares were not available. On Saturdays things were simpler with The Bee Line running three journeys all the way through. An additional short working left Swindon at 10.00 for Lambourn and worked by ECW-bodied Bristol VR 571 (OCY 905R) in this September 1988 view. Six of the type was acquired from South Wales Transport to replace vehicles lost in a depot fire at Newbury earlier that year. (Author's collection)

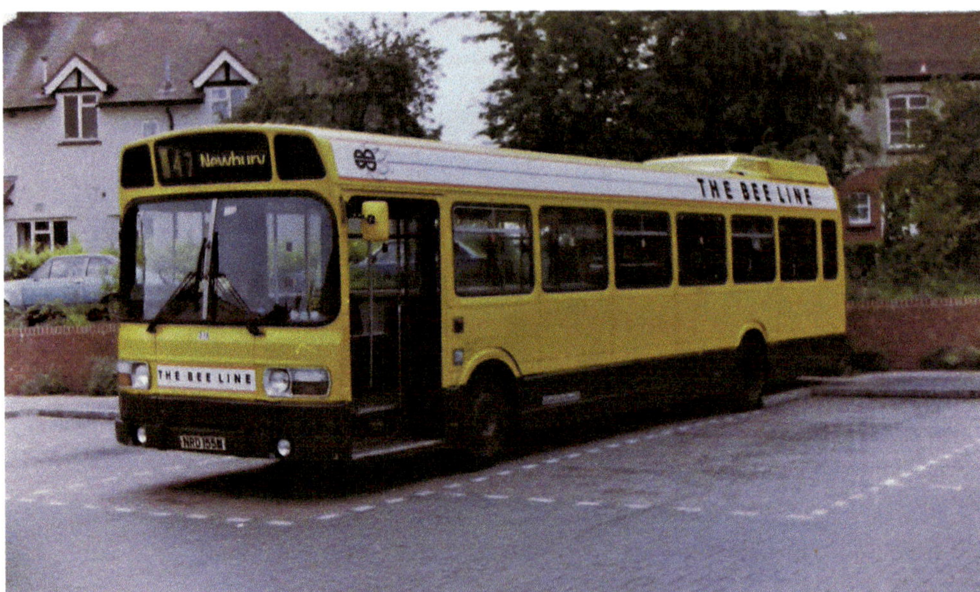

Very much the standard single-decker used by The Bee Line sixty-five Leyland Nationals were inherited from the Alder Valley split in 1986. Looking clean and smart in standard yellow and grey livery, 314 (NRD 155M) is laying over at Market Street bus station in May 1992. (Author's collection)

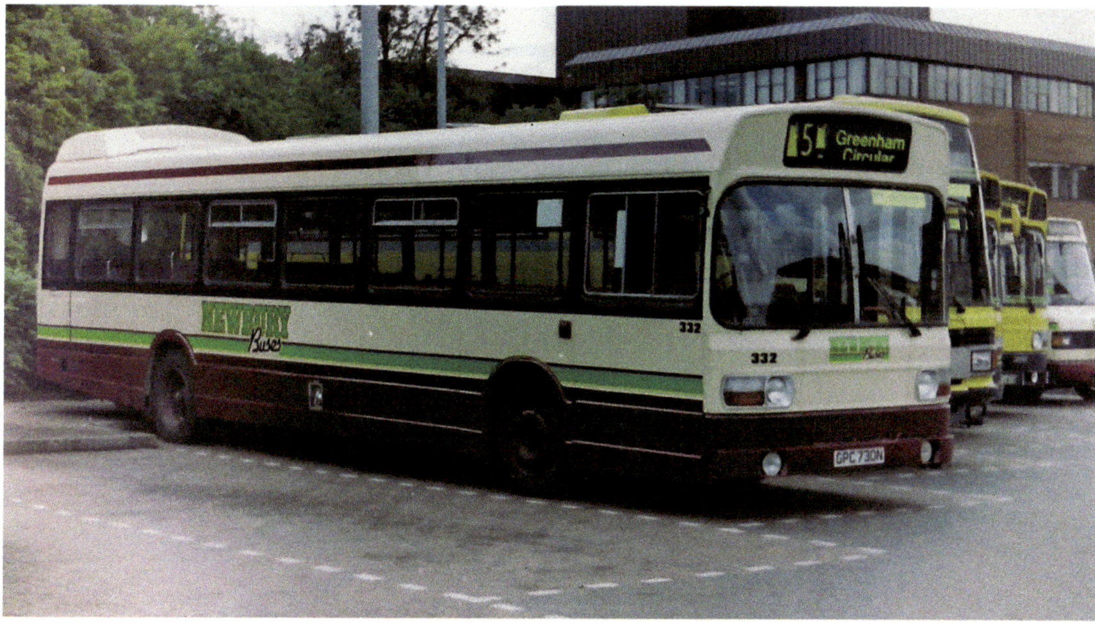

Portraying a very different appearance on 24 August 1993 is Leyland National 332 (GPC 730N), which received the Newbury Buses variation of Reading Buses livery. Along with an interior refurbishment this gave a very smart look to the eighteen-year-old vehicle. There should be no protests from the passengers of Greenham even if the N prefix isn't shown in the destination blind. (Author's collection)

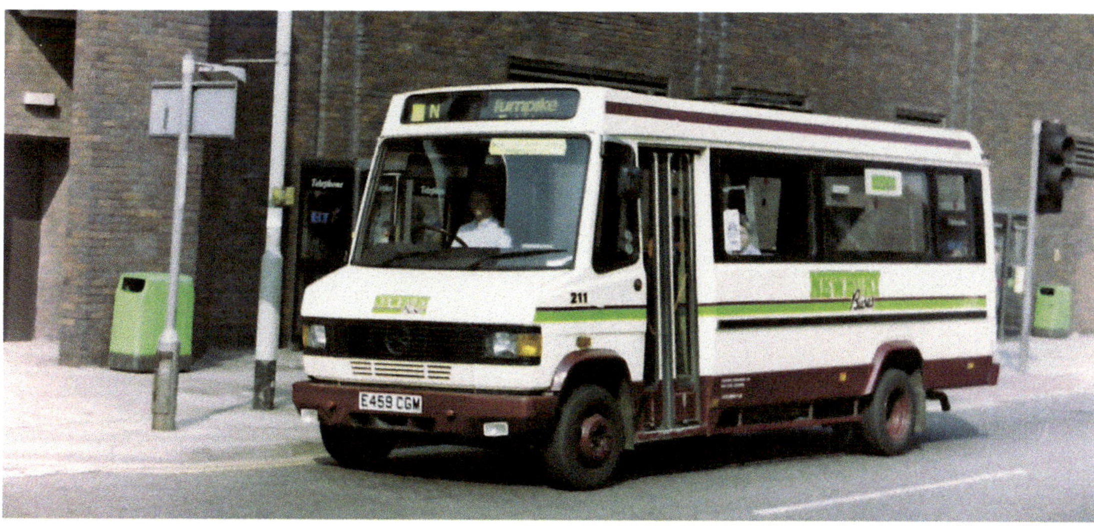

The Ford Transits proved too small, as did the six Freight Rover Sherpas used at deregulation. More successful were a batch of eighteen Robin Hood-bodied Mercedes-Benz 609D twenty-seaters, which were shared with fellow company London Buslines. Bracknell, Maidenhead and Newbury depots received these and three were taken over by Reading Buses in 1992. Carrying its new livery well, as it passes the Kennet Shopping centre in September 1993, is 211 (E459 CGM), formerly 163 and used when new on route C4 by London Buslines. (Author's collection)

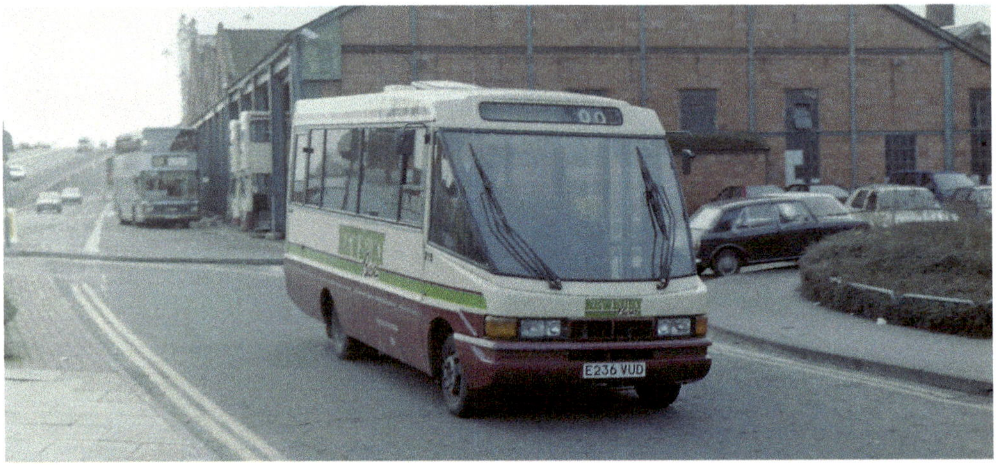

Optare CityPacer 215 (E236 VUD) was one of a pair acquired from Lancaster City Transport in 1992 when that company ceased trading but new to South Midland in 1987. After service at Newbury the bus came to Reading for use on routes competing with Reading Mainline. This location today is completely different with the Oracle shopping centre and leisure facilities built either side of the canal, just out of view on the right. Dating from 1903, the depot saw use by trams, trolleybuses and many types of bus until closure in 1998. (Author's collection)

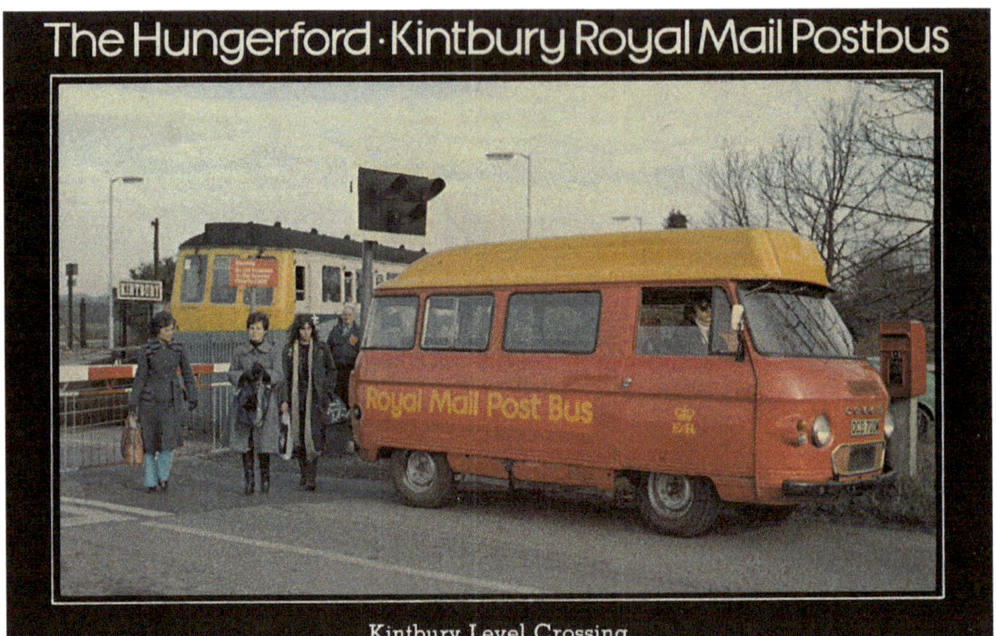

An unusual operation to be found in west Berkshire was Royal Mail's Postbus. One may associate the Scottish Highlands or Lake District with these services; however, five routes ran from the Newbury and Hungerford areas into very rural territory. These began in 1974 and ran until the late 1990s. Passengers could travel with the 'postie' on his or her round, which ran to a timetable and could mean lengthy journey times. This 1980 postcard shows one of the original Commer vans with Rootes body conversion. Will any of the passengers leaving the BR class 117 DMU at Kintbury transfer to the Postbus? (Postmaster Reading/author's collection)

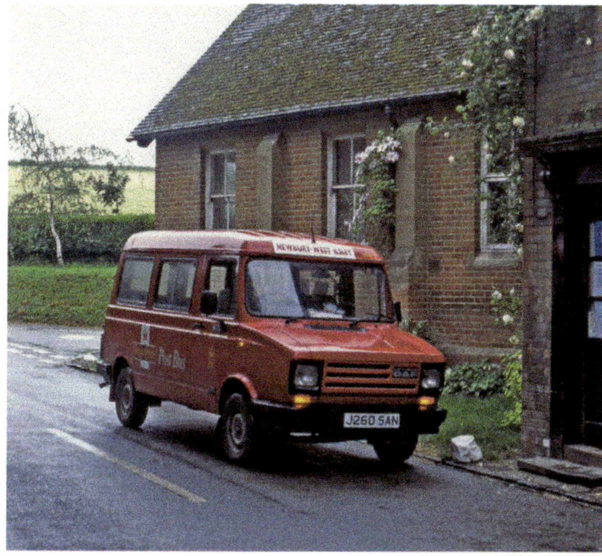

Postbus route 5 ran from Newbury to West Ilsley and was introduced on 18 July 1975. This view taken on 20 June 1996 shows one of the Commers' more modern replacements, the Leyland- DAF Sherpa. Royal Mail was a big customer for this type, which carried several different makers' badges over the years. Fares were taken by the drivers and an Almex 'A' ticket machine can be seen through the windscreen. Locally numbered NB2, J260 SAN would work the 11.10 from West Ilsley to Newbury, a fifty-minute journey. (John Law/ author's collection)

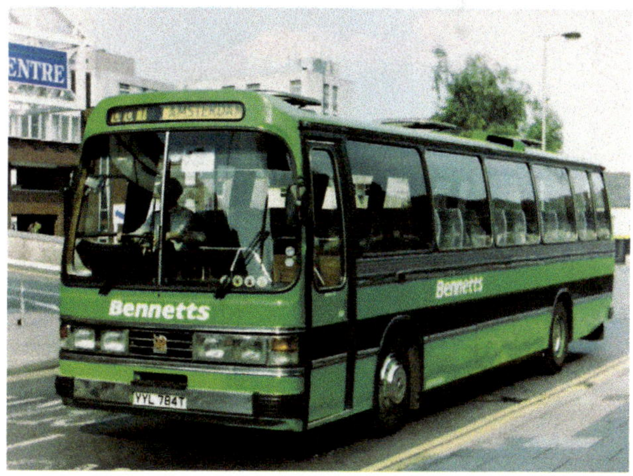

The village of Chieveley lies close to our last destination and was where Bennetts Coaches were based. Along with coaching operations a number of local contracts and bus services were operated in the Newbury area. Duple Dominant-bodied Bedford YMT YYL 784T was new to Grey Green and is where the destination blind would have originated. In this September 1993 view on Market Street, Newbury, the coach would most likely be returning to a location in west Berkshire as opposed to the capital of the Netherlands. (Author's collection)

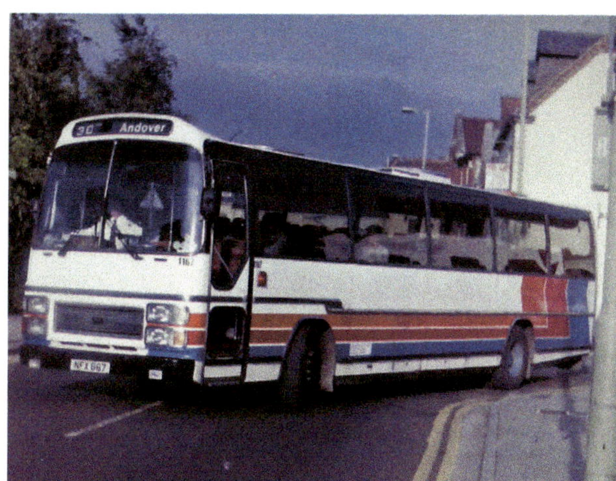

We haven't seen much of Stagecoach so far and, in fact, the Group's operations only appear at the west of Berkshire and north of Buckinghamshire. Hampshire Bus Plaxton Supreme V-bodied Leyland Leopard 1167 (NFX 667, HHC 367Y) was new to Southdown as 1367 and also carried the number 1017. Departing Market Street bus station for Andover *c.* 1990, other variations of route 30 saw some journeys extended to Winchester and Southampton. This route is now branded as the 'Activ 8' and is operated with double-deckers. The cherished registration mark is still in use with Stagecoach South. (Author's collection)

Bracknell and South of Berkshire

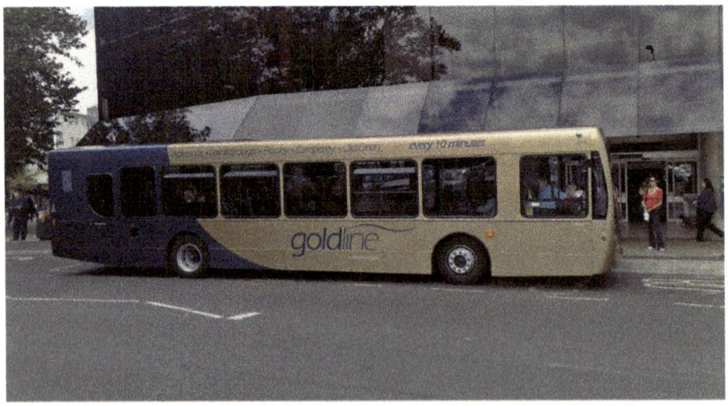

Perth and Leamington Spa were the two locations where Stagecoach's Goldline brand was launched in 2007. The concept was to 'woo the middle classes' from their cars and to give an upmarket image to bus travel. The brand was rolled out across other Group companies and Stagecoach South used it on route 1 between Aldershot and Old Dean. Wooing some passengers outside The Meads Shopping Centre at Farnborough in 2009 was Alexander Dennis Enviro 300-bodied MAN 22746 (GX58 MVK). Stagecoach acquired part of Alder Valley South in 1992 and the Goldline brand is now known as Stagecoach Gold. (Raymond Bedford)

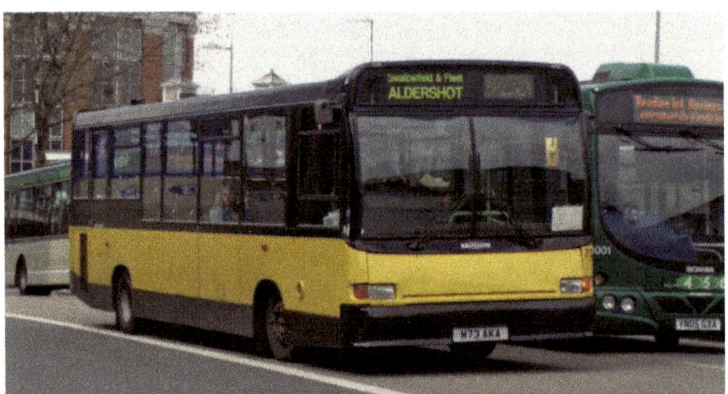

We are buzzing again in Reading and Berkshire on yellow-liveried buses, this time with Countywide Travel, established in 1995 over the border in Basingstoke. The coaching unit was sold to Weavaway in 2007, allowing the management to focus on the remaining bus operation, which was rebranded 'Fleet Buzz'. On 16 May 2008 Marshall-bodied Dennis Dart M73 AKA, one of a trio acquired from Halton Transport, is returning to Aldershot from Reading Station Hill on route 72. This link had previously been provided by Alder Valley South and Tillingbourne. Stagecoach bought the company in 2011, eventually integrating it with Basingstoke and Aldershot depots.

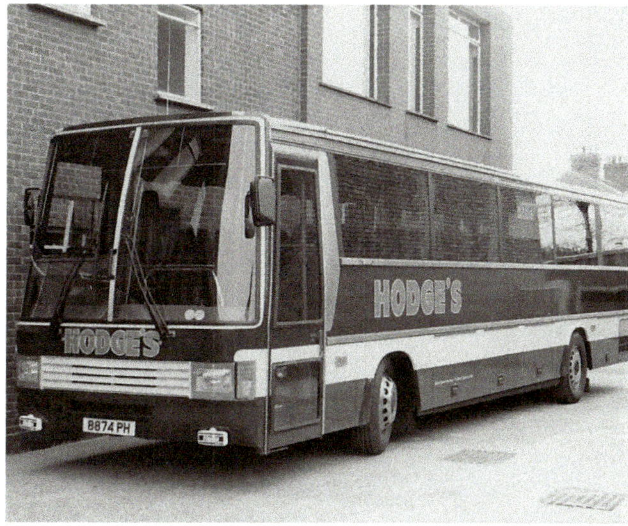

Founded in 1924, Hodge's are based at the small Berkshire town of Sandhurst, best known for its Royal Military Academy. Building up a strong business by the 1980s, the company began to purchase foreign-built coaches, the influence of European manufacturers becoming more significant around this time. In 1984 this rather unusual Bova with exotic-sounding Duple Calypso bodywork joined the fleet. Awaiting collection from dealers Moseley Continental when new, and registered 8874 PH, the coach went on to serve with several other operators until the mid-2000s carrying registrations A37 HPL, LIB 9415 and VIB 3294. (Author's collection)

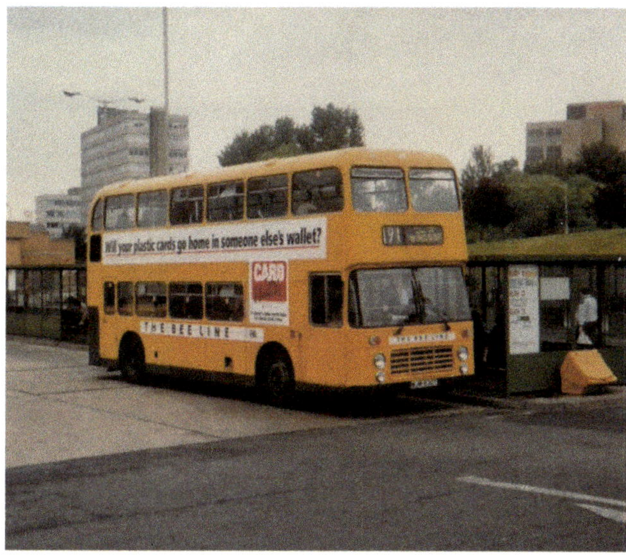

Usually, the preserve of the Northern Counties-bodied Leyland Olympians, Bristol VR 525 (WJM 830T) works trunk route 191. With the sale of Reading, Newbury and Wycombe depots The Bee Line had only thirteen former Alder Valley Bristol VRs remaining in the fleet when this view was taken on 9 July 1993 at Bracknell bus station. During First Group ownership some would transfer to other group companies.

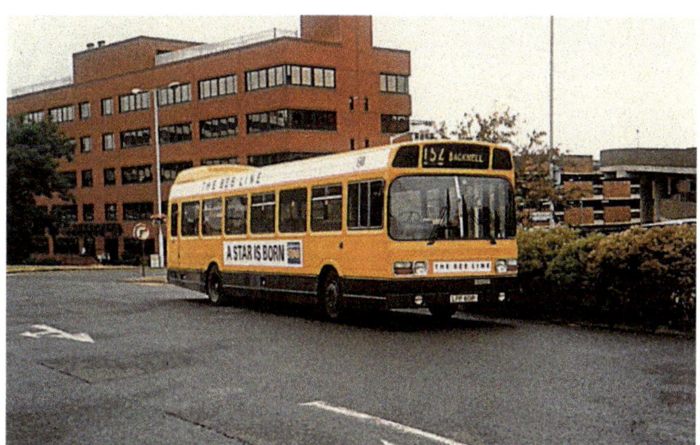

One-time Careline-liveried Leyland National 374 (LPF 601P) still retains its dual-purpose seating and wheelchair lift. It is working a town service at Bracknell bus station on 9 July 1993.

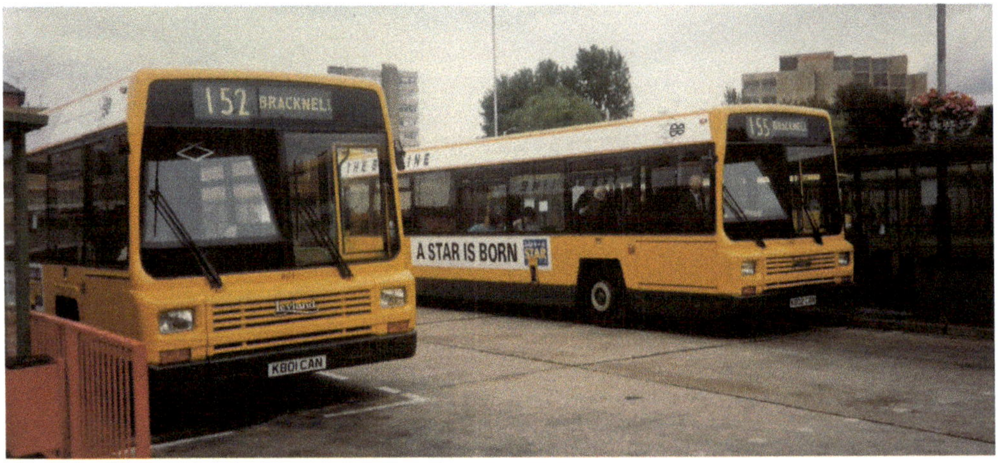

New to Alder Valley in 1992 were a pair of Leyland Lynx 2s for a tendered route in Guildford. Being non-standard to Stagecoach, when it took the company over, both were sold to The Bee Line when less than a year old. Retaining their AV fleet numbers 801 and 802, K801/2 CAN are both operating Bracknell town routes on 9 July 1993 with the vague destination 'Bracknell' seemingly a feature. Both transferred within First Group to operate in and around Southampton.

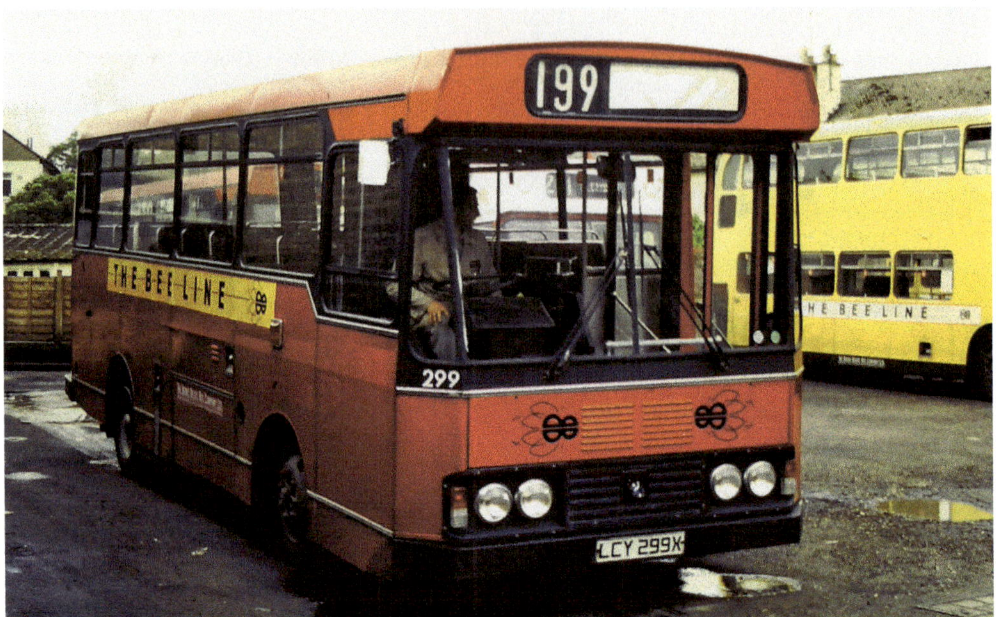

National Bus Company trialled the Bedford YMQS with Lex Maxeta thirty-seven-seat body in South Wales on rural work, and also with United Counties on town services. Alder Valley acquired five of the Welsh batch plus two new examples. The Bee Line inherited four, of which 299 (LCY 299X) based at Bracknell, is still wearing South Wales red livery and demonstrates the application of offside legal lettering, a Berks Bucks Bus Co. quirk. It is leaving the depot to work irregular route 199 to Hawthorn Hill and Billingbear. Going on to work in north London and Milton Keynes for R&I Buses, the vehicle subsequently carried several registrations before entering preservation with the Cardiff Transport Group. (Author's collection)

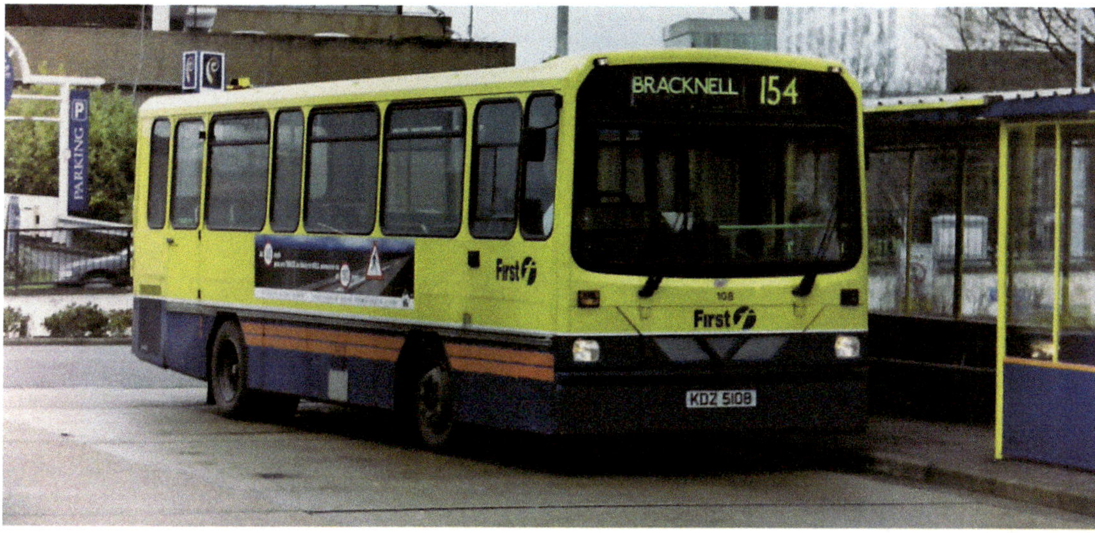

Q-Drive Group sold The Bee Line's remaining depots, along with London Buslines, to Centrewest in 1996, which was taken over by First Group soon after. Delocalising would ensue with 'The Bee Line' removed and vehicles simply showing 'First' logos. Under common ownership with London older vehicles were cascaded, with Bracknell receiving Wright Handybus-bodied Dennis Darts new to London Buses in 1989. Carrying the Northern Irish registration from new, former DW108 (KDZ 5108, now 108) has worked a service from Bullbrook on 7 February 2002. (Author's collection)

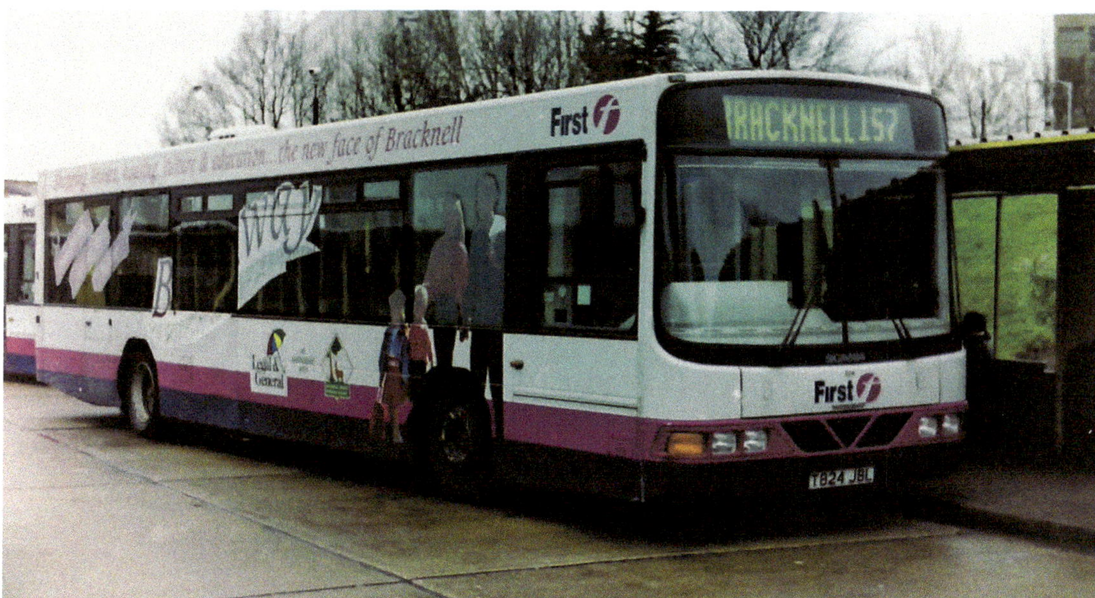

The Bee Line was a fond user of Scania chassis for buses and coaches, a trend that continued under First ownership. The smart Wright bodywork marketed as Axcess-Floline was favoured by First and was carried on Scania and Volvo chassis. Viewed on the same date as the previous photo, 824 (T824 JBL) was one of six Scania L94s received in 1999, the first new buses delivered under the new management. (Author's collection)

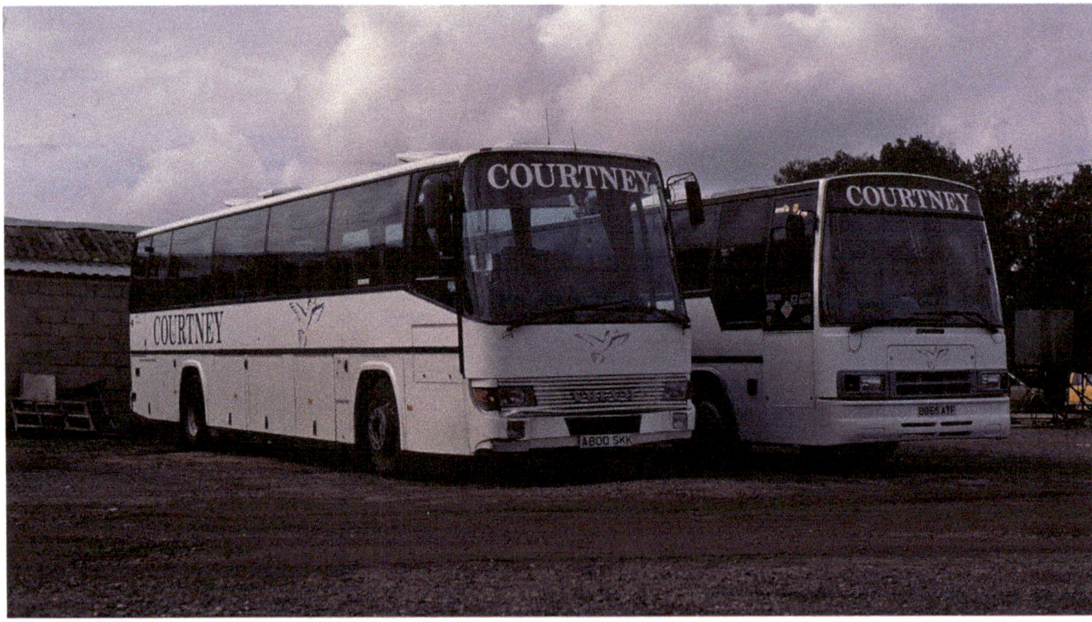

Founded in Bracknell in 1973, Courtney Coaches' origins were with taxis, coach hire being introduced in the 1980s. At Downmill Road depot we see Berkhof Everest-bodied Volvo B10M A800 SKK and Plaxton Paramount-bodied Bedford YNT D865 ATF. In 1997 the latter went on to work with Gozo Coaches in Malta, was re-registered FBY-047 and given the name *Holy Mary*. (Dave Bowman/author's collection)

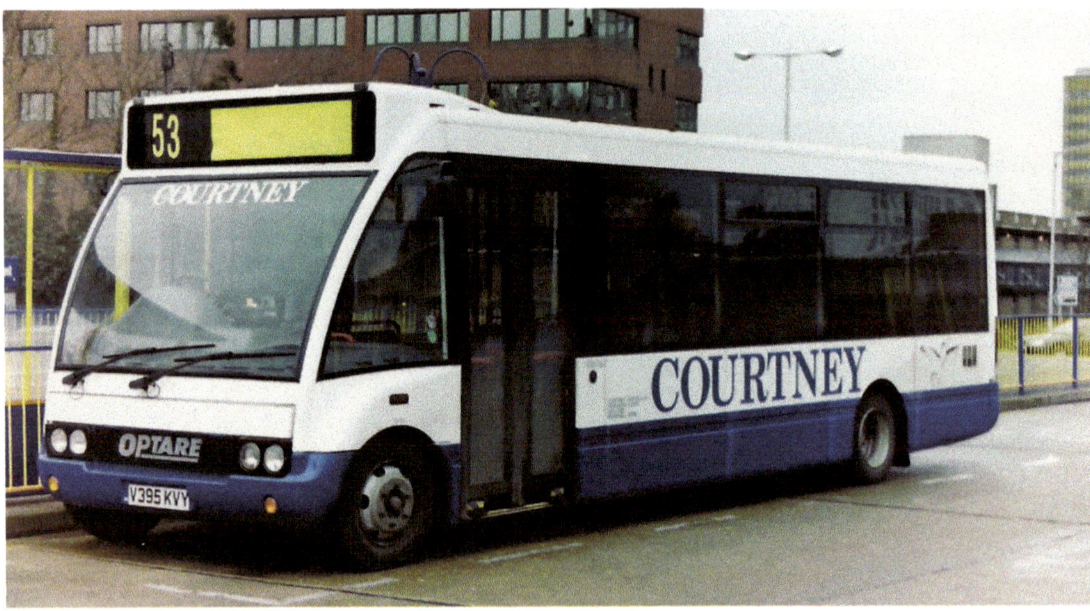

Courtney moved on to service bus work in 2000, the first local route being the 53 from Bracknell to Slough, Wexham Park Hospital via Maidenhead previously operated by Martins Coaches. Optare Solo V395 KVY was new to the company and is laying over at Bracknell bus station in February 2002. (Author's collection)

Links with London

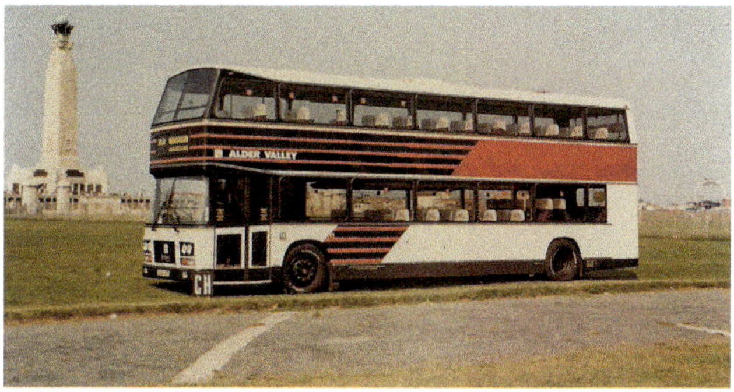

The early 1980s saw National Bus Company operators in the Home Counties receive impressive long wheelbase Leyland Olympians with ECW coach bodywork for coach services into London. Alder Valley received ten of these seventy-three seaters in 1983/4, which were initially split between Aldershot and Reading depots. Brand new 1506 (A506 GPC) is on display at the Southsea bus rally on 17 June 1984. Yet to have Londonlink vinyls applied, the coach went on to work for The Bee Line (numbered 804), its career ending prematurely being one of twenty-three vehicles lost in the 1988 Newbury depot fire. (Author's collection)

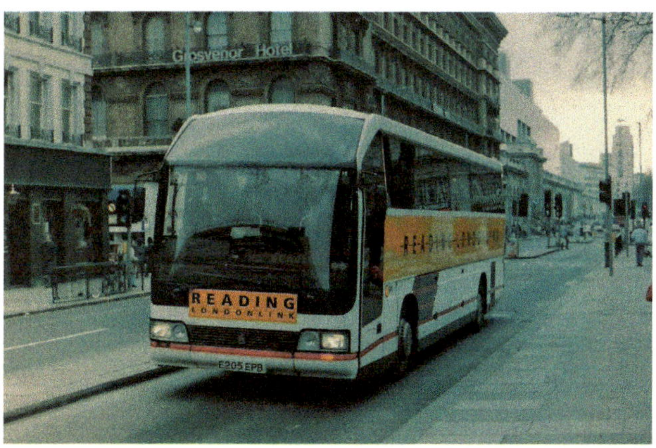

An equally smart single-deck coach was chosen for Alder Valley with six Hestair Duple 425 integral vehicles delivered in 1987. Developed to combat the ever-increasing influx of foreign coachwork designs coming onto the market, there is a noticeable family likeness to some of today's Plaxton designs. Transfers or loans between Alder Valley and The Bee Line often continued with both companies under the ownership of Len Wright. With Londonlink NBC coach-style livery, 1205 (E205 EPB) would normally work routes to and from Aldershot. With The Bee Line vinyls added and heading towards Reading the coach is about to negotiate the former road system around Grosvenor Gardens, Victoria, *c.* 1990. (Colin Lloyd/Author's collection)

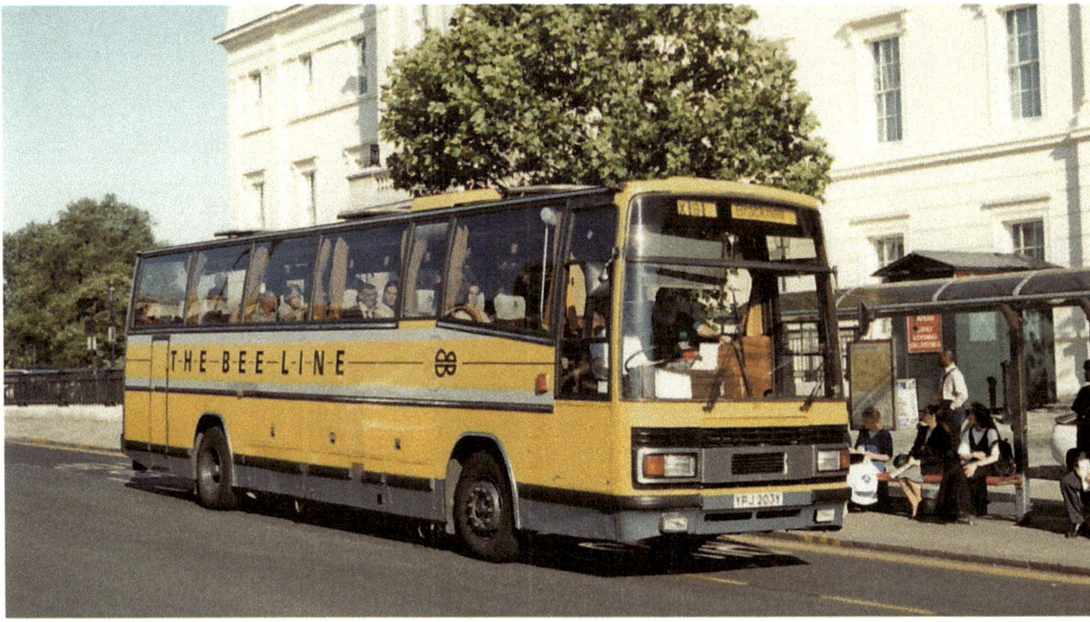

In 1983 Alder Valley received ten Plaxton Paramount 3500-bodied Leyland Tigers seating fifty. Numbered 1201–10 and initially used at Reading on the Rail Air service, they were later cascaded to coach and private hire work. The Bee Line took all but two of the batch and renumbered them into the 7xx coach series. At Hyde Park corner en route to Bracknell on the X9, 752 (YPJ 203Y) carries a respectable load and wears plain Bee Line livery. (Author's collection)

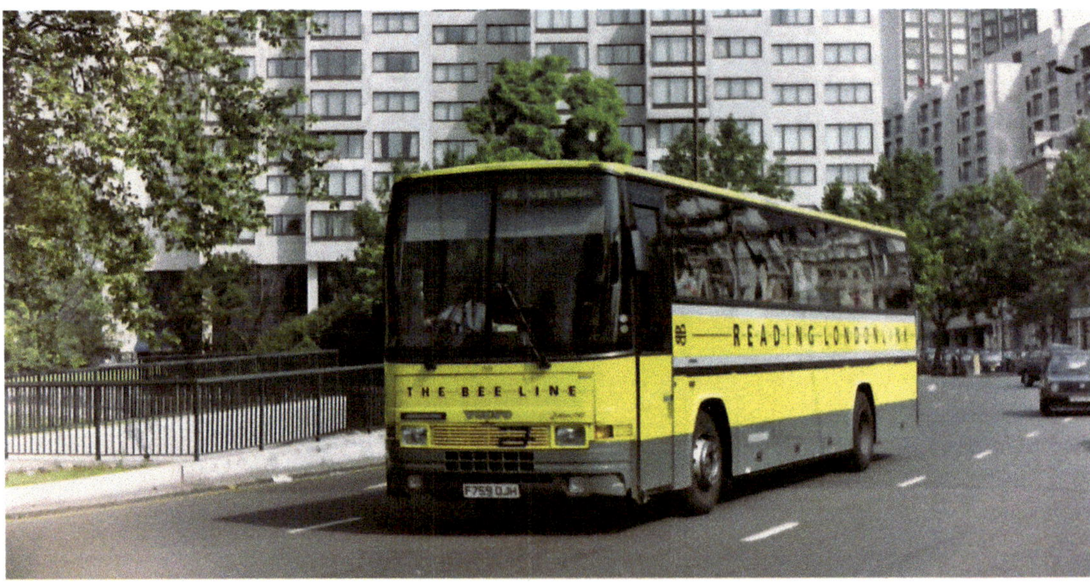

The Bee Line also operated five Hestair Duple 425 coaches, and Len Wright's coaching pedigree ensured some other interesting types would be used. Ten Jonckheere Jubilee P50-bodied Volvo B10Ms were delivered in 1989 for use on Reading and Newbury Londonlink services. 789 (F759 OJH) is rounding Hyde Park corner nearing its destination in the spring of 1992. Later the same year these routes and some of the coaches would pass to Reading Buses. (Author's collection)

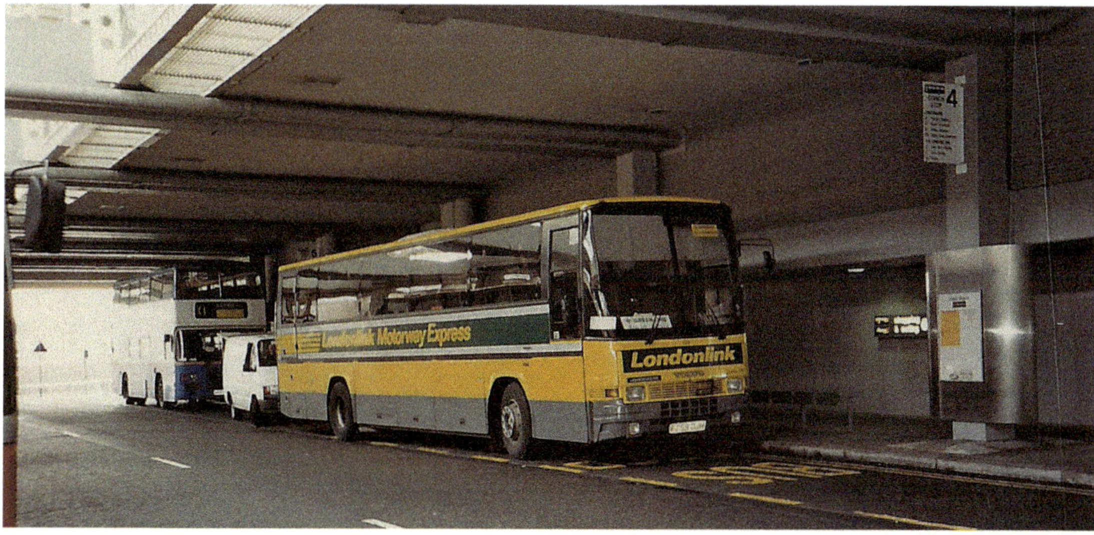

Alder Valley South's Londonlink routes were joined with those of the remaining Bee Line operations in 1992. The X7 and X9 were the main routes from Bracknell, running across Surrey towards the capital on roughly an hourly frequency Mondays to Saturdays, and every two hours on Sundays. Five of the Jonckheere-bodied Volvo B10Ms were transferred including 789 (F759 OJH), seen working the service on 23 April 1993. Originally using the main coach station at Victoria, by now the routes were Green Line-associated and set down at the terminal across the road at Bullied Way. Marketing depicted coaches in this style, although eventually the full Green Line livery would be applied.

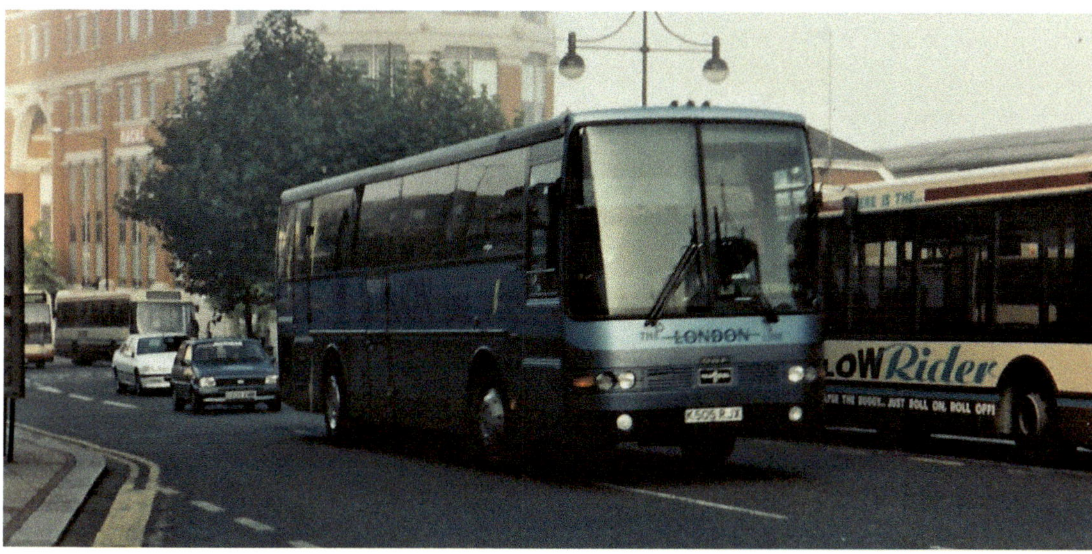

Reading Buses combined the Londonlink services with their own Goldline routes and rebranded them as The London Line in this two-tone blue livery. New for this operation was Van Hool Alizee-bodied DAF 251 (K505 RJX), passing along Station Hill in its home town on 18 October 1997. The April 1996 timetable offered five routes on roughly a ninety-minute frequency, seven days a week with enhancements at peak times. However, by May 2000 the service would be withdrawn.

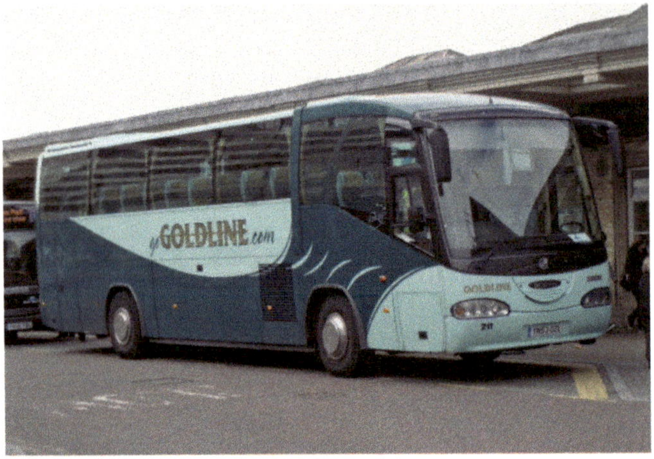

The Goldline name was first used by Reading Transport in 1980 for the joint partnership with Southend Transport. Latterly used by the coach division on a programme of excursions and tours, contracts and private hire, the last new coaches for Goldline work were six Irizar Century-bodied Scania L114s delivered in 2003. Laying over at Reading station on 16 May 2008 is 211 (YN53 OZL) three months before the Goldline operations ceased.

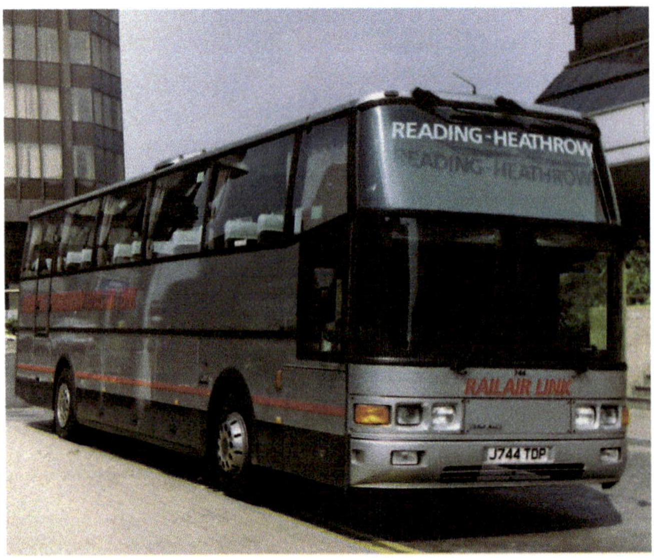

Launched in 1963, the Rail Air service linked Reading railway station with Heathrow Airport. Tickets had to be prebooked or combined with a rail ticket, and vehicles, which were fitted-out to a relatively high specification, also carried a dedicated livery. The Bee Line acquired the service, which was officially numbered X25, at privatisation. Leyland Tigers (see page 32) were replaced in 1991 with seven smart silver-liveried Berkhof Excellence-bodied Scania K112s. Q-Drive Group had an interest in Berkhof at the time. On the stand at Reading station in June 1992 is 744 (J744 TDP). (Author's collection)

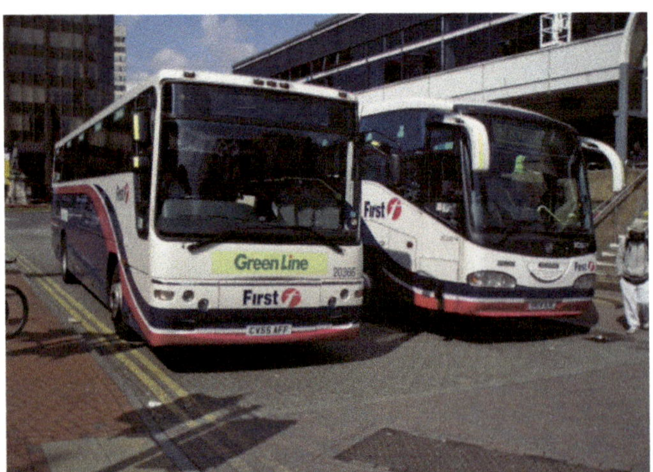

On the same stand at Reading station, this time on 16 May 2008, we see Plaxton Profile-bodied Volvo B7R 20366 (CV55 AFF) with wheelchair lift and Irizar Century-bodied Scania K114 23014 (YN04 AJX). Although outshopped in First Group-inspired liveries, the Volvo also carries a Green Line fleet name while the Scania shows the SC class code as a prefix to its fleet number, revealing the link with First London at this time.

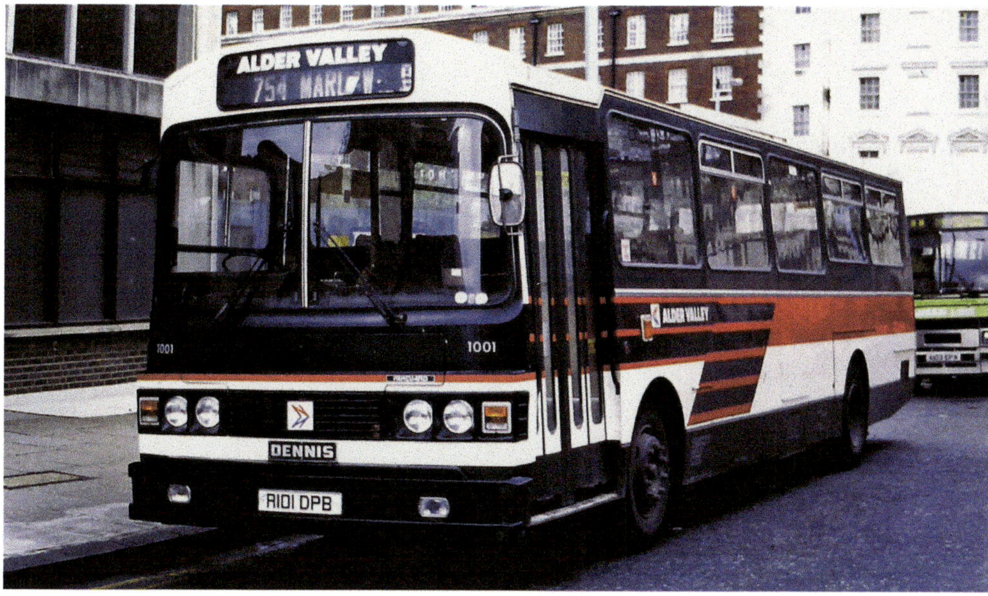

In 1983 Alder Valley received a one-off Dennis Falcon with fifty-three coach-seat Wadham Stringer bodywork. Initially used on Londonlink services from Aldershot, 1001 (A101 DPB) was transferred to High Wycombe with the pre-privatisation split in 1986. Rebuilt a year later following a fire, the vehicle was swapped in 1991, when owned by Oxford Bus Company, for two Bristol VRs from Maynes of Manchester. Caught resting at Eccleston Bridge, Victoria, soon after transfer to High Wycombe depot, 1001 awaits evening commuters for Marlow on route 754 (later X54), which ended on 27 February 1988. (Author's collection)

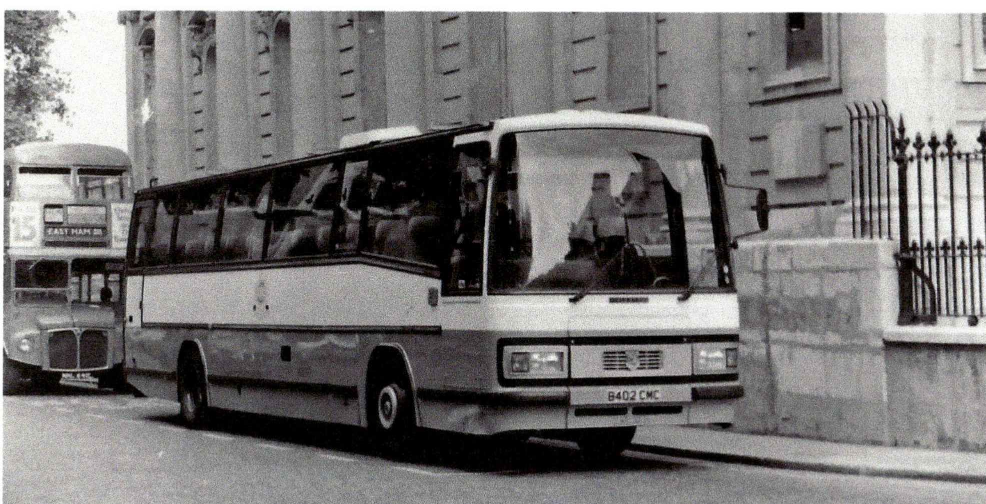

Seeing opportunities for improvement in commuter coach services from Maidenhead, Marlow and south Buckinghamshire Armchair Coaches of Brentford set up routes from these areas in 1988. Maidenhead had five return peak journeys to and from London and the City, which offered very competitive season ticket prices and local pick-up/drop-off points. Viewed in central London and exemplifying Armchair's smart fleet is B402 CMC, one of three similar fifty-five-seat Plaxton Paramount 3200-bodied Leyland Tigers. (Stewart J. Brown/author's collection)

Windsor and Maidenhead

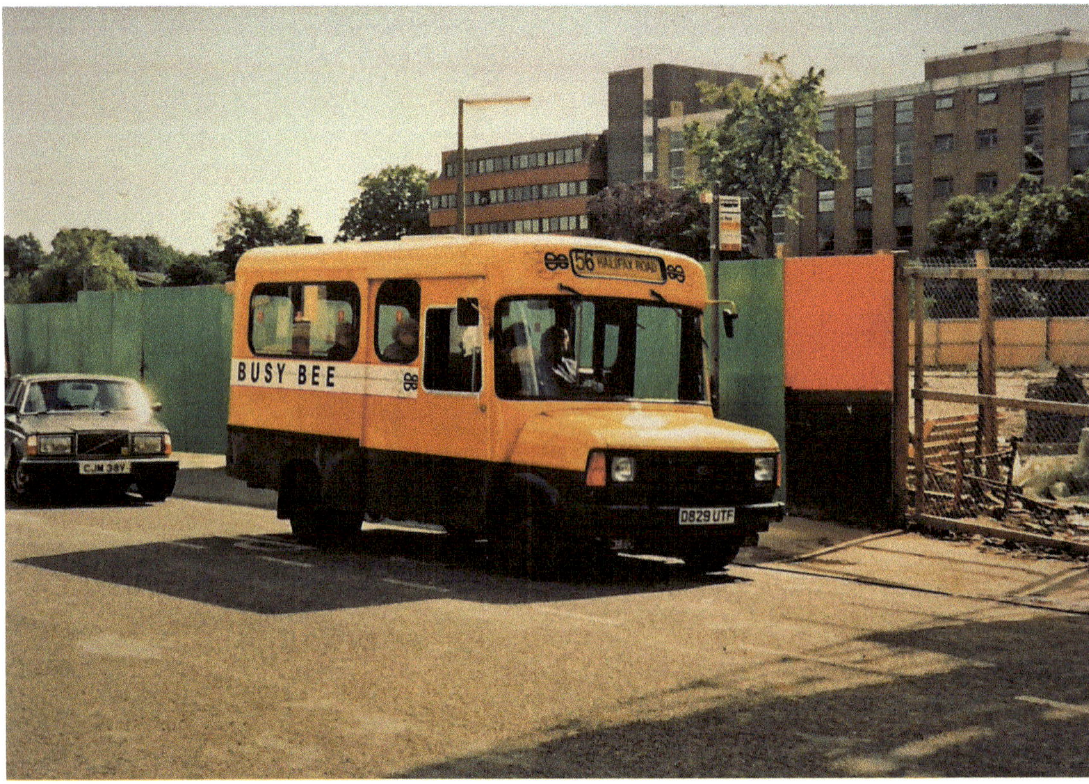

Maidenhead's once extensive bus and coach station ran the length of Bridge Avenue. By the time of this 1986 view the site has been cleared to make way for new office developments and bus stops have been relocated along the road itself. New as 329 but renumbered 108, D829 UTF originally had booked registration C329 RPE but arrived too late to carry it. Branded as Busy Bee, the buses worked the main cross-Maidenhead minibus routes 55 and 56 linking Halifax Road with Woodlands Park. (Brighton Bus Interest Group/author's collection)

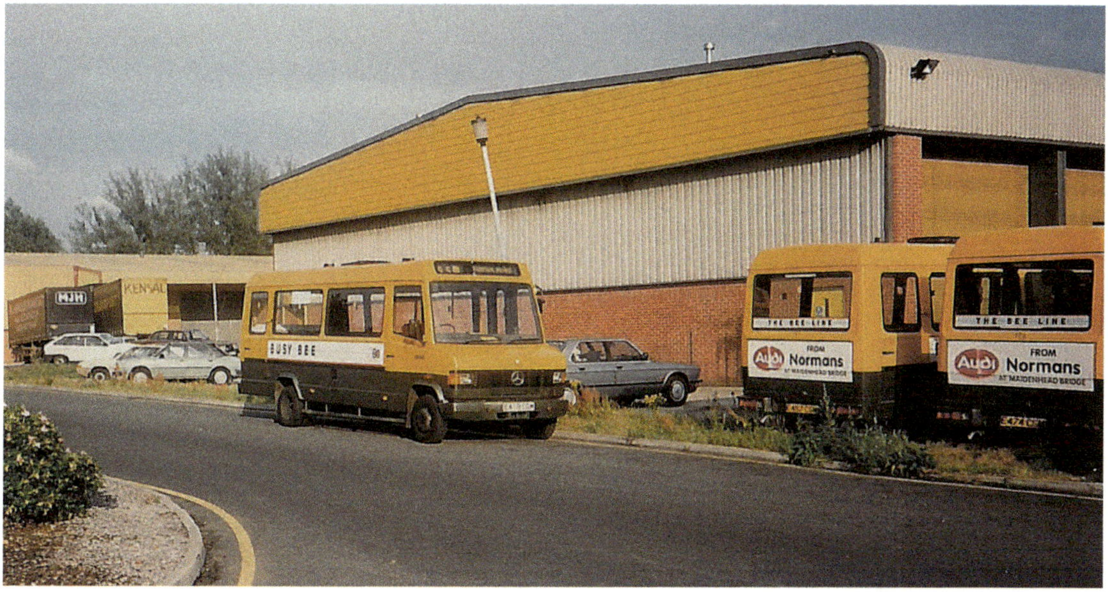

Replacements for the Ford Transits appeared quickly in the shape of Robin Hood-bodied Mercedes-Benz L609Ds with twenty seats. Maidenhead depot were recipients of several of the batch including 162 (E458 CGM) and the type enjoyed a long working life. Some were subsequently used by other operators, with this particular example going on to work in the Stroud area and clocking up nearly twenty years' service. This view of Maidenhead depot is during the evening run-in on 9 July 1993.

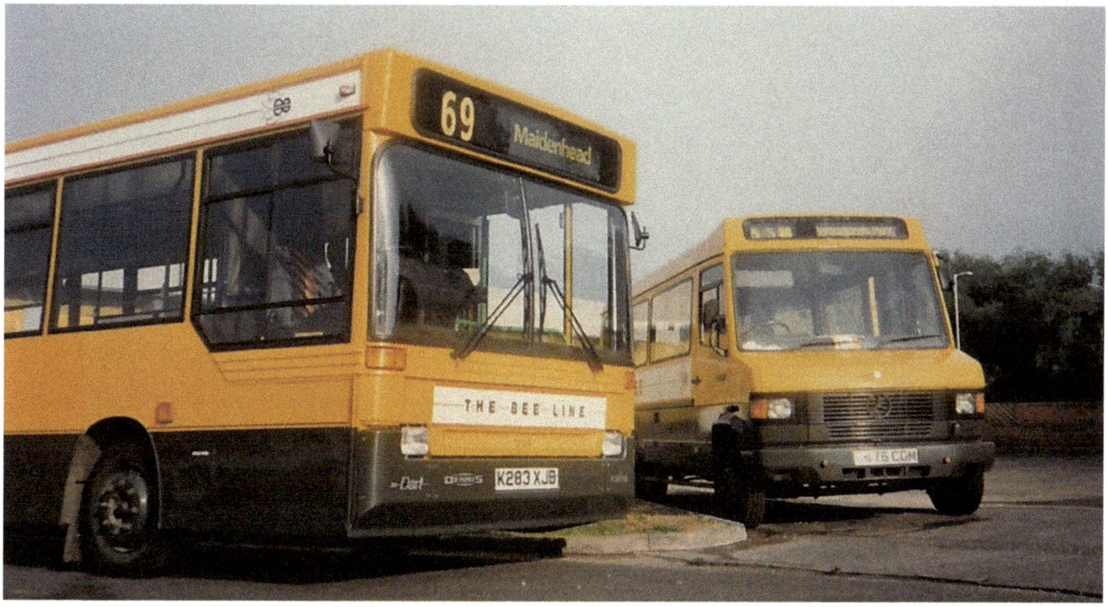

In February 1992 Maidenhead received four Plaxton Pointer-bodied Dennis Darts to replace ageing Leyland Nationals, with four more following soon after. Last of the batch 204 (K283 XJB) has arrived back at the depot from Slough and stands alongside Mercedes 180 (E476 CGM) at the end of a day's work on 9 July 1993.

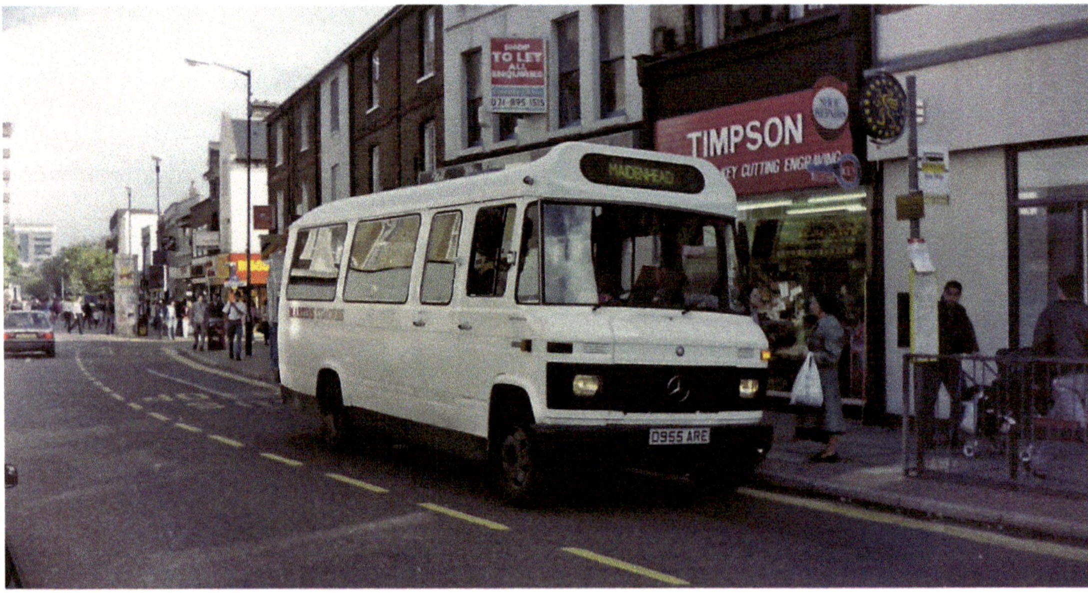

Ash of High Wycombe traded under several names, including Martins Coaches on tendered routes in the Maidenhead and south Buckinghamshire area, and also ran a number of coaches. Loading on Slough High Street for Maidenhead is twenty-one-seat PMT-bodied Mercedes-Benz 608D D955 ARE, acquired from an operator in Dereham. This area has been completely redeveloped and the buildings to the left of the Midland Bank have been demolished. (Author's collection)

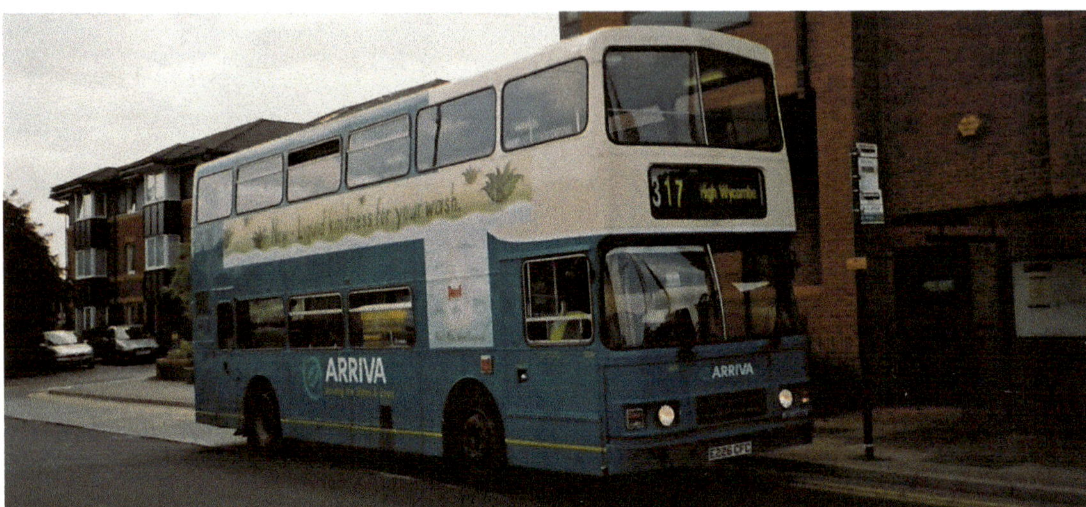

Between Maidenhead and High Wycombe the main route was the 317, operated by High Wycombe depot of The Bee Line, which, after subsequent takeovers, became Wycombe Bus Company and later, Arriva the Shires. On Bridge Avenue on 28 May 2003 is Alexander RL-bodied Leyland Olympian 5826 (E226 CFC) wearing the Shires & Essex fleet names. The driver is following Arriva's policy of the time by leaving the headlights switched on while on service. New to Oxford Bus Company as 226, and fitted with dual doors for Park & Ride duties, the bus arrived in High Wycombe mid-1999 and later worked from Aylesbury Depot.

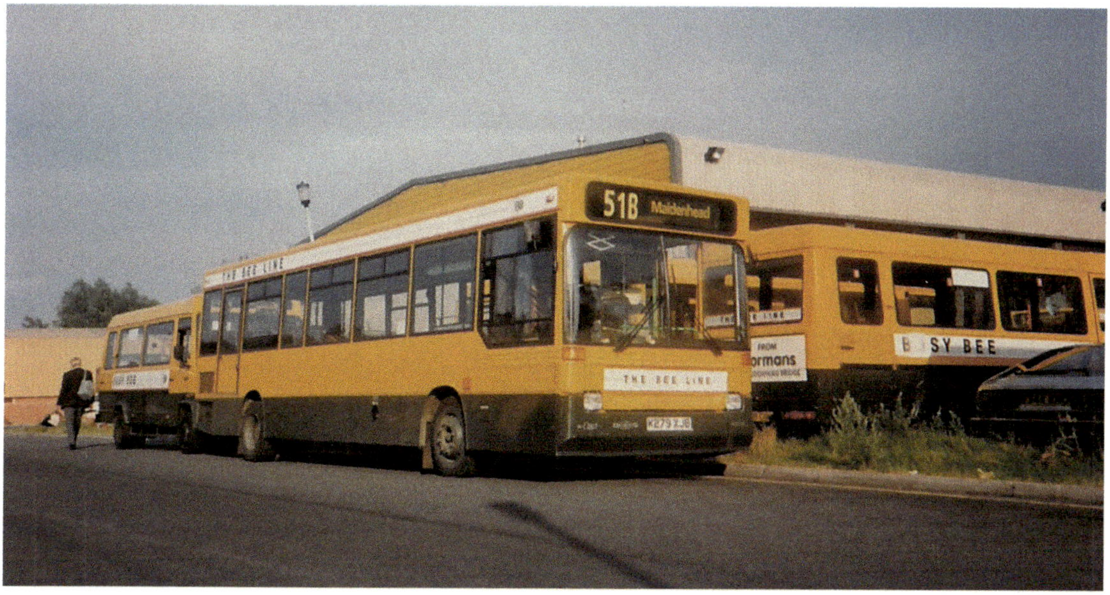

The original Alder Valley depot on Moorbridge Road was closed in 1990 and the site is now occupied by a Waitrose supermarket. A new depot was established at Stafferton Way where Dennis Dart 201 (K279 XJB) has returned from Windsor on 9 July 1993. The depot closed soon after this view was taken and operations moved to Slough. With First Group, 201 would become 46079 and later transfer to Yeovil, others of the same batch going to Norwich. The premises are now occupied by Royal Mail.

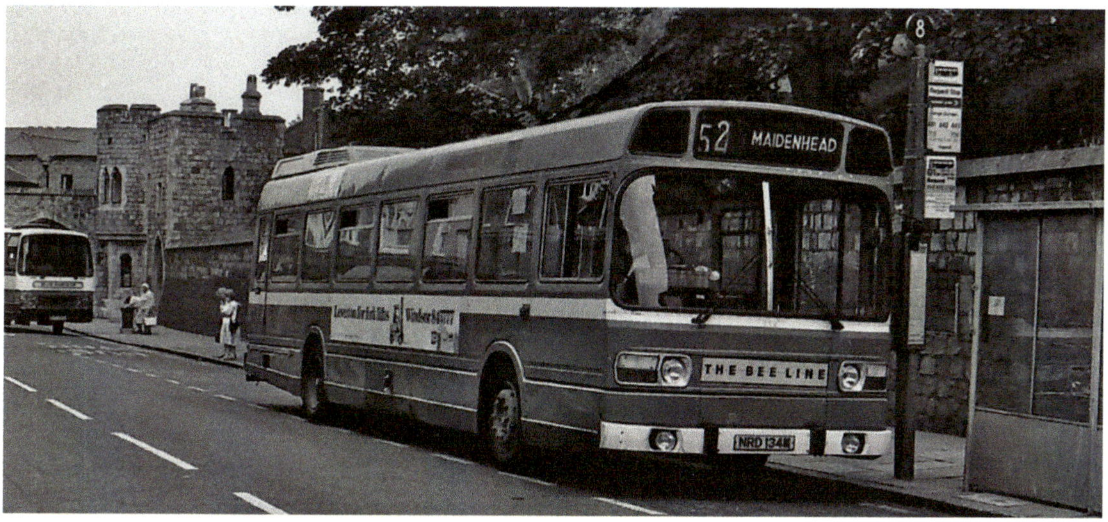

Moving on to the other town of the royal borough, best known for its castle and safari park (now Legoland), The Bee Line's Leyland National 134 (NRD 134M), later numbered 302, waits at the terminus on Thames Street, Windsor, adjacent to the castle. This 1987 view shows the vehicle still in NBC red livery with the new name applied only at the front. The bus would return to its home town via Bray and Holyport. London Country once had a substantial depot in the town and the well-decorated bus stop pole is to an LT style, also displaying Green Line services. (Brian Botley/author's collection)

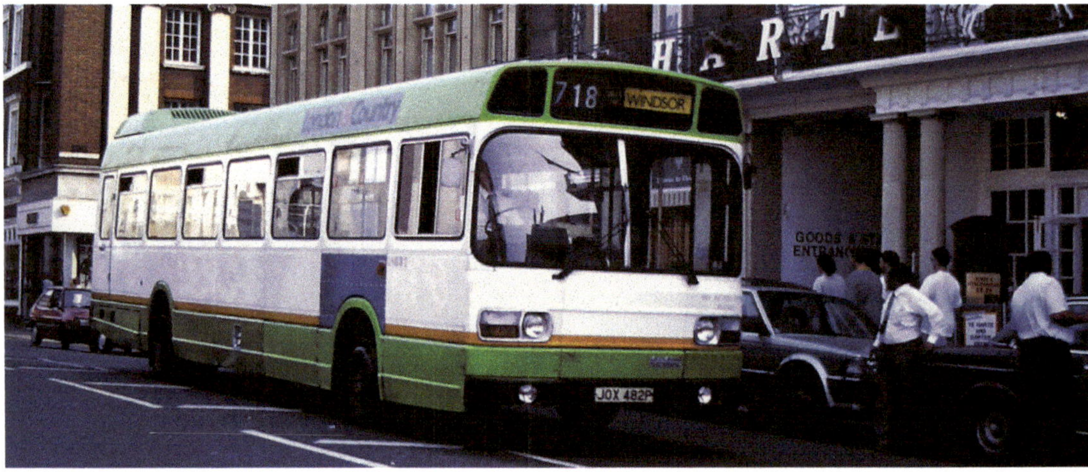

Here is another unusual livery, this time carried through Windsor on London & Country Leyland National LNB82 (JOX 482P), which was new to Midland Red at Cannock in 1975. In 1988 the vehicle passed from Midland Red to Shamrock & Rambler in Bournemouth, gaining this green and white colour scheme and Charlie's Cars fleet names for services competing with Bournemouth Transport. After only seven months it came to L&C, staying until June 1994. It was then sent to East Lancs for conversion to a National Greenway and transferred to Midland Fox. Displaying Green Line blinds in this summer 1993 view, LNB82 is making its way along High Street opposite the castle and is passing the Harte & Garter Hotel, once a fourteenth-century inn. (Rob Edworthy/author's collection)

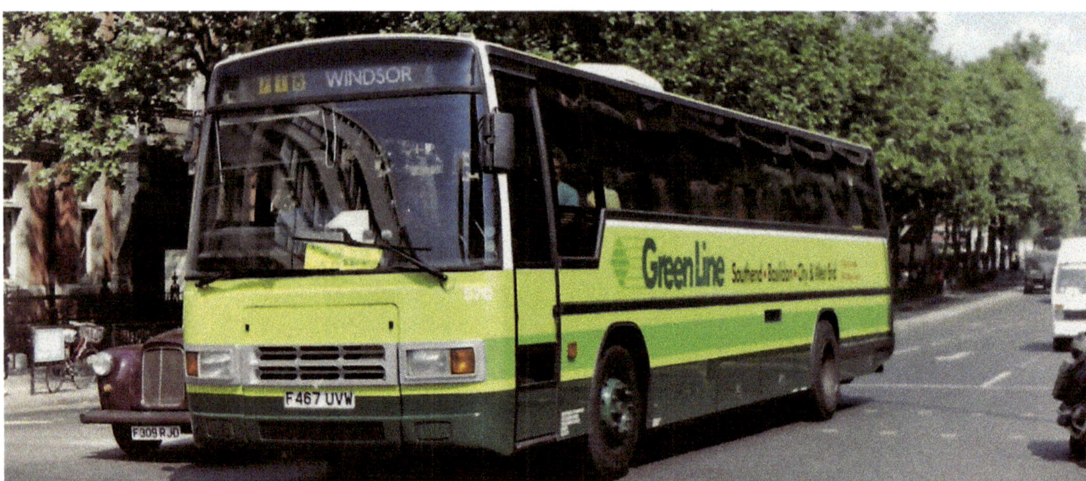

On the same route, but at the London end in Buckingham Palace Road, is Southend Transport 570 (F467 UVW), a Plaxton Paramount 3200-bodied Volvo B10M, still showing the Southend X1 branding but working for London &Country. The 718 ran from April to September with four journeys Mondays to Fridays (but only a couple at weekends) linking the capital to Windsor via Weybridge, Walton-on-Thames and Kingston, while serving other attractions en route. There was also a year-round service 700/702 operated by Bee Line, which served Bracknell, Slough and Legoland. The coach was new as F450 PSL on Stagecoach Caledonian Express work. Moving through British Bus Group companies, London & Country and then The Shires, the coach finally finished up with Emblings. (Colin Lloyd/author's collection)

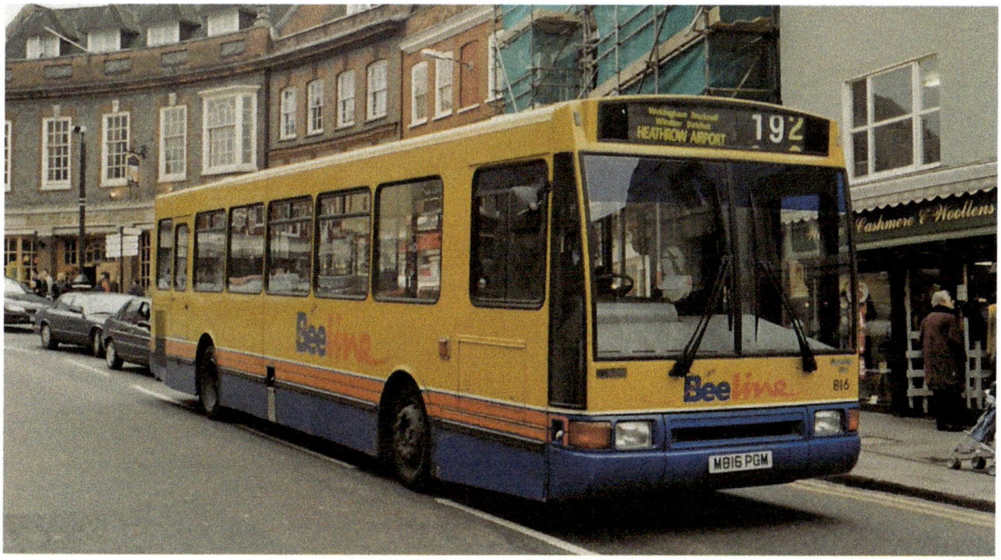

We see again the 19x group of services from Reading and Bracknell, now serving Slough and Heathrow Airport. In 1994 Bee Line's Bracknell depot received what would be the last new step-entrance vehicles, ten Scania L113s with Northern Counties fifty-one-seat bodywork. Wearing the last version of Bee Line livery and fleet names before First corporatism took hold, an 'f' sticker is just visible in the front nearside window. 816 (M816 PGM) heads along High Street, Windsor, towards Heathrow. (Author's collection)

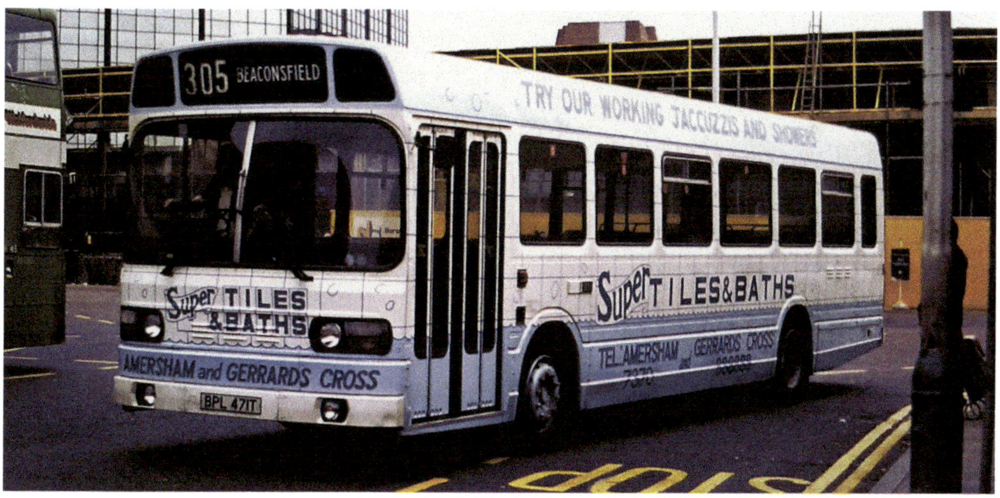

We are now at the eastern edge of Berkshire and south Buckinghamshire where both counties neighbour the boroughs of Greater London. This was London Country North West territory and two of its vehicles are seen in Uxbridge on 18 May 1984. Emerging from the left a Watfordwide branded AN-class Leyland Atlantean heads for its home town while Amersham's SNB471 (BPL 471T) works the rural 305 route. Eleven SNBs at this time carried overall adverts for various local businesses. The 305 linked High Wycombe with Uxbridge via some salubrious locations, with several route variations. One such example was this one to Beaconsfield, which so far seems devoid of passengers. Perhaps the offer to try a working jacuzzi or shower has taken their fancy. (Hugh Jones/author's collection)

Slough and London Heathrow

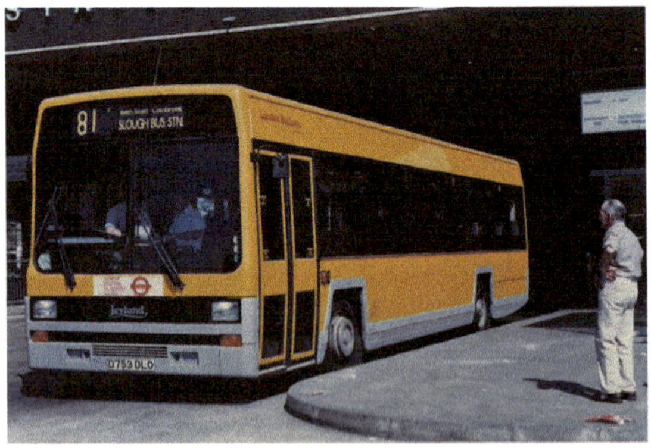

Now in the Berkshire town of Slough, only some 20 miles from central London, we meet London Transport 'red bus' operations. From 1985, LT's underperforming routes were put out to tender among private operators. One such route in the first tender round of 13 July 1985 was the 81 between Slough and Hounslow, which Len Wright's London Buslines operation won and kept for ten years. Nine ex-LT Leyland Fleetlines were initially used, the majority being displaced by the arrival of six Leyland Lynxes in 1987. We see that familiar yellow livery once more, which the vehicles would keep post-1995 following transfer to Bee Line's operation in that town. With the crew being scrutinised on 5 July 1987 by the waiting passenger, 53 (D753 DLO) would soon head towards Hounslow. (Ian Pringle/author's collection)

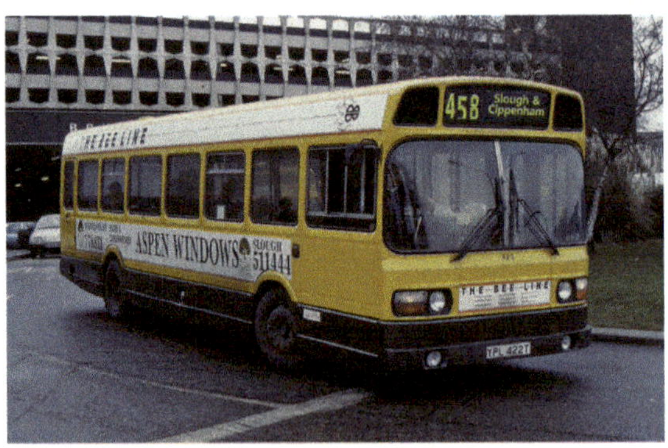

London Country North West was taken over by Luton & District in 1990, with their smart green and grey livery inspiring a red and cream L&D version. Slough depot was sold to The Bee Line in 1993 and soon afterwards the standard yellow and grey livery was applied. Former SNB422 (YPL 422T), now just 422, was one of twenty-two of the Leyland National B series variant to be acquired. Departing Brunel bus station in late 1993 on the 458, a route number from a series used by London Country across this area, the bus had worked through from Uxbridge. (John Law/author's collection)

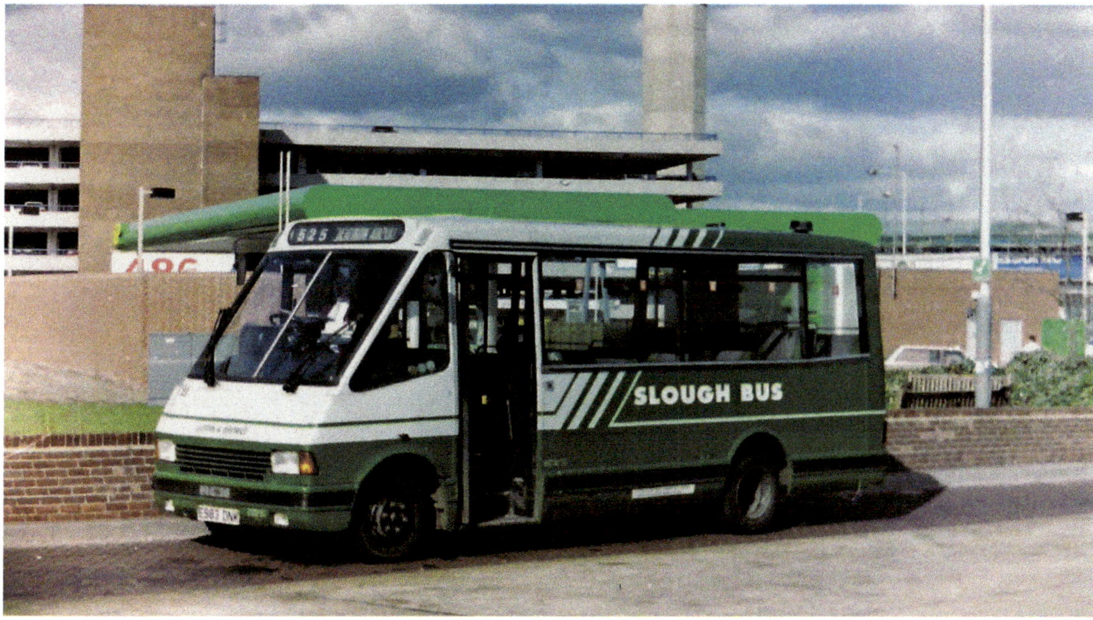

Representing the L&D era is one of two MCW MetroRiders allocated to Slough. MCW13 (E983 DNK) wears the green and grey livery with Slough Bus fleet names. It is laying over at Heathrow Central bus station after working the 525 from Slough, only 7 miles away. Forthcoming investment and improvements would see Mercedes-Benz Citaro vehicles operate services from this and other local towns. (Author's collection)

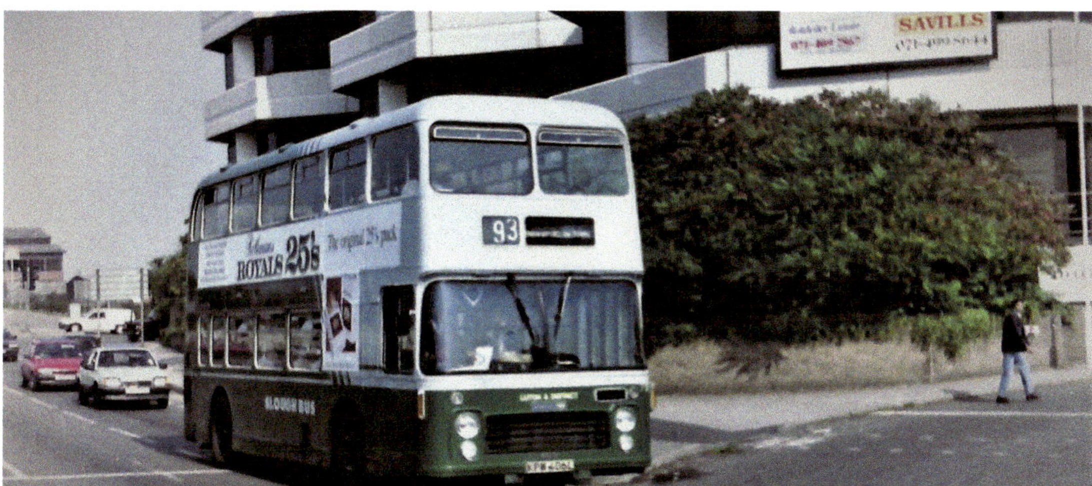

In 1991/2 Luton & District acquired a number of elderly Bristol VRs, which were mainly allocated to the former London Country North West depots. One of eight to arrive from Cambus was VR714 (KPW 406L) making its way along Stoke Road on the 93 not far from the bus station and depot. Note the small print on the destination blind, which from a distance would be hard to view. This area, along with much of the town centre, has since been redeveloped. The bus had a dramatic ending, being used in a low bridge crash test on 15 October 1996 for a training film. (Author's collection)

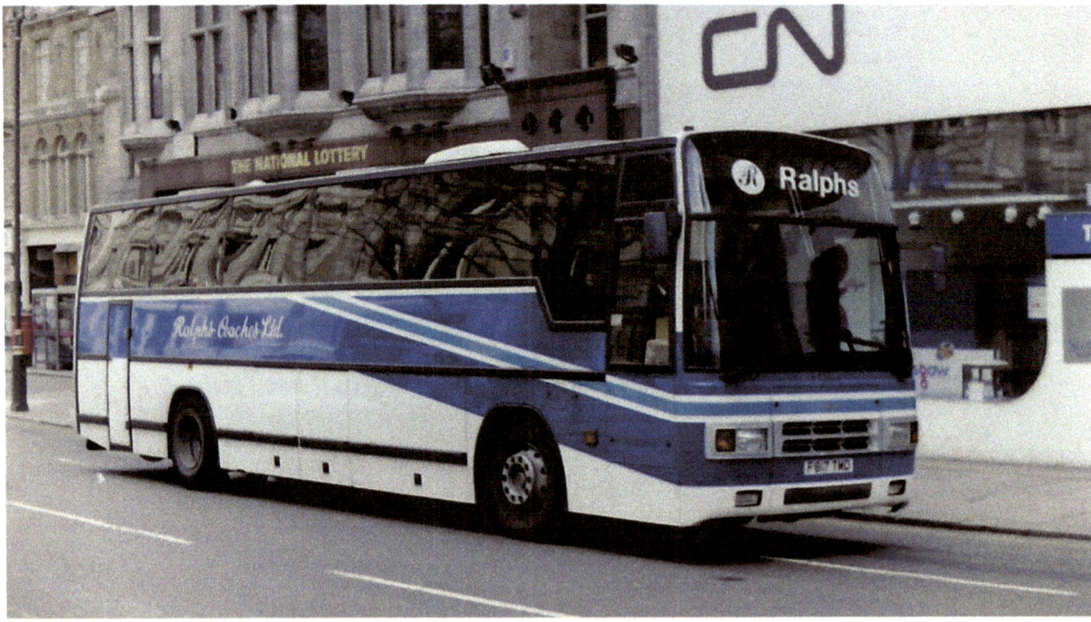

With Heathrow and London in close proximity to its base, private hire work for Ralph's Coaches of Langley ran in tandem with its airport operations. New in 1989, F817 TMD, a Plaxton Paramount 3500-bodied Volvo B10M, was one of a trio that seated fifty-six and is viewed running through central London at Cockspur Street near Trafalgar Square. (Colin Lloyd/ author's collection)

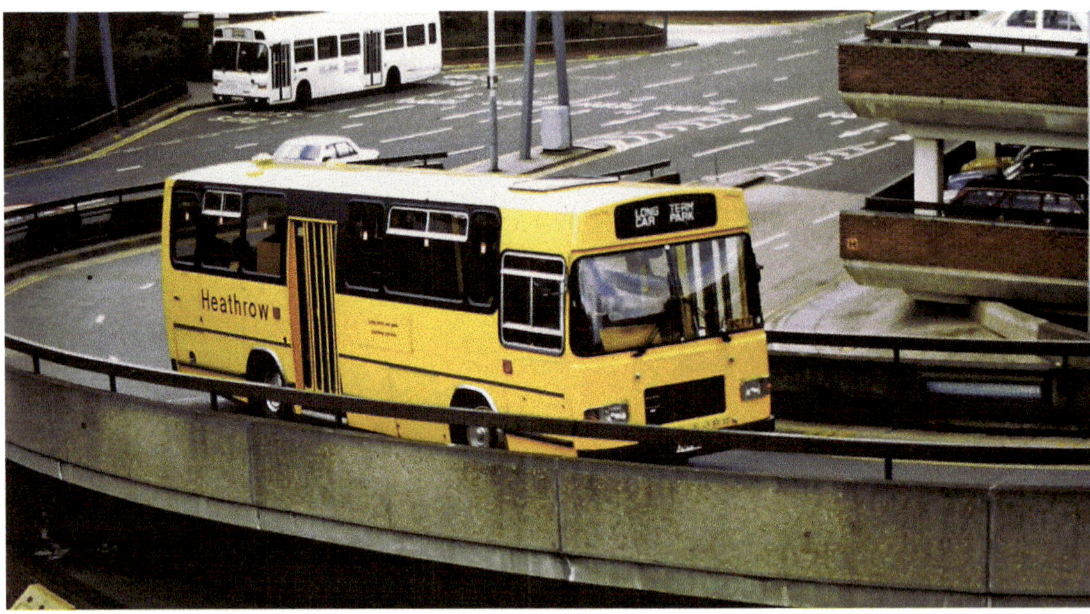

Showing the unusual specification on some airside vehicles, Ralph's XNK 198X is a Plaxton Bustler-bodied Ford R1014. It is ascending the ramp to Terminal One while working long-term car park shuttle duties on behalf of BAA Heathrow. In an unusually quiet central area a British Airways-liveried Leyland National can be seen laying over on the bus stand. (Author's collection)

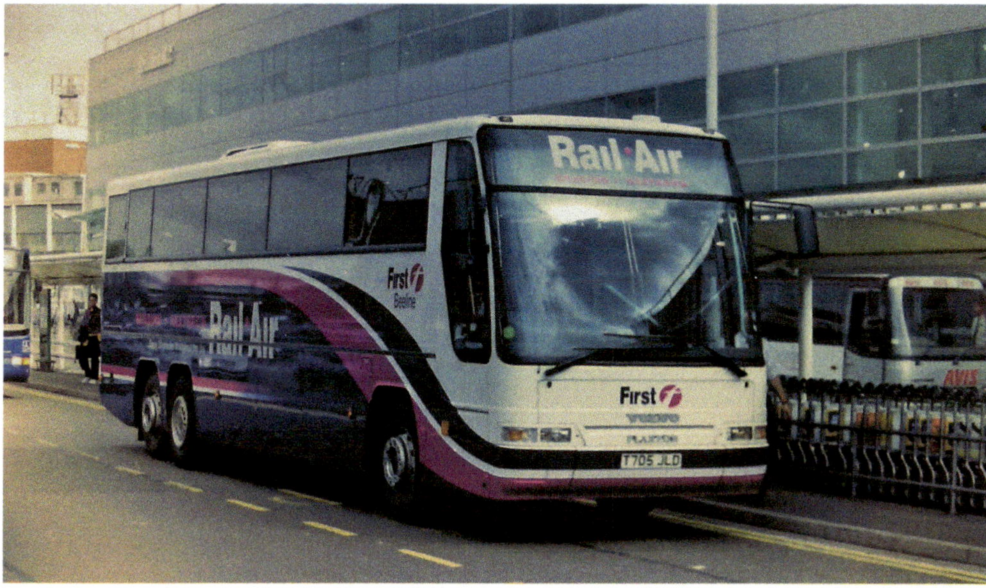

Having earlier seen unusual coaches on the Reading Rail Air service, First Bee Line kept the tradition going in 1999 when seven tri-axle Volvo B12Ts arrived fitted with Plaxton Excalibur fifty-three-seat bodies. At terminal two on 22 September of that year is 705 (T705 JLD). Once their use on the route was complete they went on to work for the rail replacement division of First. (Author's collection)

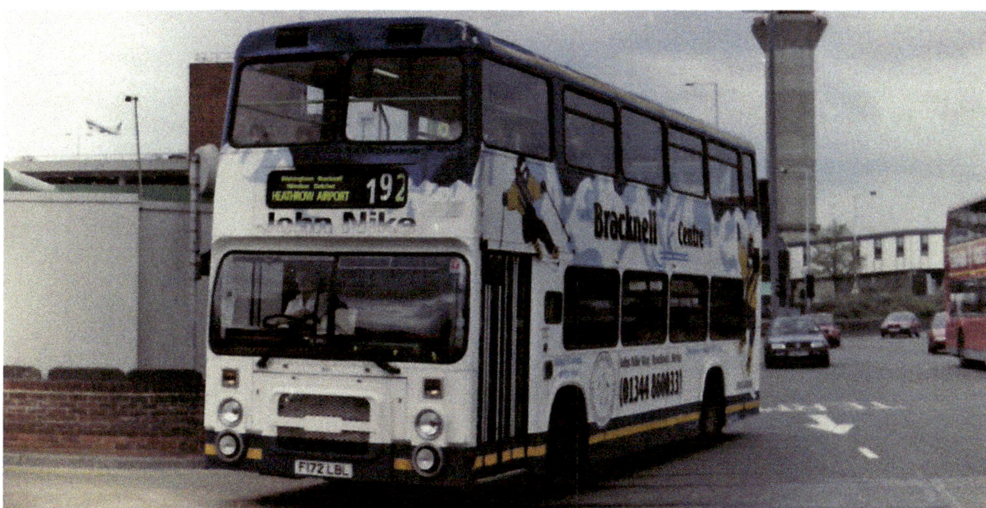

Framed between a departing plane and Heathrow's main RADAR tower is Bee Line's Northern Counties-bodied Leyland Olympian 501 (F172 LBL), renumbered from 601 and arriving at the Central bus station. Route 192 was extended to serve Heathrow as part of the enhancement of services funded by BAA. Carrying an updated version of the overall advert for John Nike Leisure Centre, the red T logo in the corner of the nearside windscreen stood for Transmo. This was the multi-operator smart card system, the reader for which can be seen on top of the Wayfarer ticket machine. The bus moved with First to Eastern Counties and a vehicle of the same batch is now preserved. (Author's collection)

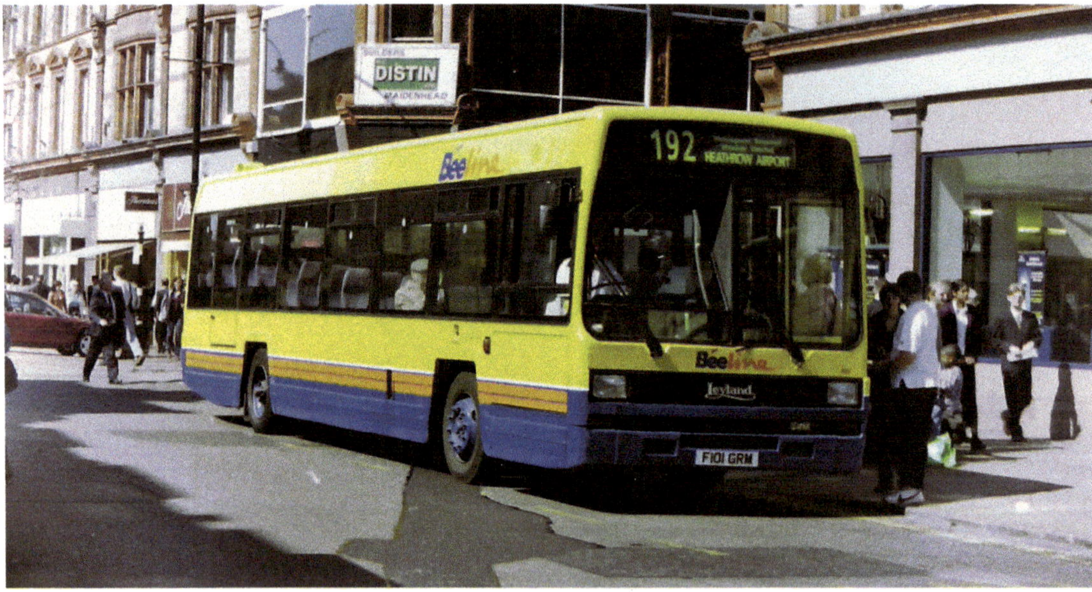

Q-Drive Group sold The Bee Line and London Buslines to First, joining them to Centrewest, once a London Buses division. New at Uxbridge for Hillingdon route 128, F101 GRM was numbered LX1 and later saw use on express route 607 for which the forty-eight coach seats were fitted. When acquired by Bee Line in 1997 it took number LX800 in the series with similar Lynxes from London Buslines and Alder Valley's Mk 2 pair. It is loading in Broad Street, Reading, also on the 192. (Author's collection)

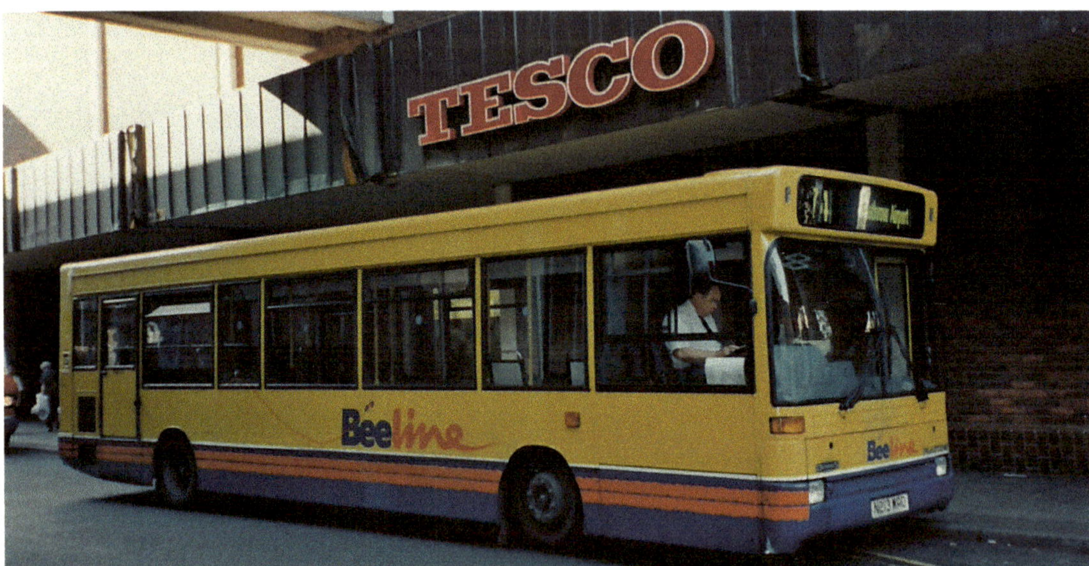

Bee Line were early recipients in 1996 of the Dennis Dart SLF with Plaxton Pointer bodywork. Delivered in this livery, they were the company's first low-floor vehicles, all seven initially working routes from Slough depot. This included the 74 (previously the 704) between High Wycombe and Heathrow Airport, jointly operated with Luton & District. Laying over at High Wycombe bus station on 19 October 1997 was 213 (N213 WRD).

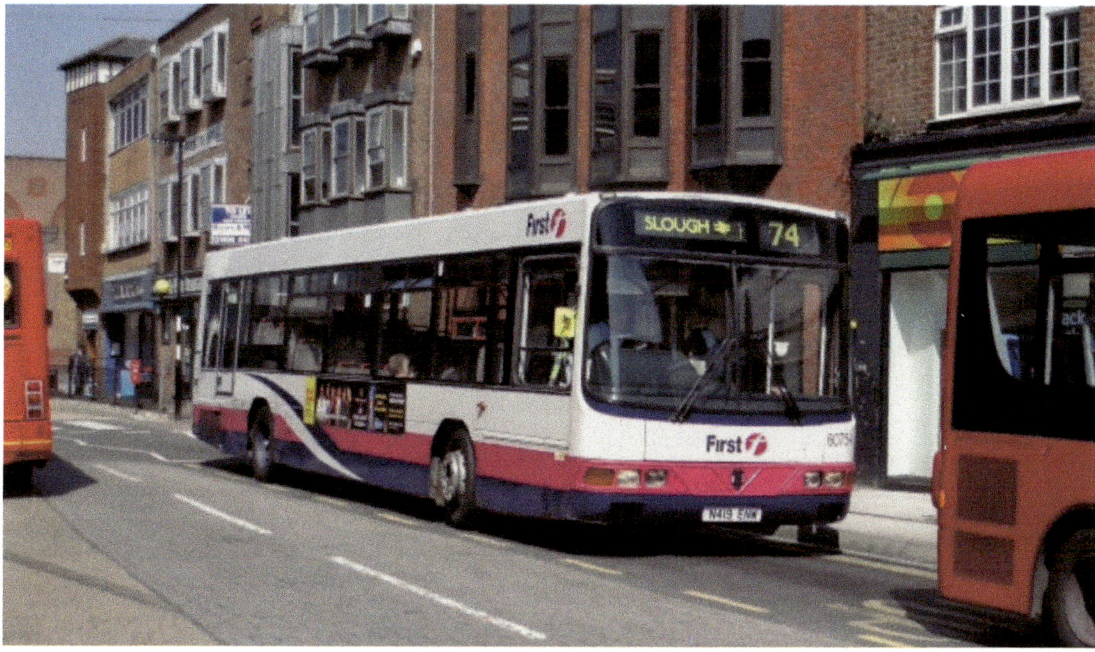

Operating the same service in First Group corporate livery is 60754 (N419 ENW), a Scania L113CRL with Wright Access Ultralow body. New to First York as 8419 in a P&R livery, it also served with South Yorkshire before joining Bee Line. Here it is loading at Oxford Street in High Wycombe on 7 May 2008.

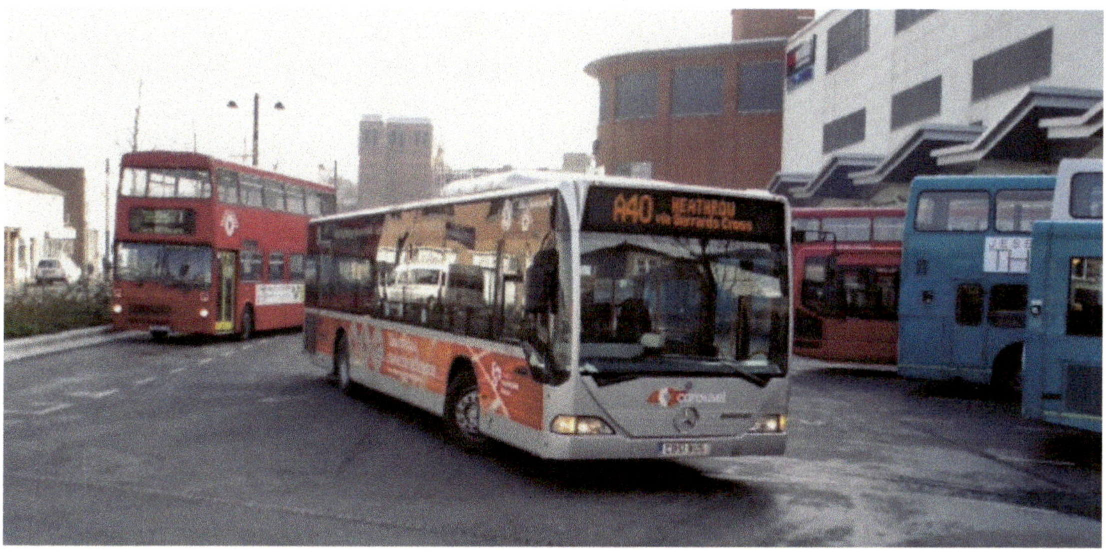

Formed in 2000, Carousel Buses began operations in and around High Wycombe initially using MCW Metrobuses mainly of London origin (rear left of the picture). Route A40 to Heathrow Airport commenced in August 2003 using former Armchair Leyland Olympians. A trio of new Mercedes-Benz Citaro vehicles arrived in April 2004 branded for the service. MB51 (CB51 BUS) was numerically the first and is departing High Wycombe's new bus station on 16 April 2008. These smart vehicles matched those used by other operators at the time.

High Wycombe

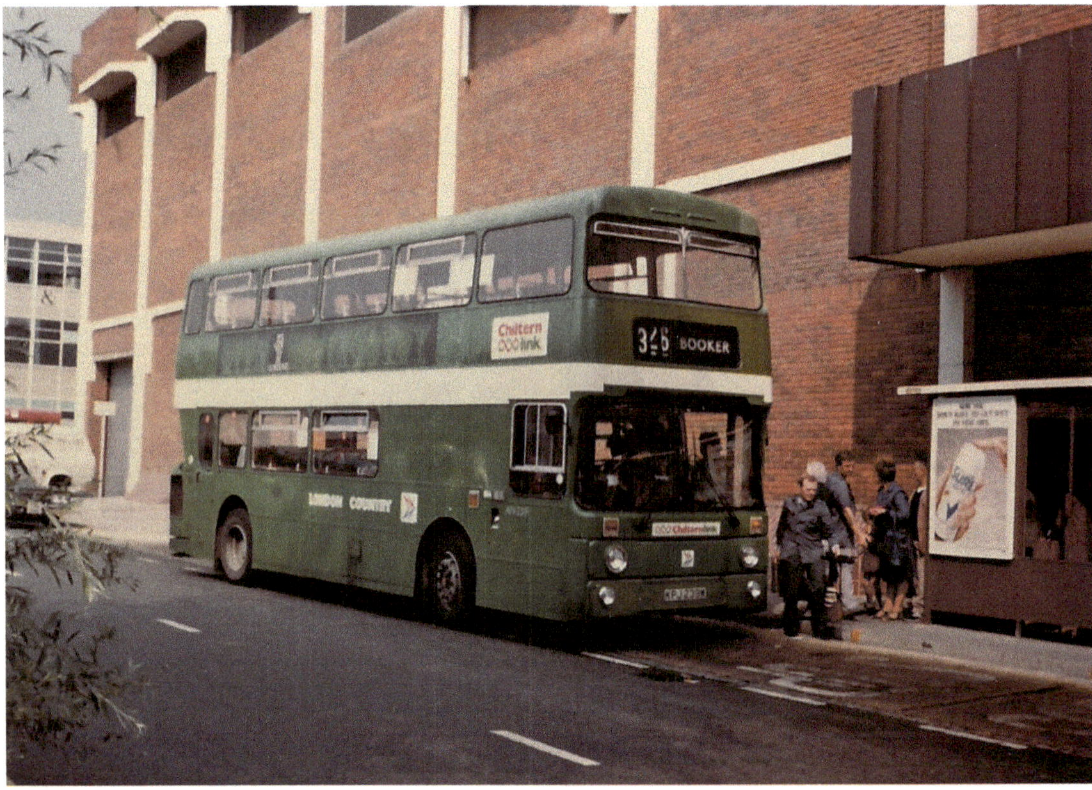

Staying at High Wycombe this pre-privatisation scene shows the Market Analysis Project (MAP) 'Chilternlink' name used on services in this area by London Country and Alder Valley. Amersham's Leyland Atlantean AN239 (KPJ 239W), bodied by Roe to the style of the older Park Royal examples, is on Union Street by Newlands bus station. At this time cross-town routes used this for Booker and Desborough Castle. The Alder Valley Leyland National, the roof of which is just visible on the left, is loading in Temple Street, which was used by services eastbound to Totteridge and Micklefield. A crew change has just taken place with a driver eagerly heading towards the bus station for his break. (Author's collection)

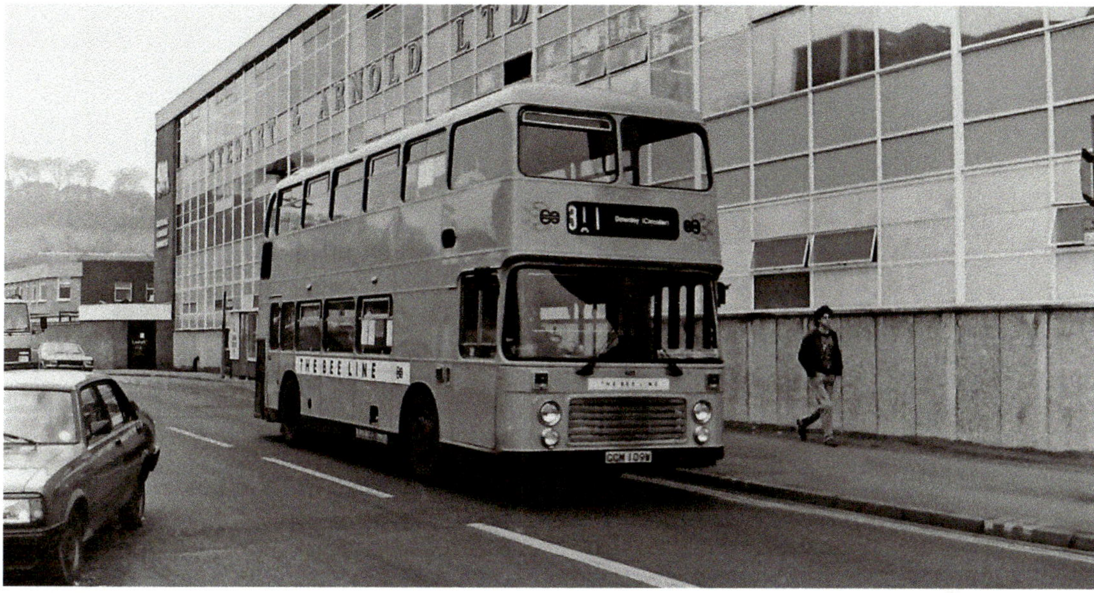

Working the 311 Downley circular in 1987 is GGM 109W of The Bee Line, still numbered 629 but soon to become 542. The bright yellow bus works along Temple Street with the previously mentioned cross-town services stop visible behind the bus, outside Stewart & Arnold's chocolate factory. That company relocated to Banbury in 1992, the same year the bus moved to Walls of Manchester. Four years later it passed to Stephensons of Rochford. This whole area now forms part of the Eden shopping complex. (Kevin Lane/author's collection)

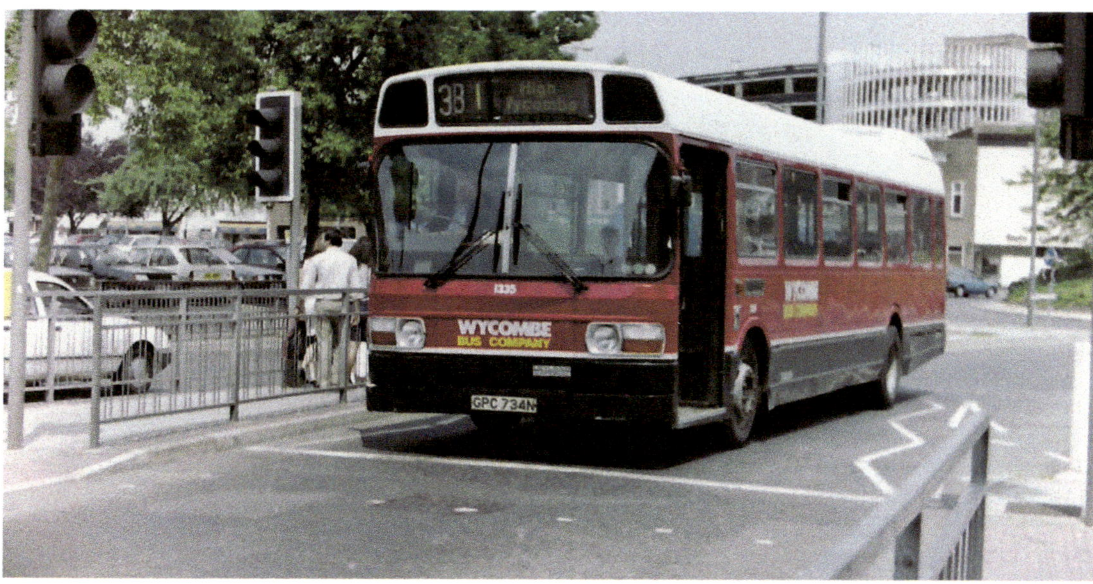

On 23 November 1990 The Bee Line's High Wycombe depot of fifty-one vehicles was sold to City of Oxford Motor Services (COMS). That operator had never previously run Leyland Nationals but seventeen came with the purchase. First to be repainted into Oxford's red livery was 1335 (GPC 734N), which in this June 1992 view was returning from Thame. Oxford simply prefixed the existing Bee Line fleet number with a 1. (Author's collection)

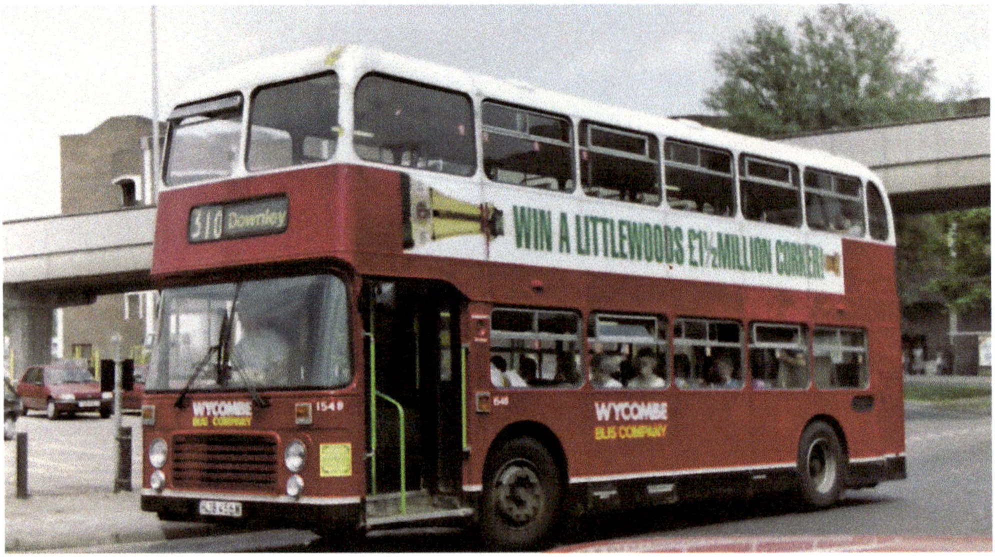

The standard Wycombe Bus Company double-decker was the ECW-bodied Bristol VR, which included all fourteen of Alder Valley's final batch registered HJB-W. Originally numbered 636, HJB 456W was 1549 when captured in June 1992 departing the bus station for Downley via Hughenden Road. The vehicle would go on to work for Hedingham Omnibuses in 1996. (Author's collection)

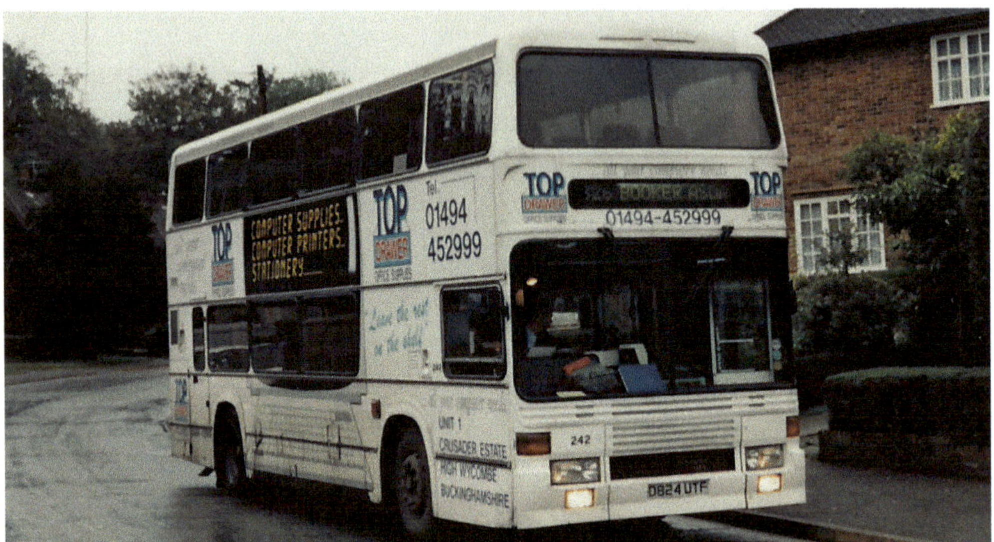

Shortly before the divestment of High Wycombe depot The Bee Line transferred the trio of short wheelbase ECW coach-bodied Leyland Olympians from Bracknell. These elegant vehicles were ideally suited for longer routes and not the hilly terrain of the town services upon which they spent much of their lives. All three had a mid-life refurbishment during 1994 at Oxford's Cowley Road workshops. At Woodside Road, Micklefield, on 17 October 1997 last of the batch D824 UTF works town route 326. Then numbered 242 and wearing an overall advert, the vehicle also carried the numbers 1624, 824 and 1824 (see page 83) and later saw service with Western Greyhound in Newquay.

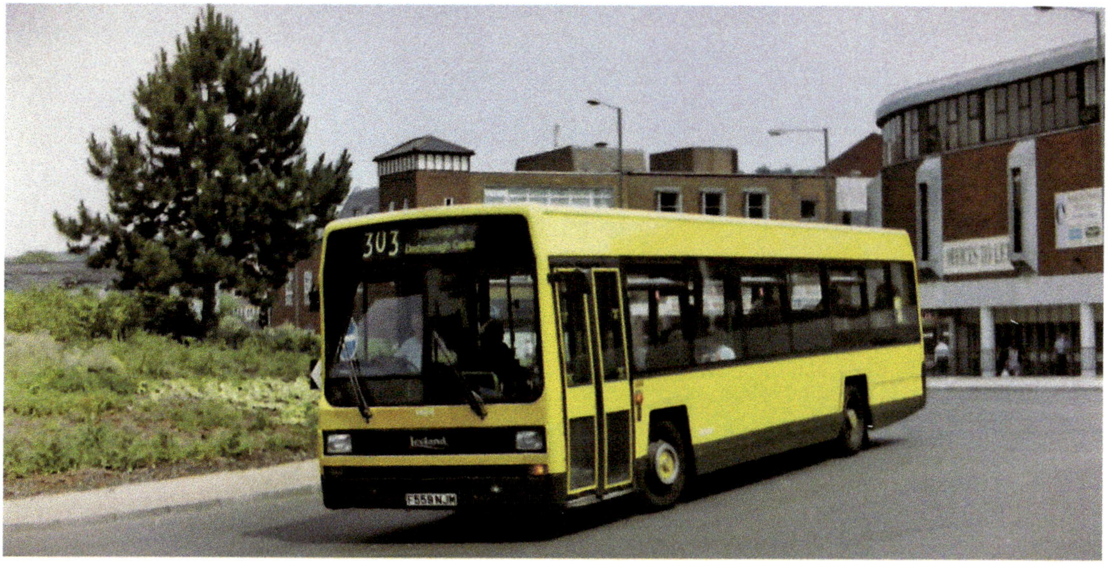

In 1988 The Bee Line received five smart Leyland Lynxes, which were allocated to High Wycombe. Their five-speed ZF gearboxes were well suited to interurban routes and the powerful Cummins engines made light work of the town's grueling gradients. Surprisingly they were some of the last buses repainted into Oxford's red livery and ran in the condition shown by 1404 (F559 NJM), making its way around the Oxford Road/Abbey Way roundabout in June 1992. It is on cross-town route 303 to which two of the type were regularly allocated. The lazy blind was inspired by earlier joint operation with London Country. (Author's collection)

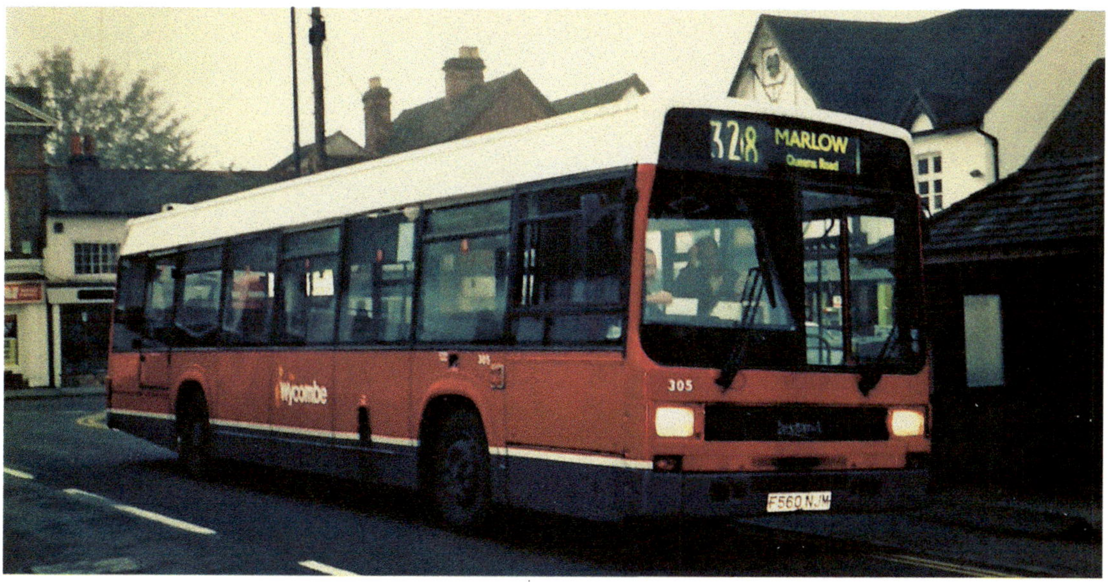

In December 1995 the Wycombe fleet was renumbered into a three-digit series in common with Oxford Bus Company. Leyland Lynx 305 (F560 NJM), the last of the batch of five, is at Queens Road, Marlow, on 18 October 1997 on a Saturday morning 328 short working from High Wycombe. The bus will return at 07.39, this time on route 329. The Lynxes also received mid-life refurbishment at Cowley Road, being re-trimmed and re-panelled.

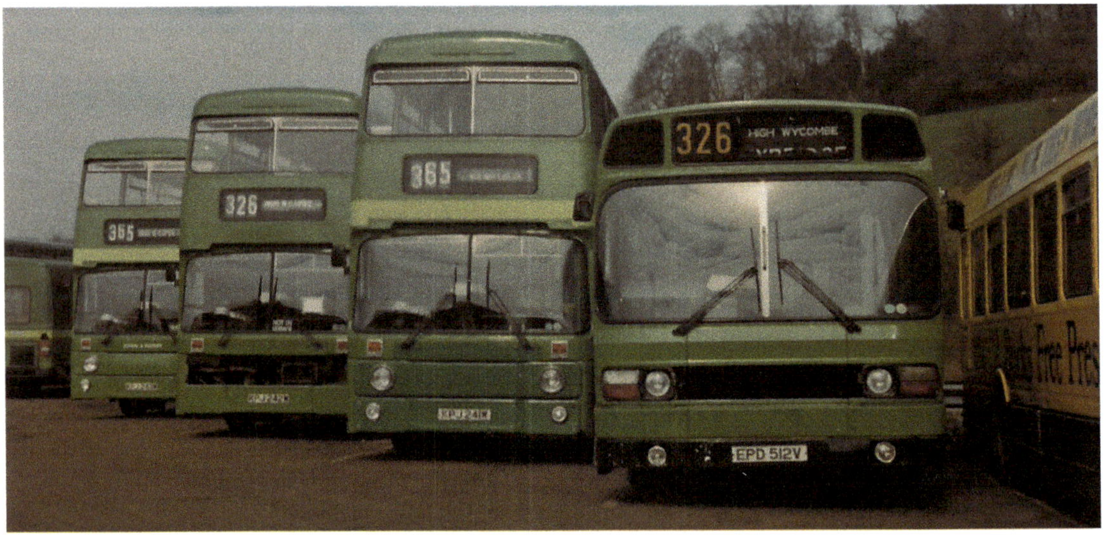

An outstation of Amersham in use from 1990 was a yard at the site of the old West Wycombe railway station, which was shared with BRS Trucks. Coded HW, this facility was pushed to capacity when Amersham closed. Despite this 1992 view dating from the Luton & District era, the scene could have been from NBC days with AN and SNB class vehicles dominating in leaf green livery. All were long-standing Amersham and Wycombe vehicles, and two of the town's local service route numbers can clearly be identified. SNB506 (EPD 506V), with Bucks Free Press overall advert, is just visible on the right. SNB512 (EPD 512V) would soon wear a scheme for a local VW dealership. In later years Heyfordian would use this yard. (Author's collection)

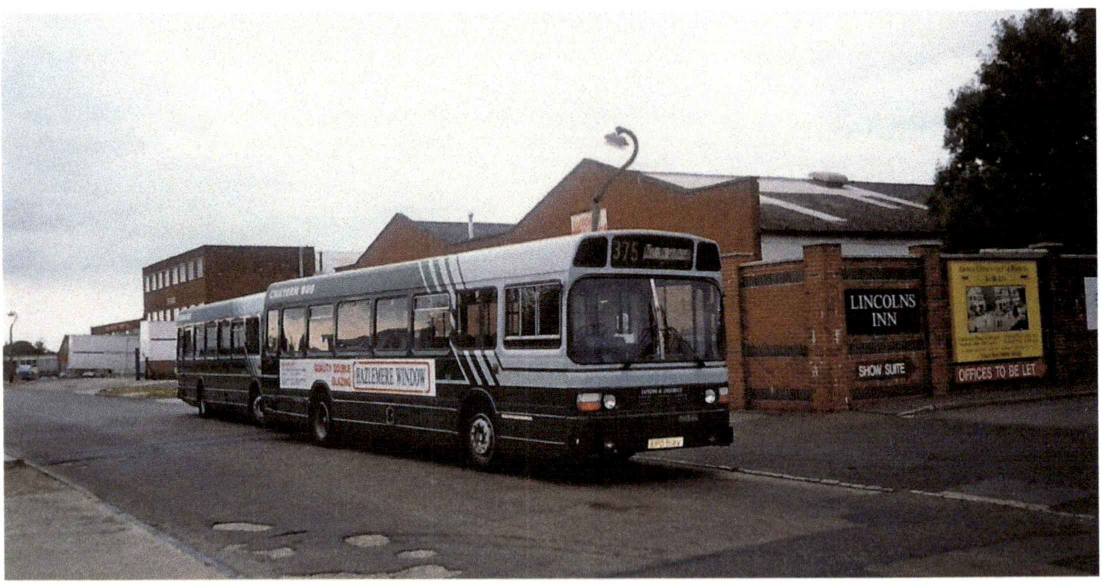

By April 1992 facilities at Lincoln Road, Cressex, were used. This industrial building was adapted for its new role with limited undercover parking, bus wash and offices. On 8 July 1993 SNB514 (EPD 514V) has returned for the night after working the infrequent 375 service between Beaconsfield and Amersham. In November 1992 it was fitted with forty-one dual-purpose seats, a luxury shared with sister vehicle SNB515, both long-term residents of the area.

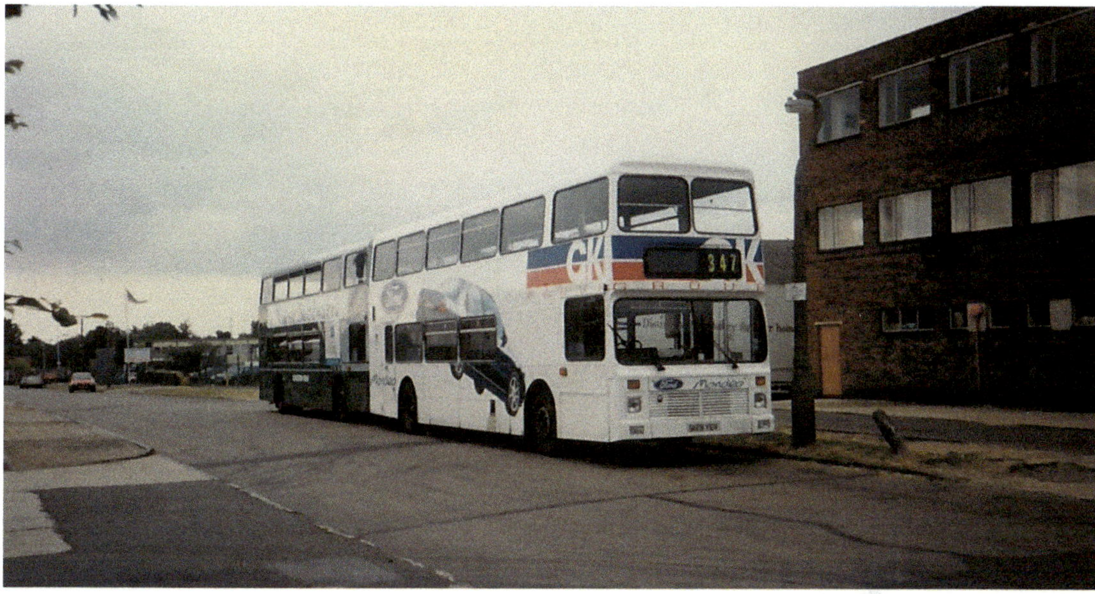

On Lincoln Road itself, after being fuelled and washed, Northern Counties-bodied long-wheelbase Leyland Olympian LRL29 (G129 YEV) is waiting to be parked in the depot with one of its fellows behind. Four of these vehicles were acquired by London Country NW in 1991 from Ensign Bus when only a year old, their previous owners using them on London sightseeing work. After a brief spell at Watford all four would serve at Amersham and High Wycombe for nearly twenty years.

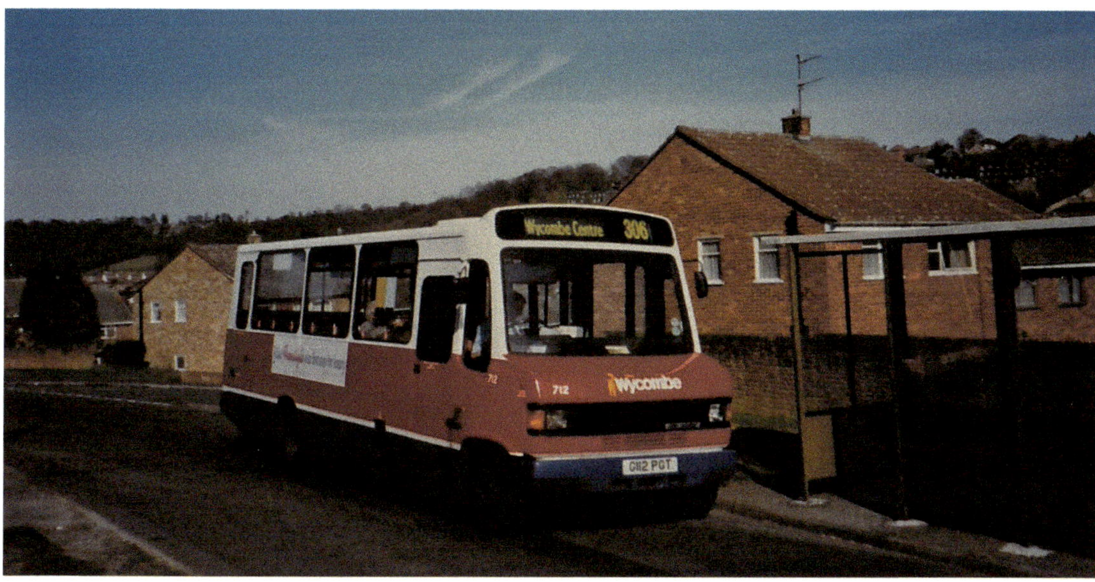

From July 1995 long-standing London Country route 365 to Hicks Farm Rise became the 306 and 307, and additionally served estates across town off Desborough Road. From the same date a blue skirt and change of logo was implemented by the Wycombe Bus Company. Pictured at Roebuck Avenue on 7 April 1997 is 712 (G112 PGT), one of fourteen Alexander AM-bodied Mercedes-Benz 811Ds new to London General.

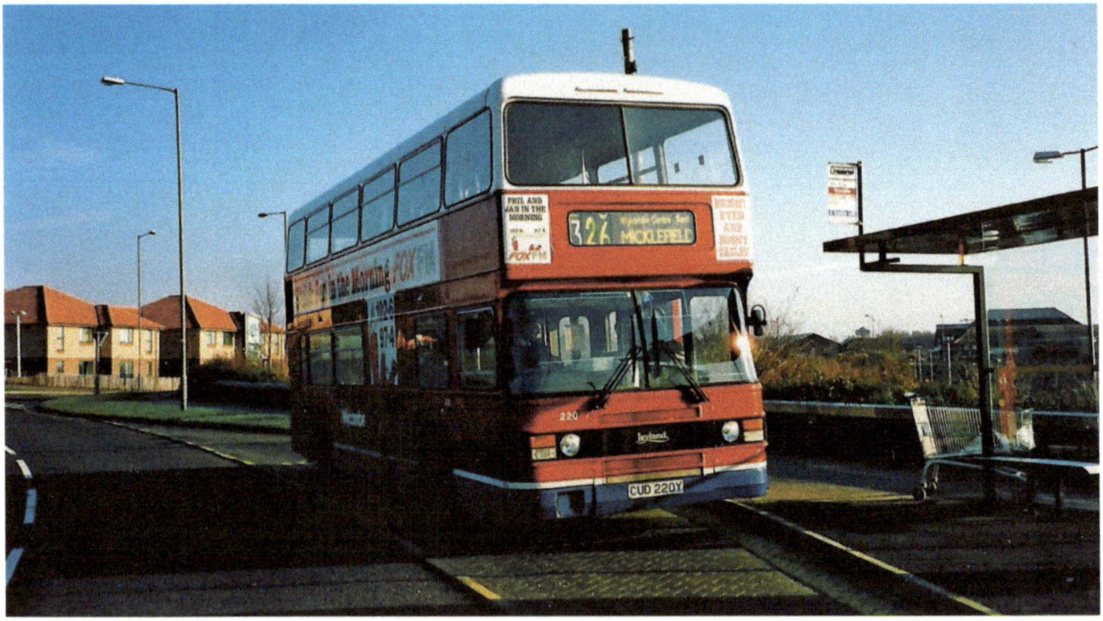

Vehicle hires and transfers from the main Oxford fleet were common, as needs dictated. With minibuses and coaches in earlier days Leyland Olympians and Titans would appear in the latter days of the operation. From Oxford's last batch of ECW-bodied Leyland Olympians 220 (CUD 220Y), with Wycombe fleet names, was at Holmers Farm Road, Booker, the Asda terminus of route 326, on 30 November 1998.

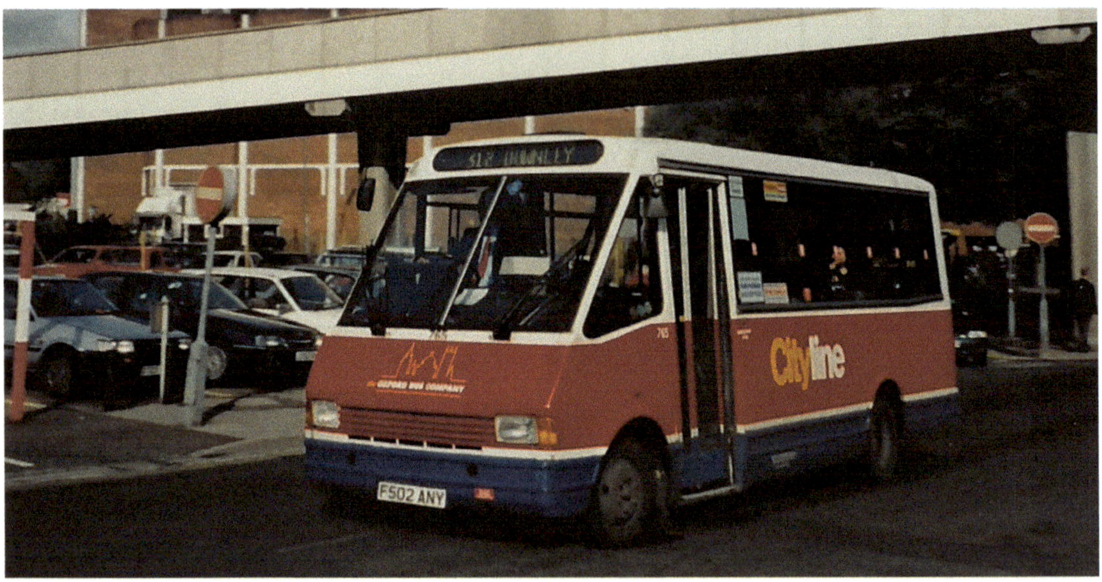

Eight MCW Metroriders, which would be replaced relatively shortly by Mercedes-Benz 811Ds from London, were used from April 1995 in Wycombe. On loan from Oxford, and carrying that depot's Cityline branding of the time, 765 (F502 ANY) has at least had its destination blinds programmed for its stay. Viewed on 17 October 1997, this bus is one of five that Oxford Bus Company had acquired from Merthyr Tydfil Transport.

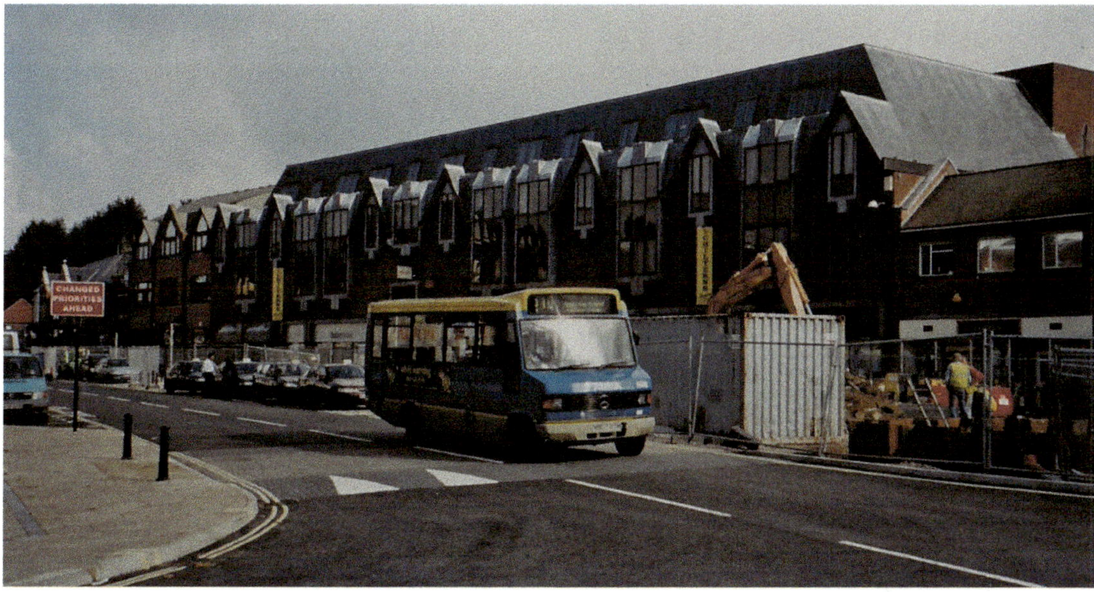

Also returning from Downley, on 20 September 2001, is Plaxton Beaver-bodied Mercedes-Benz 709D 2127 (N907 ETM) of Arriva the Shires. Evidence of past history can be seen; route 310 is of Bee Line/Wycombe Bus origin. The bus is first of the batch new to Hemel Hempstead as MP257 in September 1995, The Shires yellow and blue livery is still worn but with the addition of an Arriva logo and a black-on-white new fleet number sticker on the bonnet. Frogmoor is the location and is under redevelopment. Historically this area was the bus terminus.

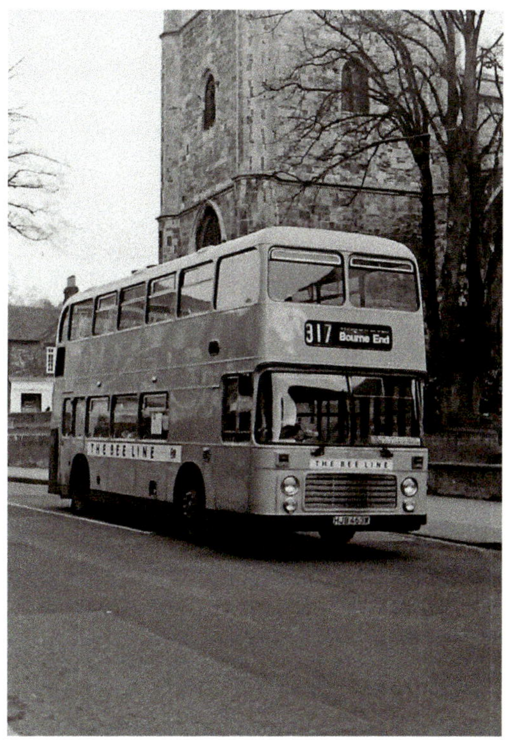

Passing All Saints Parish Church in 1987 is The Bee Line's 556 (HJB 463W) on a street that is now pedestrianised. The 317 at the time offered three journeys per hour, one to Maidenhead or Reading and two as far as Bourne End where the ECW-bodied Bristol VR is heading. The route followed a similar path to the disused railway, which once ran to the latter destination from High Wycombe. In 1992 the bus was sold to Partridge of Hadleigh before moving on to Walls of Manchester. By 1995 it was with Alpine of Llandudno and was eventually scrapped in 2007. (Kevin Lane/author's collection)

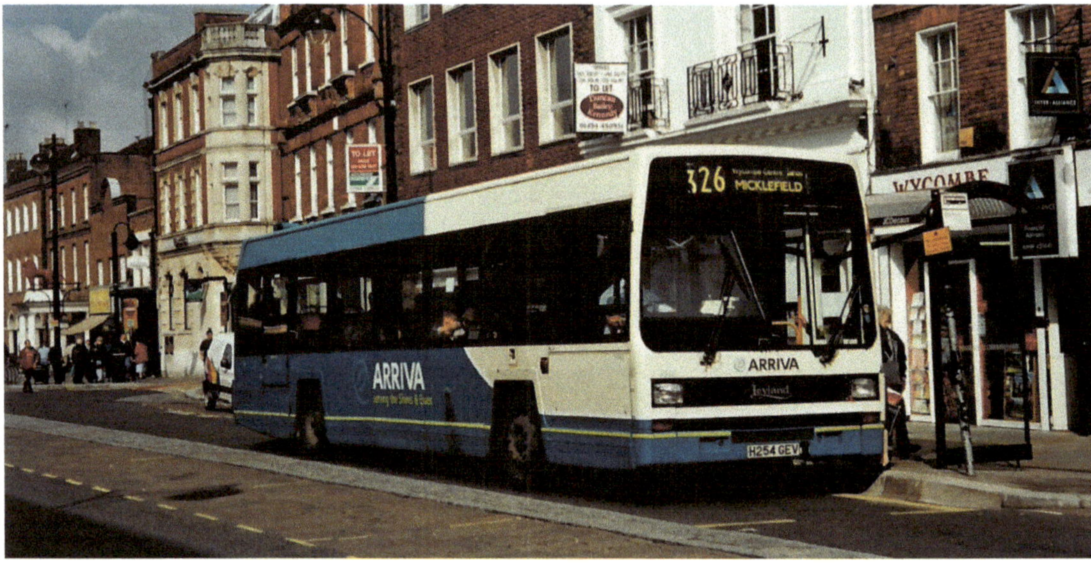

Under Arriva ownership High Wycombe depot amassed a collection of Leyland Lynxes from various sources. New to County's Harlow depot as LX254 in August 1990, H254 GEV was by now numbered 3344 in the combined Shires & Essex fleet. With the main section of the High Street now pedestrianised buses used Corporation Street to access bus stops at the eastern end. The marked centre parking bays were for queuing taxis. The Red Lion on the left of the picture once guarded the entrance to the hotel bearing that name. However, by the time of this 20 September 2001 view the building was occupied by a branch of Woolworths.

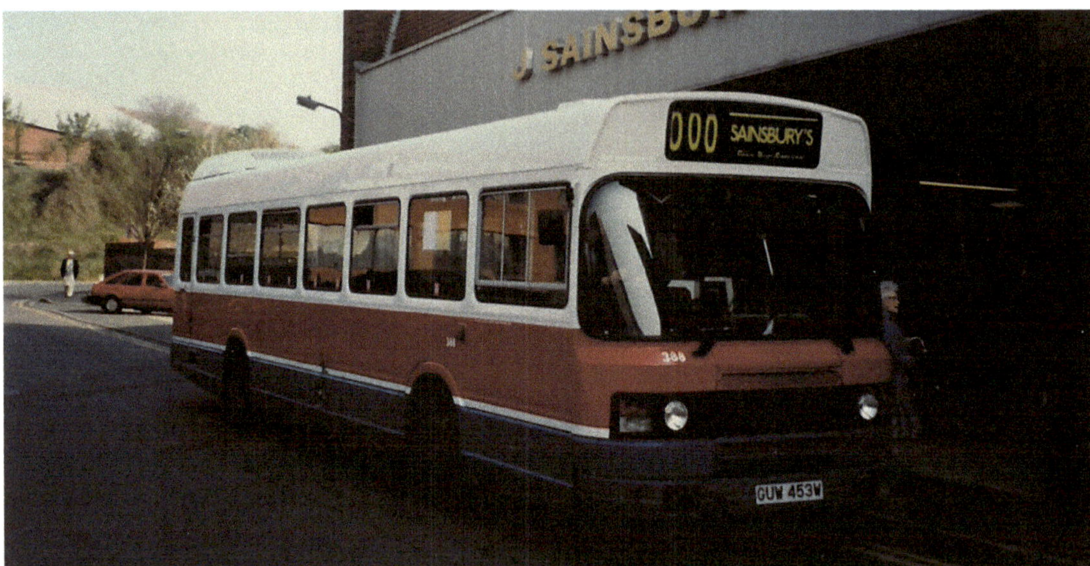

Former London General LS453 (GUW 453W) was 388 and on 10 April 1997 was working the Sainsbury's free bus service to the store located at Dovecot. The route, which originated with Alder Valley North in 1986, was about a half-mile round trip and ran Monday to Friday off-peak, usually worked by a minibus. Today's Eden bus station is roughly parallel to where 388 is standing and the Sainsbury's store has been rebuilt to front Oxford Road.

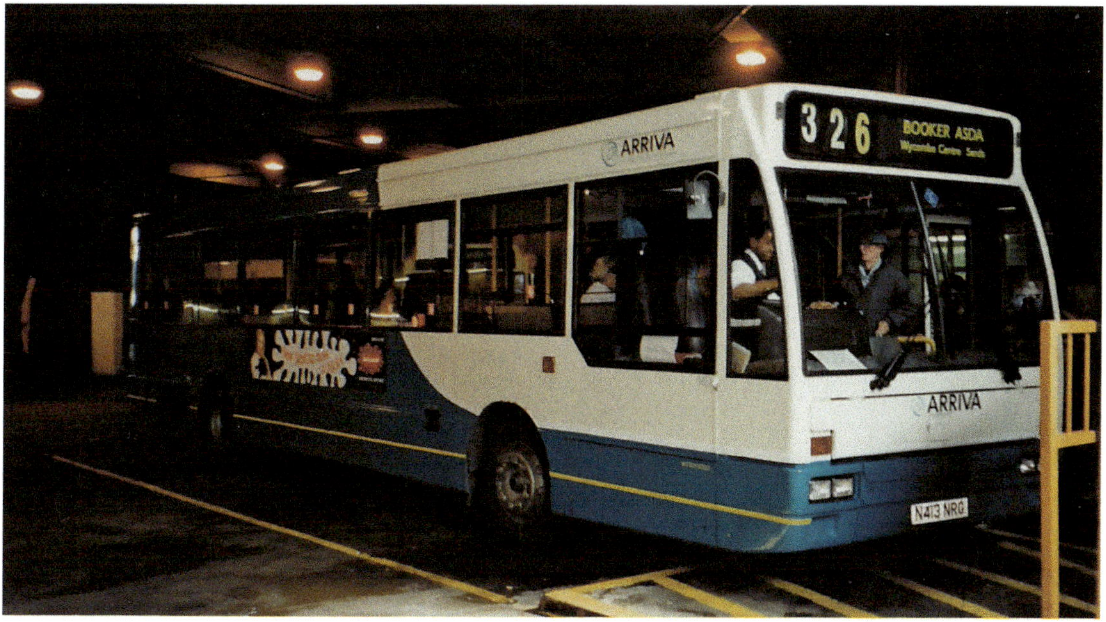

With Union Street no longer being used by cross-town routes all departures were now contained within Newlands bus station. Plaxton Verde-bodied Volvo B10Bs 621–627 were acquired from Oxford in April 2000 to replace the Leyland National 2s. Now under Arriva ownership 3853 (N413 NRG), formerly 625, loads for Booker on bay C. Some refurbishment has occurred over the years, but the gloom of the bus station can be appreciated from this 20 September 2001 view.

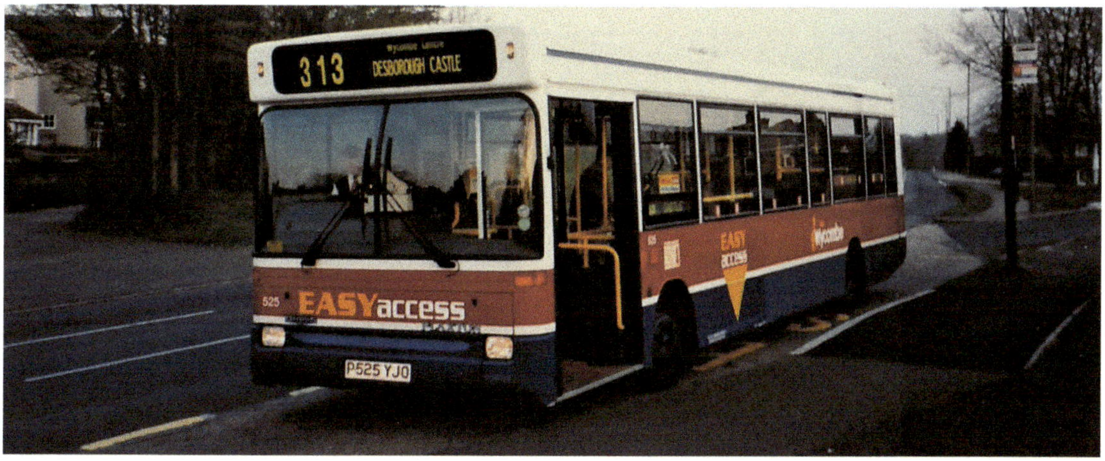

The first new vehicles for High Wycombe since the Leyland Lynxes arrived in June 1996, 521–527 were Plaxton Pointer-bodied Dennis Dart SLFs similar to those delivered to The Bee Line at the same time. All seven were branded 'Easy access' and used on routes 303/313 between Desborough Castle and Totteridge. These routes were altered as part of the July 1995 changes and followed a loop to Totteridge via Bowerdean estate, the 313 as shown running clockwise. On 10 April 1997 525 (P525 YJO) stands at Totteridge Lane/Tyzack Road, once the terminus used by London Country route 360 before the MAP survey revisions. The loops were not a success and the route reverted to using this location as a turning point, access to the stop being gained from the road on the right.

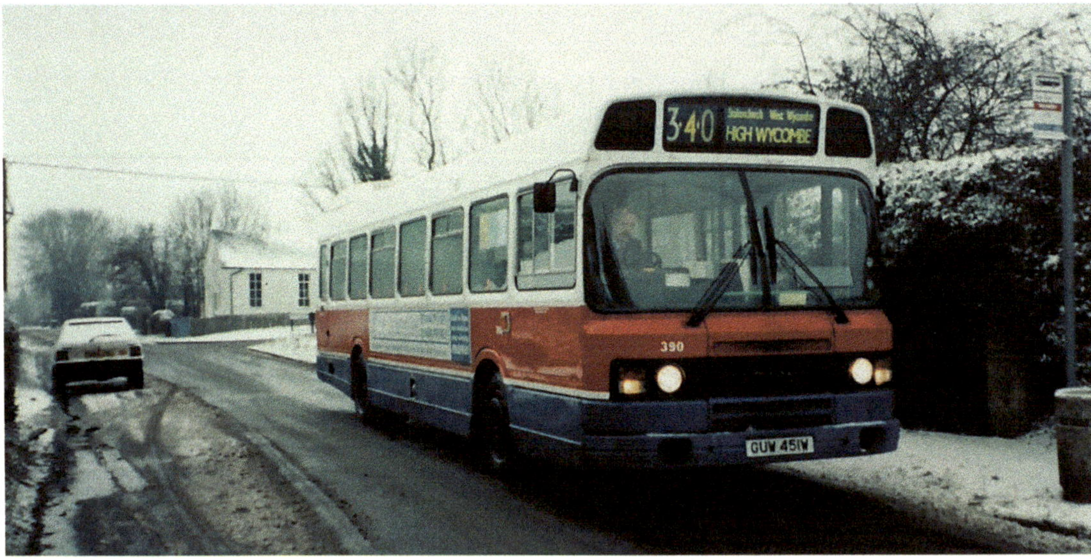

One of the trio of Leyland National 2s from Uxbridge, 390 (GUW 451W) stands in very different surroundings to those in its past life as LS451 on express route 607. This is the rural Buckinghamshire village of Radnage in wintry conditions on 17 December 1997, the bus about to work the 15.05 back to Wycombe on the last of the five Monday to Friday journeys. The rectangular frame in the nearside windscreen was a common feature of many operators' vehicles around this time and was intended for rail replacement boards or signs.

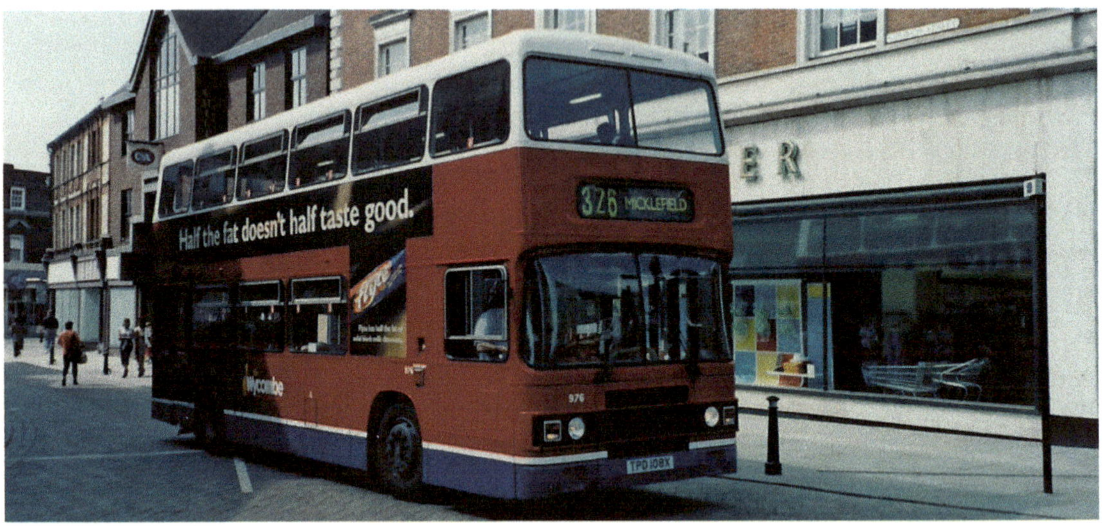

Five Roe-bodied Leyland Olympians were acquired in February 1999 from Arriva Londonlinks. These had been used in the Croydon area and were once part of the London Country LR-class. Numbered into Oxford's highbridge 9xx series, 976 (TPD 108X) was once LR8. Used on all routes at Wycombe their stay was brief and all were sold before the Arriva takeover. Ironically, members of the same class used by Arriva the Shires would be used on these routes once more when Wycombe Bus Co. was taken over. On 1 June 1999 the bus makes the turn from Church Street to Castle Street via the bus gate bollards, lowered by the transponder mounted on the pole to the right of the picture.

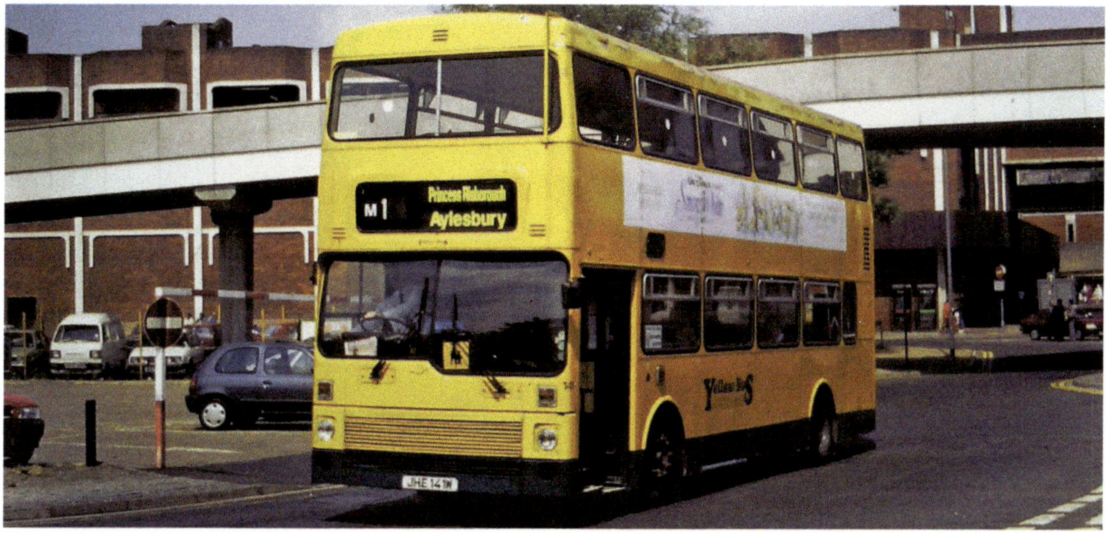

Motts Travel's route M1 was established to compete with Wycombe Bus Co. on two of its main corridors, namely Aylesbury and Lane End. The M1 also had journey variations as far south as Reading. The main double-deckers used were MCW Metrobuses with Rolls-Royce engines, new to South Yorkshire PTE. In this 1994 view JHE 141W displays two fleet numbers and that familiar yellow livery. Initially, random numbers featured, although in late 1993 those matching the registration numbers were used. The destination blinds are smart and in good condition, unlike the roof, which betrays the fact that many of the roads served had low trees! All five Metrobuses were sold to Cardiff Bluebird in July 1995. (Stewart J. Brown/author's collection)

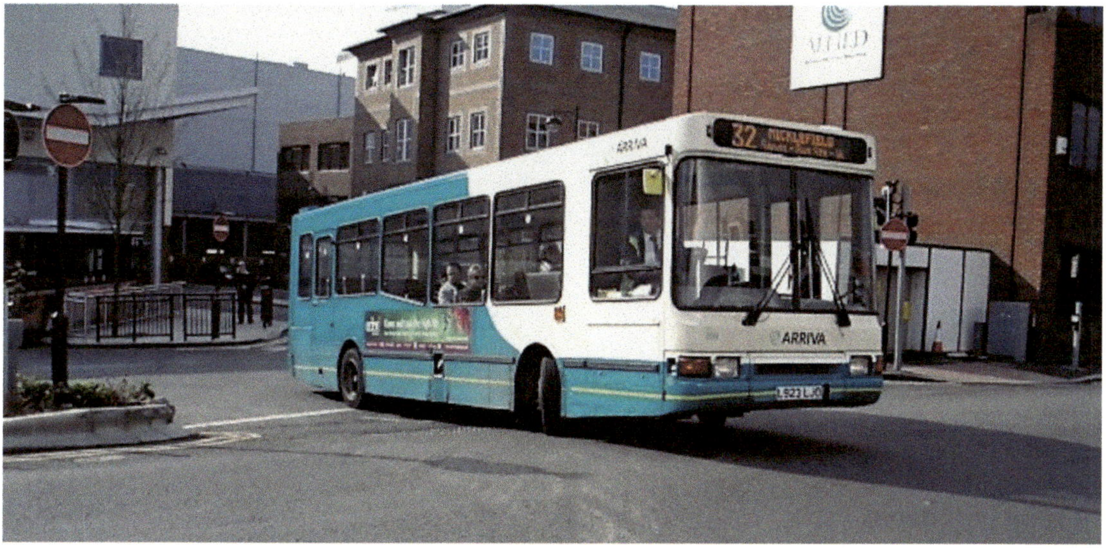

In 1994 Motts' Yellow Bus received its only new single-deck vehicles, two Northern Counties Paladin-bodied Volvo B6s. Both passed to the Shires in July 1995, slotting in well with similar examples in their fleet. The pair worked from High Wycombe depot on routes they had previously competed against. L923 LJO, formerly 923 but now numbered 3139, had received a new LED destination blind when observed on 16 April 2008, making the tight right-hand turn from Eden bus station. Route 32 was previously numbered 326.

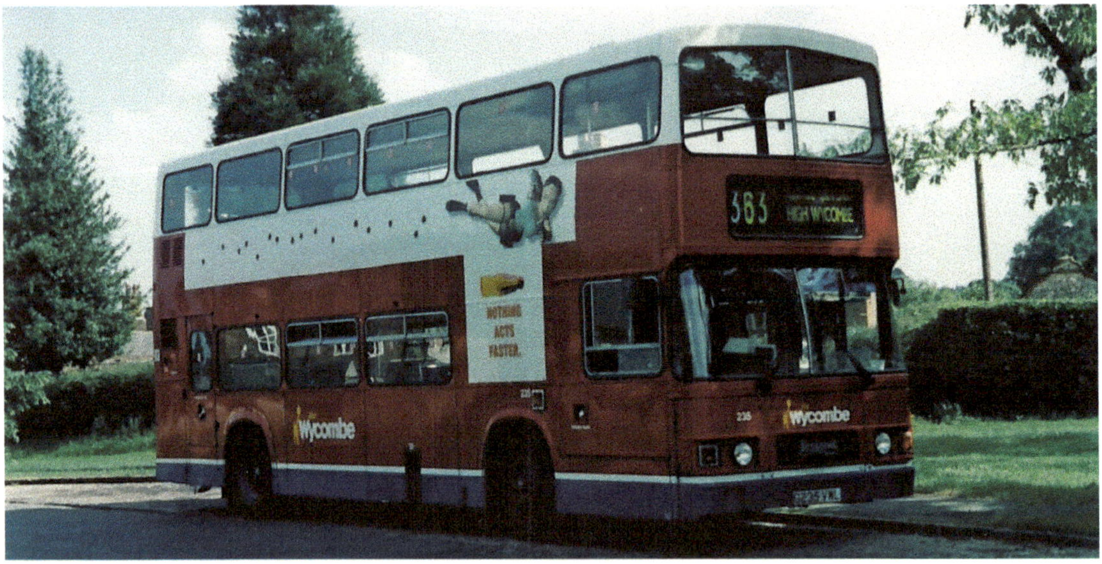

In March 1996 three of the batch of six G-registered Alexander RL-bodied Leyland Olympians were transferred from Oxford. All were converted to single-door configuration with a Bristol VR rear bench seat placed where the exit door had been. Last of the batch 235 (G235 VWL) was at Penn terminus of route 363, in what was once London Country territory, on 1 June 1999. All of this batch would eventually work from Wycombe, passing to Arriva in 2000. They transferred to other Shires depots, Luton in this case, and clocked up twenty years' service before sale to private operators.

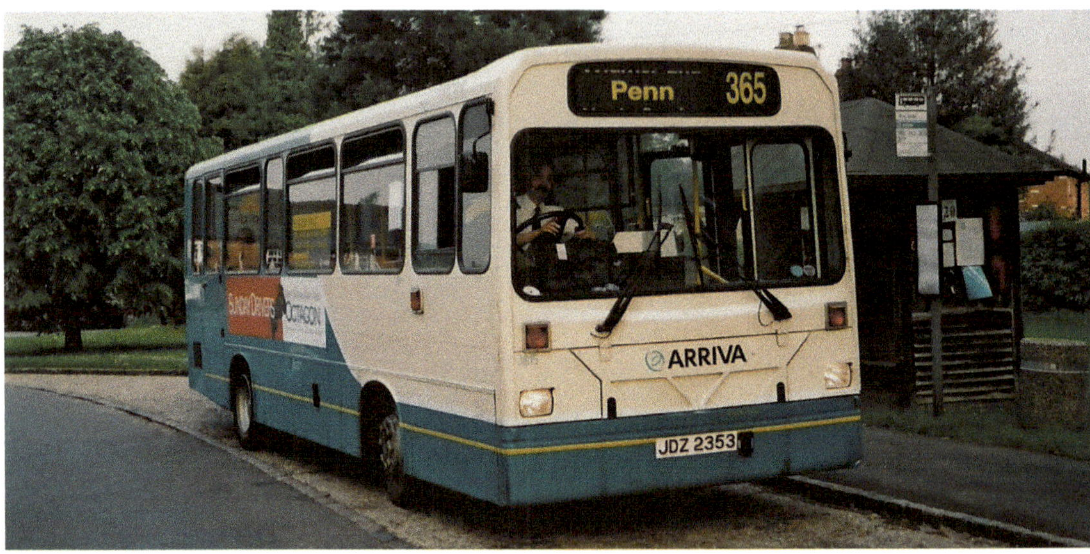

Acquired from fellow Go-Ahead companies London Central & London General in December 1999 were seven DW-class Dennis Darts with Wright Handybus thirty-seat bodies. All would pass to Arriva and remain at High Wycombe, acquiring the nickname 'bouncy castles' because of their lively riding characteristics. Formerly London Central DW53, JDZ 2353 was numbered 525 then 3825 with Arriva the Shires & Essex. It is laying over at Penn on 28 May 2003 while working the evening and Sunday route 365, which also served Widmer End.

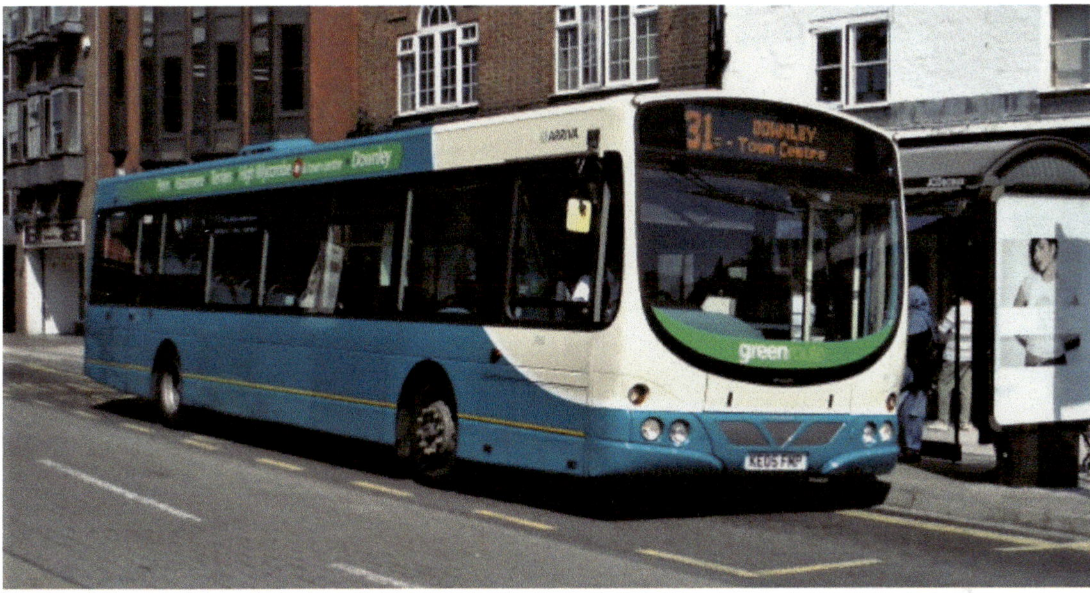

In 2005 Wycombe depot received some much-needed new vehicles: seven Volvo B7RLEs with Wright Eclipse Urban bodywork. Branded for green route 31, linking Penn to Downley via the town centre, 3865 (KE05 FMP) has been numbered into the series reserved for former Wycombe Bus vehicles, identified by the presence of the number 8 as the second digit. Loading at Oxford Street on 7 May 2008, the bus is heading for Downley. The batch would later be transferred to Luton.

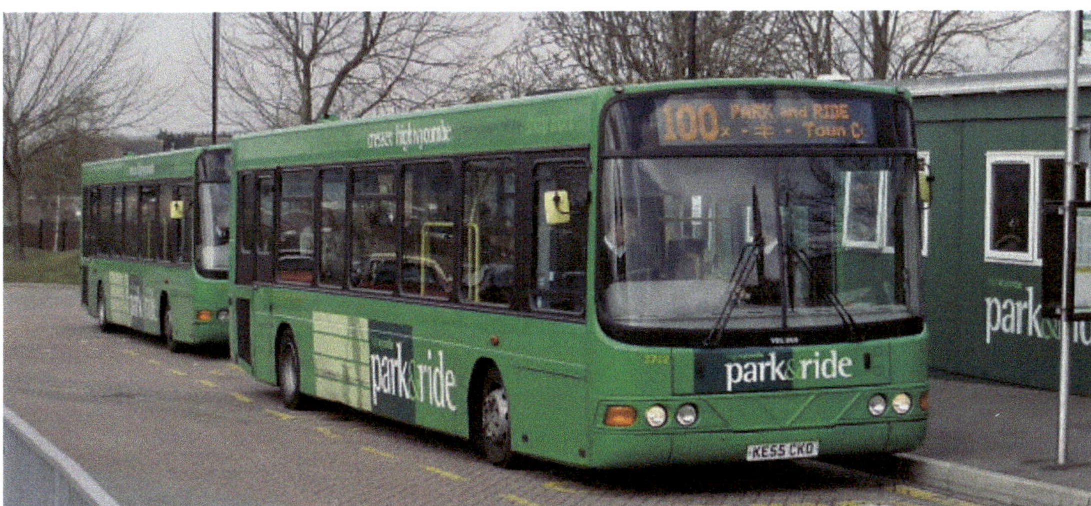

Also arriving in 2005 were a trio of Wright Cadet-bodied VDL SB120s for a new P&R service, which was launched on 5 September 2005. Initially using a car park off Crest Road, Cressex, the route ran to the town centre via the hospital and railway station. Loading for the town centre on 16 April 2008 is 3702 (KE55 CKO) with a similar vehicle behind and passenger facilities seen on the right. The site closed when a new coachway facility was opened at Handy Cross leisure centre. The bus would later become a driver training vehicle with Arriva Midlands, numbered 9553.

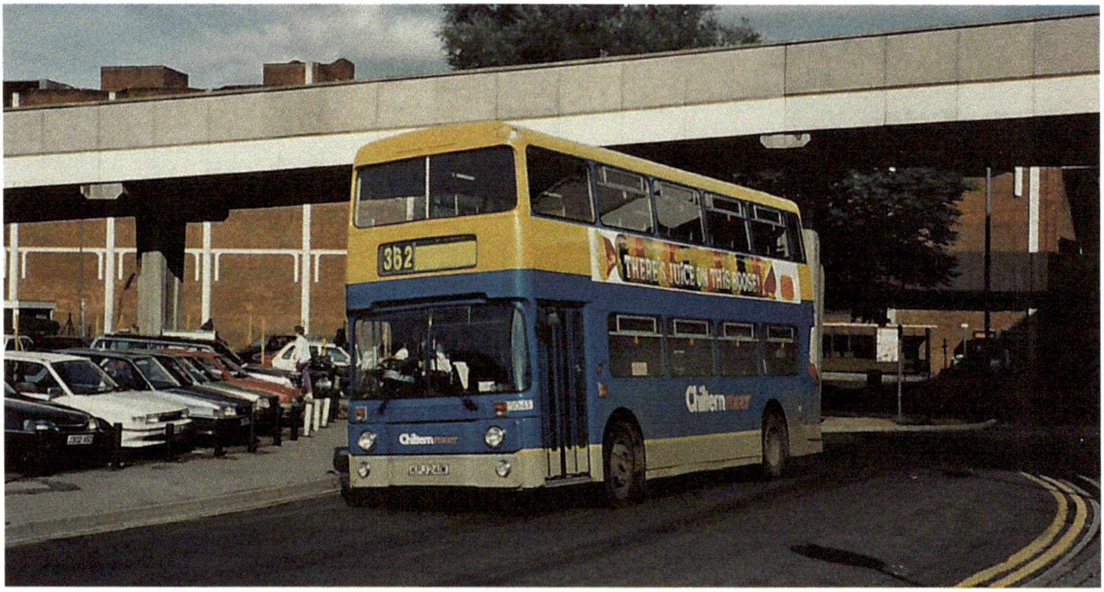

Despite being the backbone of the High Wycombe allocation, the Leyland Atlantean AN-class spent some fifteen years in adapted London Country NBC green before any were treated to a new coat of paint. The Shires yellow and blue livery was in use by this time and 5041 (KPJ 241W), previously AN241, shows off the scheme at Newland Street while heading for Amersham and Chesham on 17 October 1997. By the end of 1998 the last ANs were withdrawn, three becoming open toppers for Guide Friday sightseeing work, one of which went to Madrid.

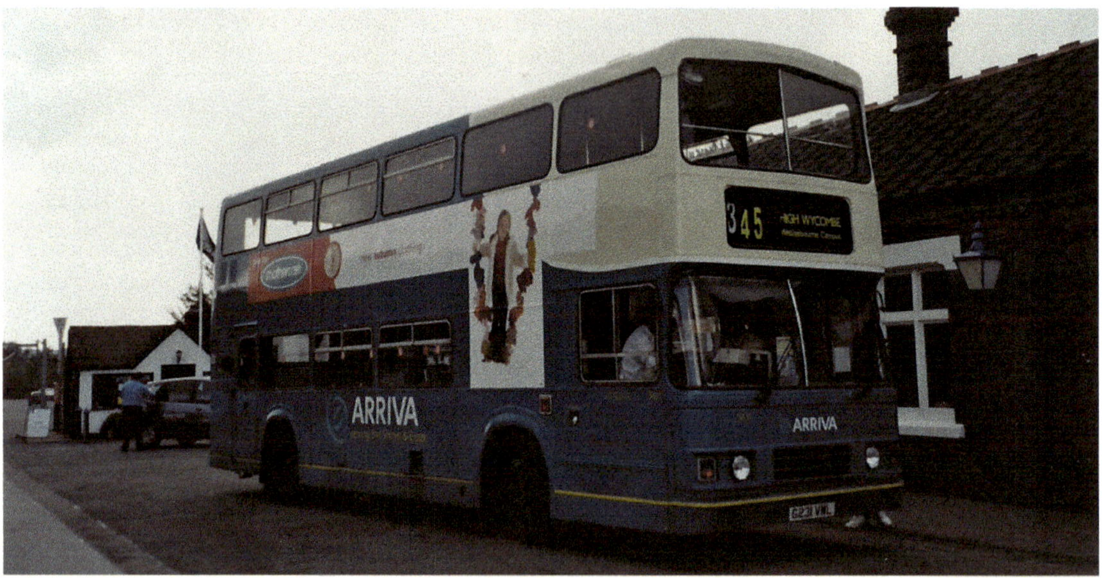

The Metropolitan Railway opened Great Missenden station in 1892. It was later served by the Great Central and today by Chiltern Railways. Buses served the forecourt where Arriva the Shires & Essex 5831 (G231 VWL) has terminated on 20 September 2001, having run from High Wycombe on the main 345 route. This Leyland Olympian with Alexander RL body was new to Oxford Bus in 1990 as 231 and was later transferred through Arriva to Luton depot.

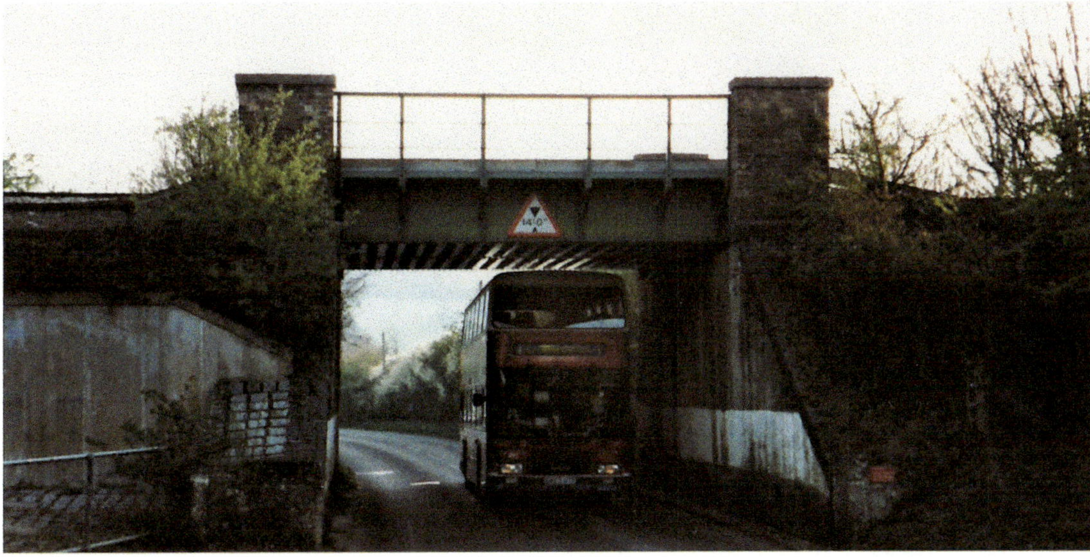

Making a similar journey, this time on the less frequent 344 route, is ECW coach-bodied Leyland Olympian 241 (D823 UTF). On 9 April 1997 it had departed Great Missenden at 07.40 and was working along Nags Head Lane, Little Kingshill, where there was little clearance under the Aylesbury to Marylebone railway line. Three of these coaches were ordered by Southern Vectis but instead delivered to Alder Valley. Arriving at Wycombe depot from Bracknell in 1990, the bus would later become 5823 with Arriva.

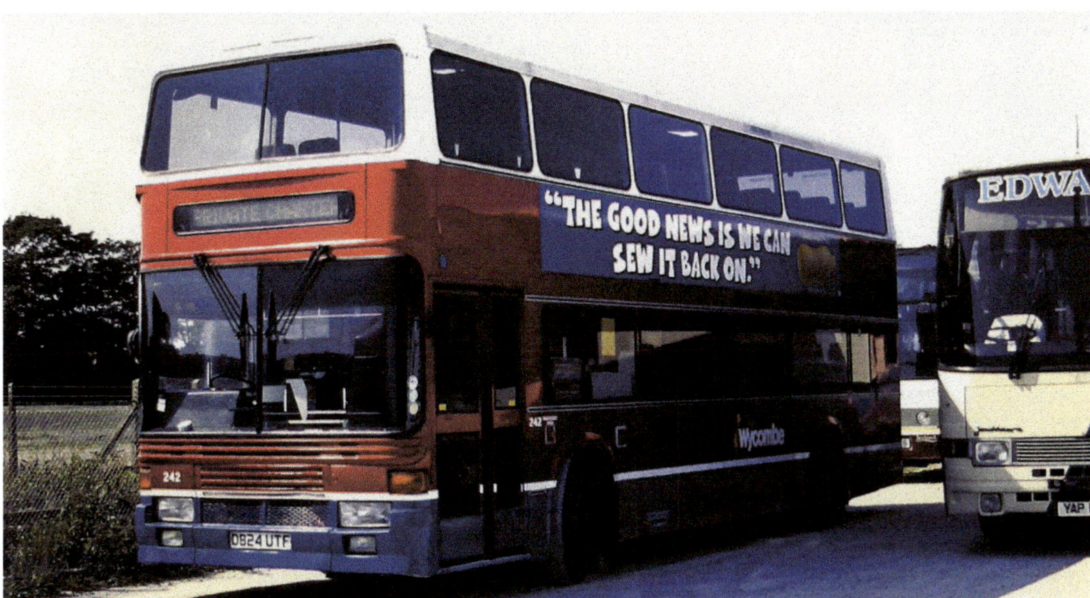

Sister vehicle 242 (D824 UTF) is doing what it does best: working a long-distance journey. The Bee Line had seasonal express routes from various depots to coastal resorts, which Wycombe Bus kept running until 1992 and on occasion members of the trio were loaned to Oxford for coach work. Wearing standard Wycombe Bus livery, 242 is parked up in Weymouth on 16 August 1998 working a private hire. (Author's collection)

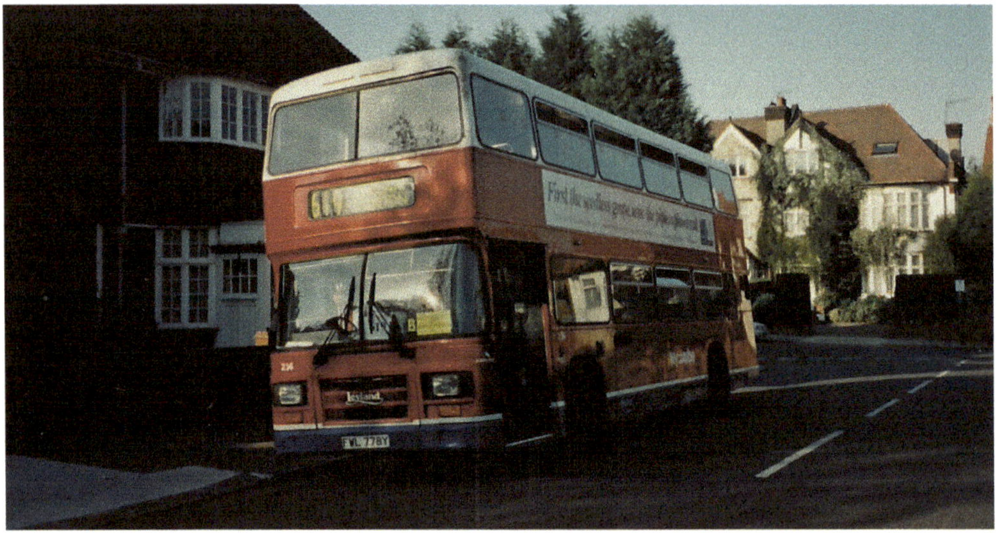

In 1991 Oxford Bus Co. acquired four ECW-bodied Leyland Olympians from AERE Harwell where they had been used on staff transport. These single-door vehicles, new in 1983, had low mileages and were used on various city and interurban routes. From September 1995 all four were progressively transferred to Wycombe after internal refurbishment. First of the batch, FWL 778Y was initially numbered 1778, then 1825, and by December 1995 its Oxford number 236 was again in use. From 1997 Wycombe Bus Co. became heavily involved in rail replacement work on behalf of London Underground, and on 19 October the bus was spotted laying over at Coverdale Road, Kilburn, while working a Jubilee Line replacement.

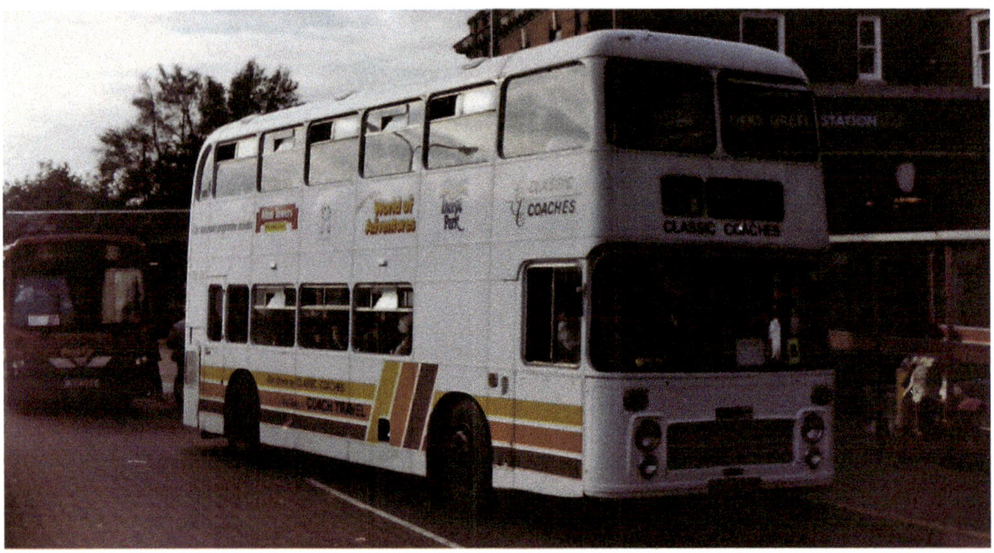

Established in 1992, Classic Coaches built up a varied fleet of heritage vehicles. These were used on contracts, heritage services and an excursion programme. Service work and rail replacement was later undertaken and one-time Southern Vectis ECW-bodied Bristol VR NDL 637M replaces the Northern Line at Golders Green. The vehicle was acquired in February 1996 and ran for four years. It is now preserved in Solent Blue Line livery at the Isle of Wight Bus Museum. (Colin Lloyd/author's collection)

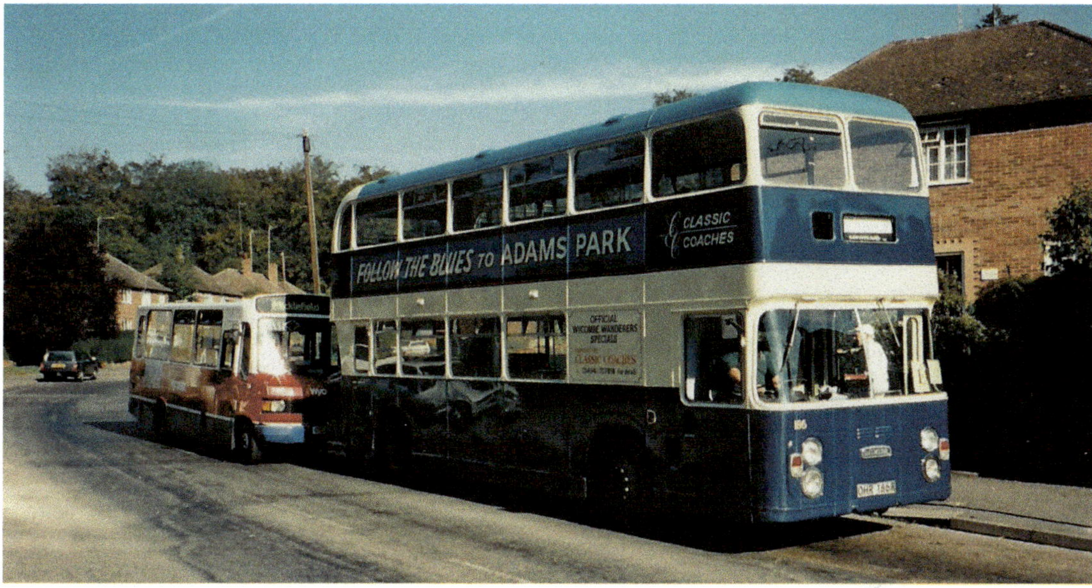

Closer to its operating base is former Thamesdown Transport ECW-bodied Daimler Fleetline OHR 186R, one of a pair joining the fleet in June 1996 from Jacobs of Fair Oak. Classic Coaches and Motts Travel ran a number of match day buses for Wycombe Wanderers FC at Adams Park, for which the bus is sign-written. Picking up at Woodside Road, Micklefield, on 18 October 1997 for a match against Bristol Rovers, the home team would win 1-0.

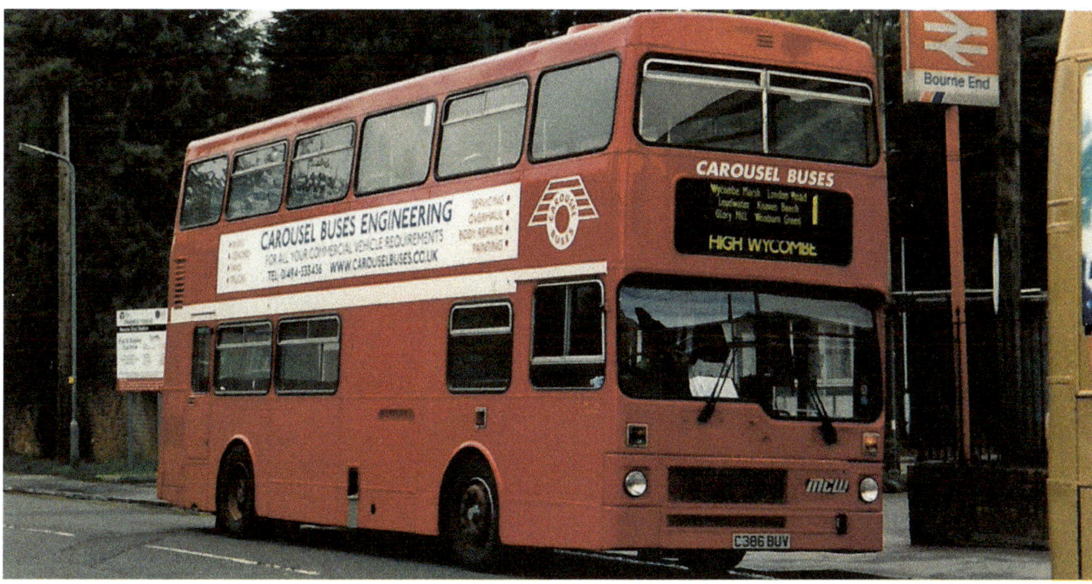

Carousel built up a good reputation in High Wycombe. Early contract wins were college route 400, schools work and rail replacement, alongside some commercial services. Route 1 ran from High Wycombe to Holtspur with certain journeys diverted via Bourne End to serve the railway station. M1386 (C386 BUV) has arrived at this location on 26 May 2002. At this time the fleet consisted of nine Metrobuses all smartly turned out in a red livery, with a full set of blinds and London Country-inspired logos.

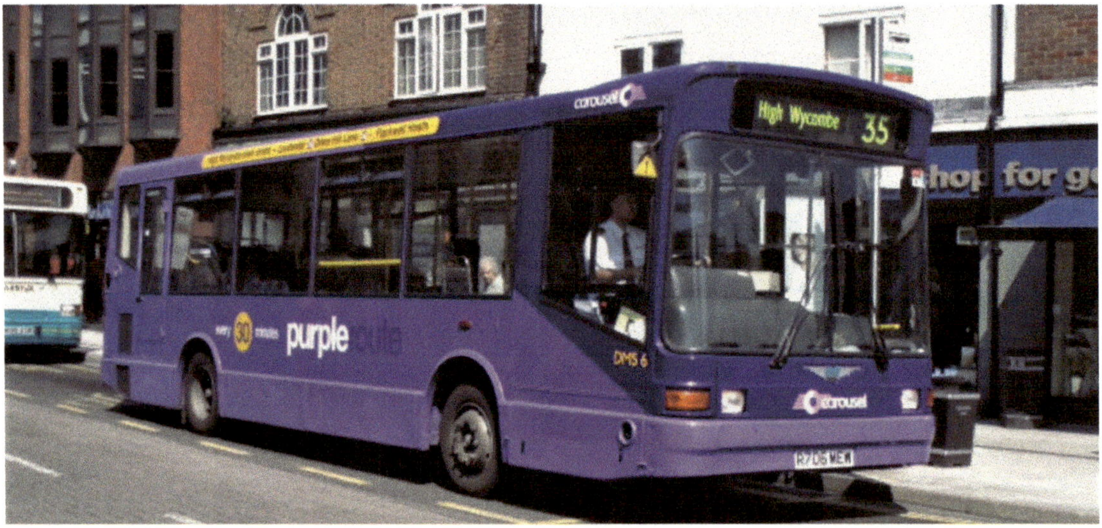

By the time this view was taken on 16 April 2008 Carousel had just over fifty vehicles in its fleet. Of London origin once more is former Metroline Marshall Capital-bodied 9.3-metre Dennis Dart SLF DMS6 (R706 MEW). It is branded for the Flackwell Heath route upon which it is operating on Oxford Street, High Wycombe. The 'rainbow route' was part of a network sponsored by Buckinghamshire County Council. The bus later carried standard red livery and was scrapped by ASM of Aylesbury in 2011.

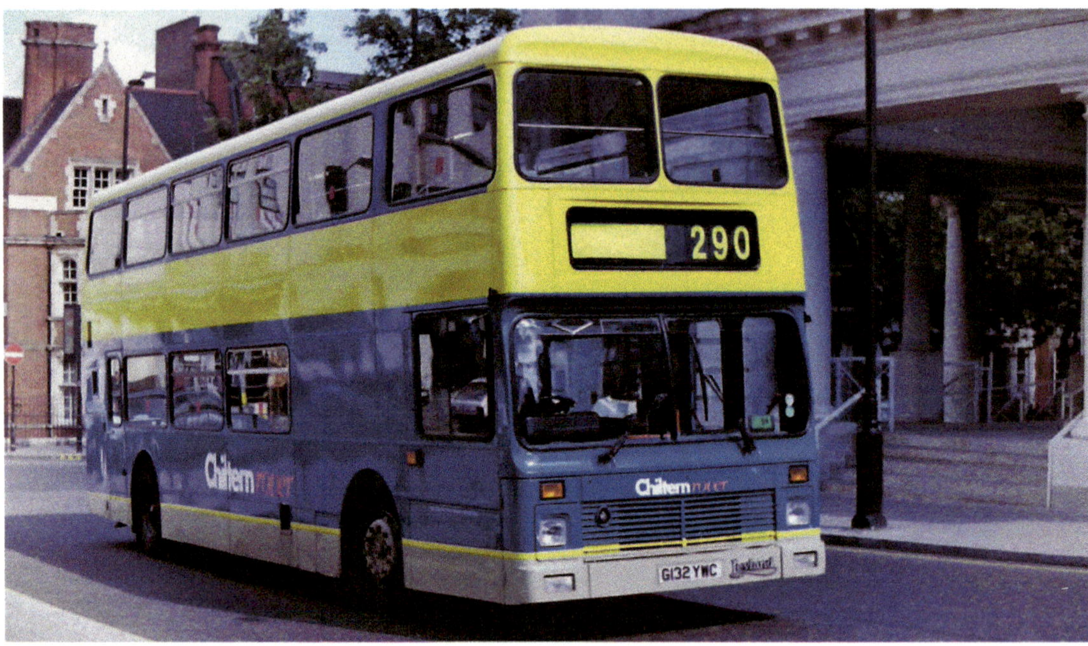

The four Northern Counties-bodied long-wheelbase Leyland Olympians were often used on Green Line routes including the seasonal ones to the coast. In 1995, LRL32 (G132 YWC) is at Bullied Way, Victoria, on the main 290 route wearing newly applied the Shires livery and still displaying its running number in the nearside windscreen. This long-term Wycombe-based vehicle was later numbered 5135 with Arriva. (Colin Lloyd/author's collection)

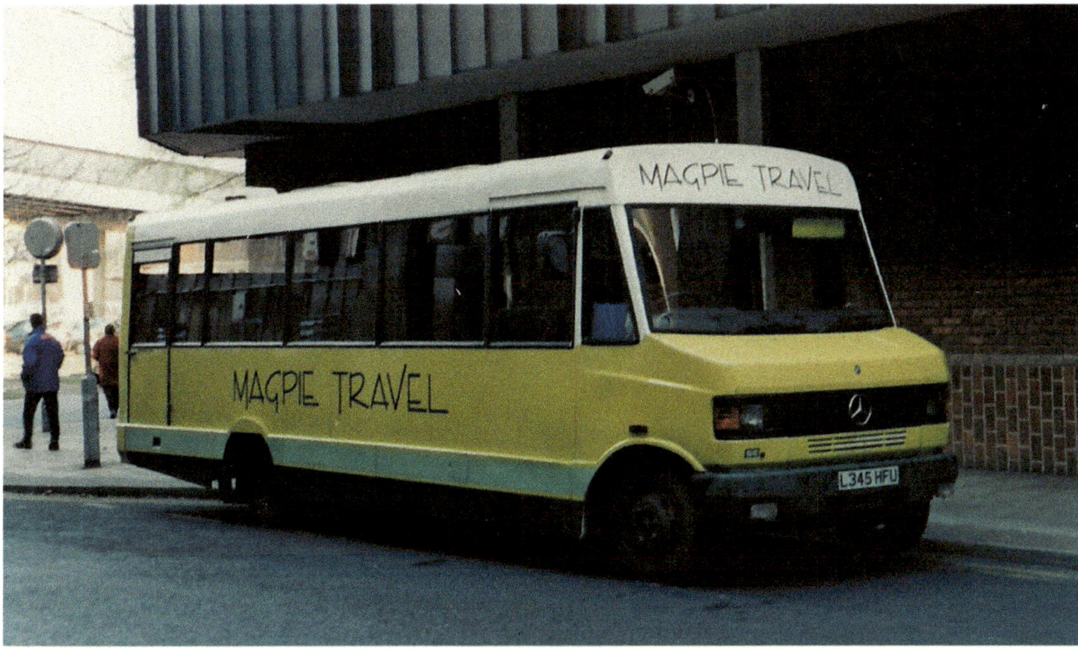

By 1998 the 290 was down to just a couple of journeys operated by Magpie Coaches and later Beckwith Coaches, both of High Wycombe. Magpie applied Green Line livery to ex-Aztec of Bristol Autobus Classique-bodied Mercedes-Benz 0814D L345 HFU, seen waiting outside Newlands bus station in Wycombe on 30 November 1998.

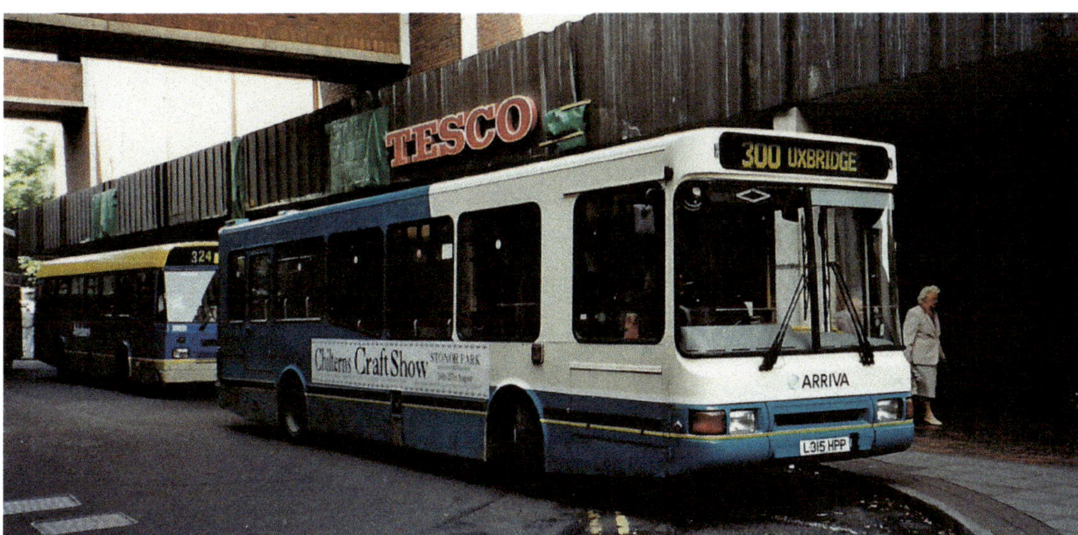

The Uxbridge to High Wycombe route 705 was renumbered 300 in April 1996 and ran hourly. Occasional journeys ran beyond Wycombe to Oxford via the A40 serving Stokenchurch, Tetsworth and Wheatley. Northern Counties-bodied Volvo B6 3115 (L315 HPP) of the large Luton & District batch waits outside Newlands bus station to take up a journey to Uxbridge on 20 September 2001. The route number 300 would later be applied to the Aylesbury service on which the vehicle behind, a Leyland National Greenway, is operating.

Amersham, Chesham and Buckinghamshire Coach Operators

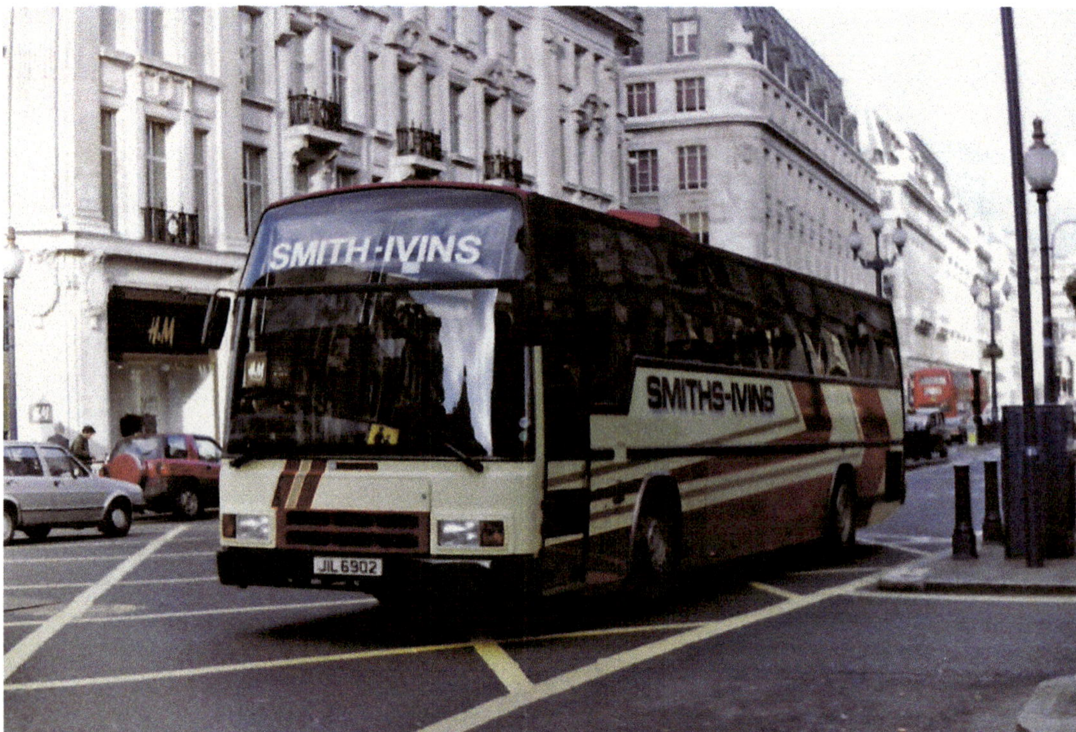

Smith-Ivins was an operator based in High Wycombe and Maidenhead, and was formed of several smaller companies including Carters and Martins Coaches. Plaxton Paramount-bodied DAF JIL 6902 was new as F214 RJX to Chambers of Stevenage in December 1988, and is operating along Regent Street by Oxford Circus in Smith-Ivins' distinctive livery. (Colin Lloyd/author's collection)

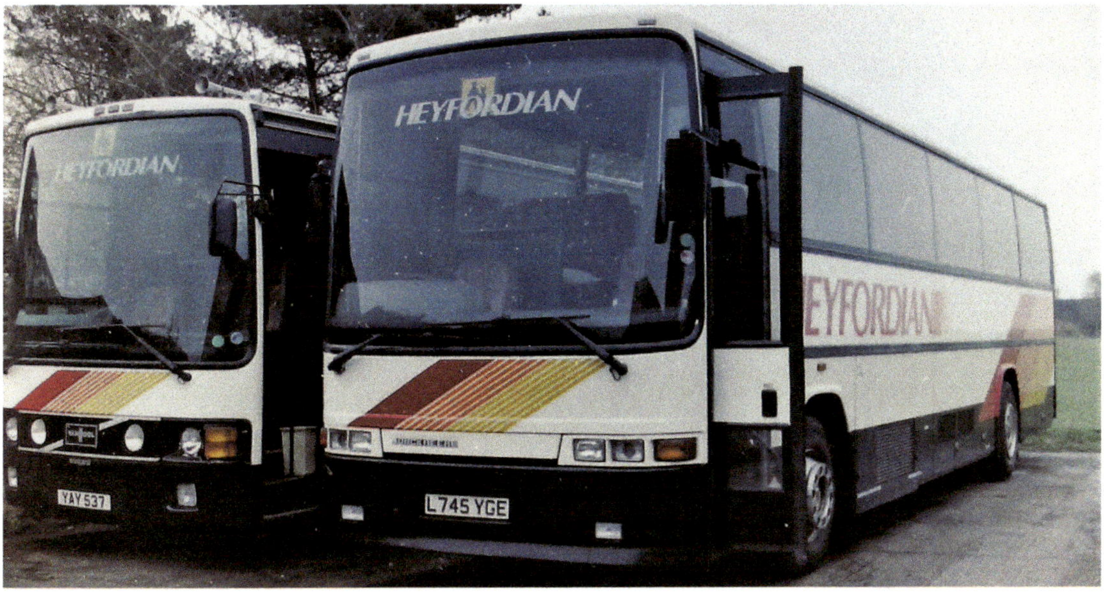

Heyfordian Travel was established in 1947 and built up a large fleet of coaches and buses which ran from five depots in Oxfordshire and Buckinghamshire. Differing European coach styles can be compared on these two Volvo B10Ms: Van Hool Alizee-bodied YAY 537 (F483 OFT), ex-Durham City Coaches, and Jonckheere Deauville L745 YGE, new to Parks of Hamilton. The latter would go on to be re-registered C15 TCL and saw use from January 2007 in the Tappins Coaches division.

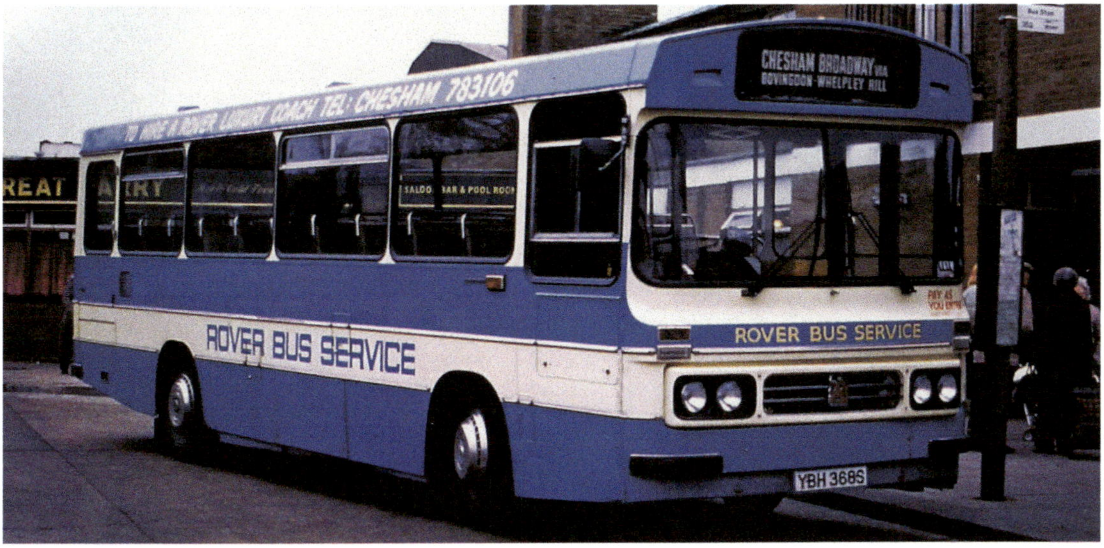

The hamlet of Lye Green is situated in the Parish of Chesham. It was home to long-established firm Rover Luxury Travel, founded by the Dell family in 1928. Two bus services were operated between Chesham and Hemel Hempstead, one jointly with London Transport until 1964. Buses for the routes were mostly bought new such as Bedford YLQ with Duple Dominant bodywork YBH 368S, later re-registered OJR 338, at Hemel Hempstead bus station. It has a detailed set of blinds, although a route number is not shown. (Author's collection)

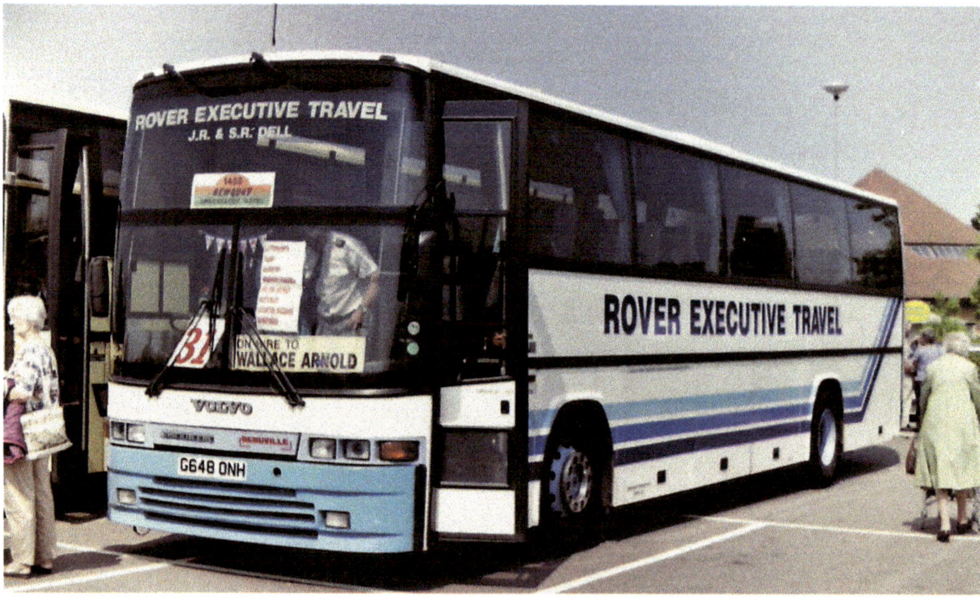

Coach feeder work was a good source of income with much of it performed on behalf of larger tour operators. Rover's immaculately turned out Jonckheere Deauville-bodied Volvo B10M G648 ONH, later re-registered TJI 8299, was new to Tellings-Golden Miller and acquired in 1994 from Redwood of Hemyock. On behalf of Wallace Arnold the careful transfer of luggage and passengers for destinations in the south midlands is taking place. The coach lasted with Rover until the company closed in 1999 and the Ambassador Hotel, Newquay, where the passengers had holidayed, is also now only a memory having closed in 2004. (Colin Lloyd/ author's collection)

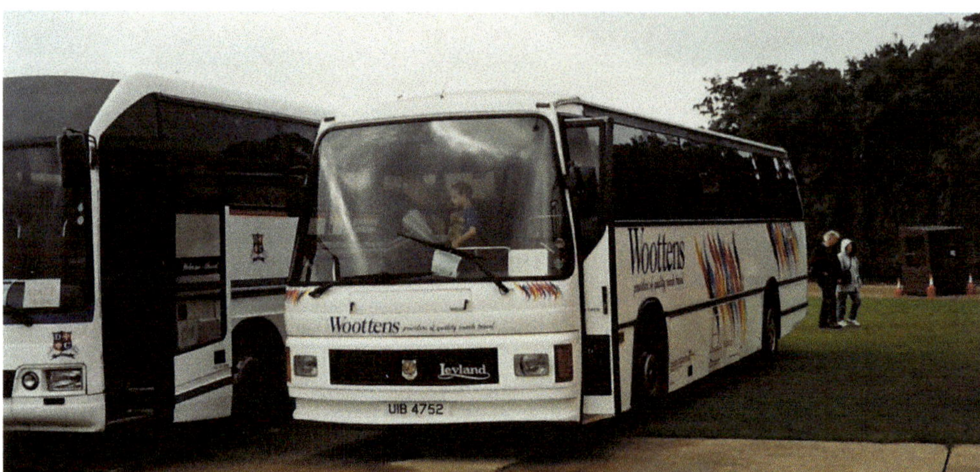

As Rover closed and vacated the Lye Green premises the site's phoenix was Woottens Coaches, established in April 1999 and moving there in August of that year. Continuing the tradition of immaculate vehicles running from the site, Woottens built up an excellent reputation and bought many new coaches for their operation. Leyland products were a favourite, an early acquisition being Duple Laser 2-bodied Leyland Tiger UIB 4752 (C913 XEO), new to Barrow-in-Furness Transport. It was at Showbus on 23 September 2001, the firm being a big supporter of the rally.

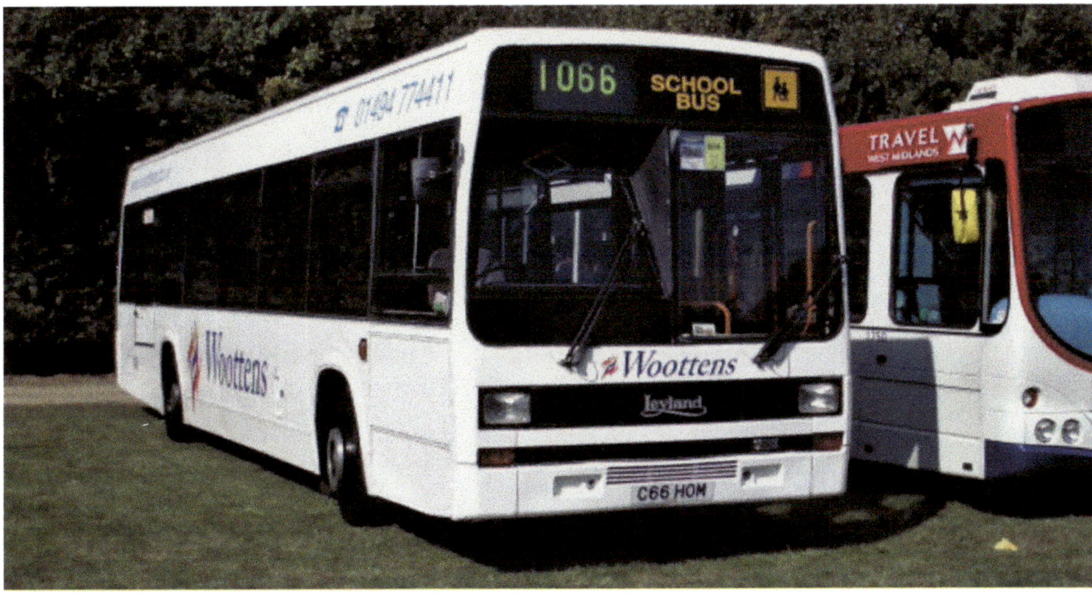

A number of buses were used by Woottens, many of which had been acquired from Oxford Bus Company. This included three early production Leyland Lynxes new to West Midlands Travel, who eventually operated 256 of the type. Following extensive refurbishment C66 HOM became trainer 972 at Oxford. Acquired in 2004, Woottens restored them internally to original condition. Perhaps travelling schoolchildren would associate 1066 with this Lynx, as well as the event in Hastings. Here it is basking in the sunshine at the 2008 Showbus event at Duxford.

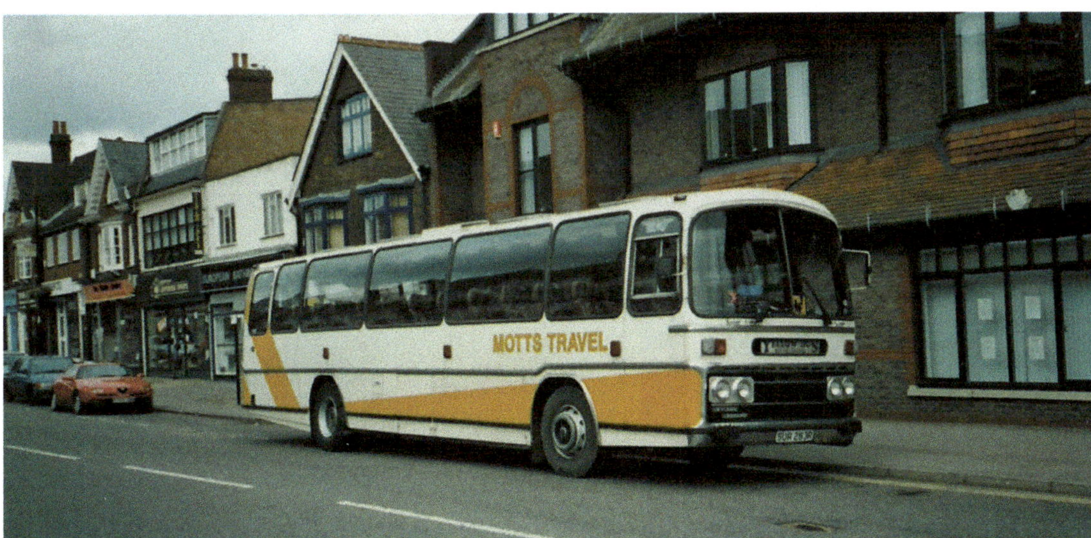

Ever-popular rail replacement work was also undertaken by Motts Travel and here Plaxton Supreme-bodied Leyland Leopard SUR 283R is a stand-by vehicle for Chiltern Railways faces Amersham station on 1 April 2001. Acquired from Clarkes of Southall in 1987 when ten years old, the coach saw regular use on Yellow Bus work as the destination blind and Wayfarer machine indicate. Painted in pseudo-1970s Motts livery the coach was a likely candidate for preservation, but which sadly never came to be.

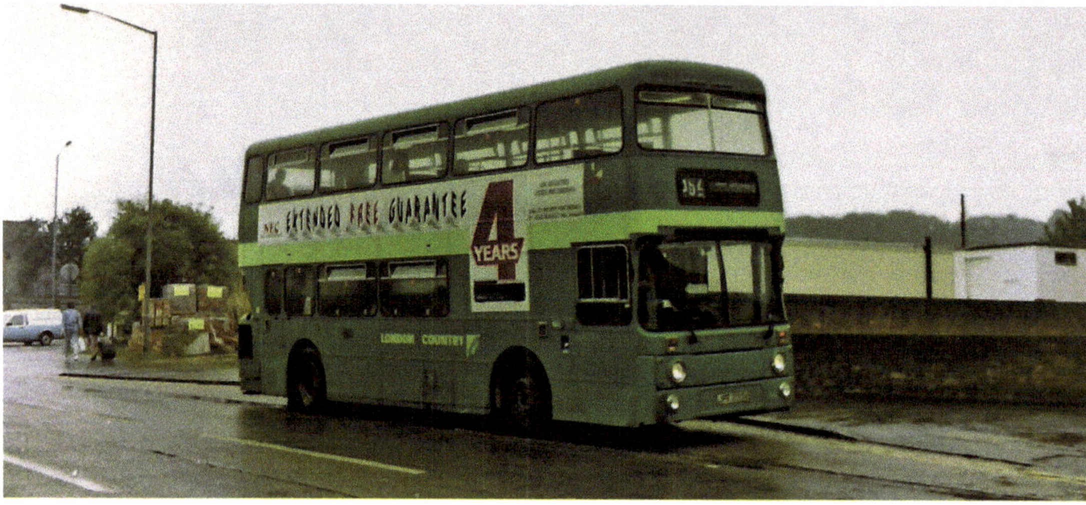

Down the hill at Amersham Old Town we are on The Broadway opposite Amersham garage, coded MA by London Country. Roe-bodied Leyland Atlantean AN233 (JPE 233V) stops to allow a crew-change while working the main trunk route to High Wycombe. London Country's AN-class Leyland Atlanteans totalled 293 examples delivered across all divisions between 1972 and 1980. Upon privatisation the North West operation received sixty-one of these original ANs, along with some examples LCBS had acquired second-hand from other operators. Amersham garage operated vehicles at both ends of the age range. With London Country North West fleet names the bus would remain a long-term resident of the area, moving to High Wycombe depot when Amersham closed in April 1992. (Author's collection)

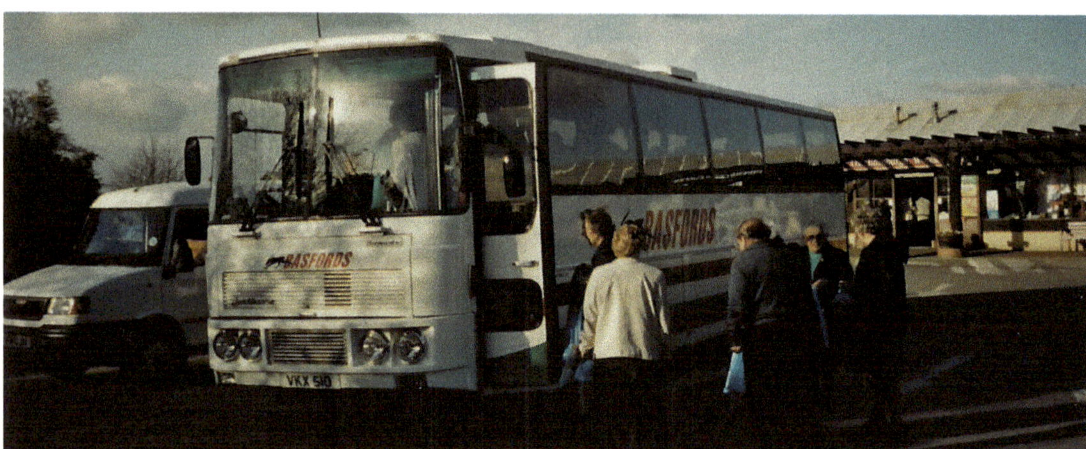

Jeffs Coaches was another company built as an amalgamation of several smaller firms operating in Northamptonshire, Oxfordshire and Buckinghamshire. All vehicles wore the standard livery of white with red and green stripes and leaping deer logo, but local company names appeared on the sides. Jonkheere Bermuda-bodied Volvo B10M VKX 510 (XNV 145W), once exhibited at the 1981 Commercial Motor show, was an uncommon type when new. Displaying Basfords fleet names and based at their depot in Greens Norton, Northamptonshire, the coach was caught on 26 March 2002 at the Worlds End garden centre in Wendover. Having filled the boot with plants, shrubs, and garden ornaments the group are boarding the coach for their return journey to Brackley.

Aylesbury and The Vale

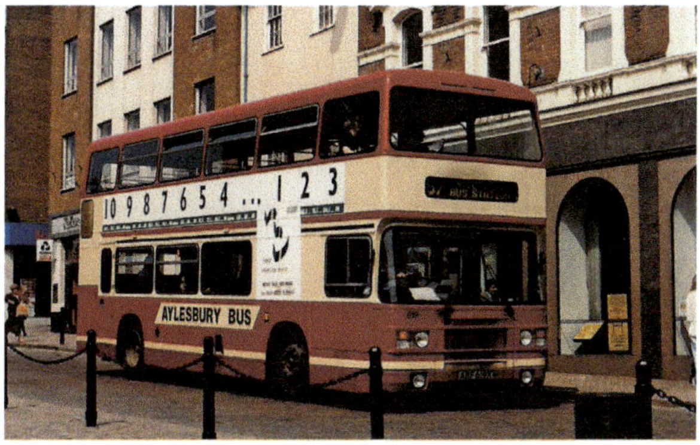

United Counties received twenty early production ECW-bodied Leyland Olympians in 1981. Nine were initially allocated to Luton and all transferred in 1989 to Aylesbury depot where they remained long-term residents. In full Luton & District livery, 619 (ARP 619X) skirts around Market Square, which was restricted to buses only by the time this summer 1993 view was taken. The original Transign destination equipment was replaced early on, the new screen showing the bus to be working unusual route 67. Only one Monday to Friday journey ran into Aylesbury bus station, the 07.41 from the village of Swanbourne via the Horwoods. Other odd journeys linked outlying villages. (Author's collection)

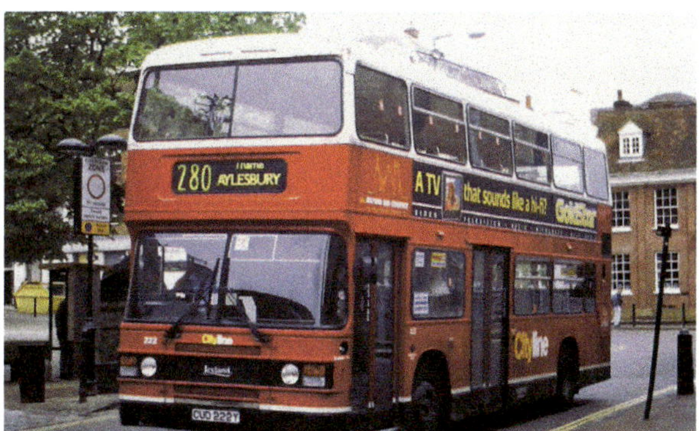

Further around Market Square and about to enter Friars Square bus station is 222 (CUD 222Y), a similar vehicle type belonging to Oxford Bus Co. That company's South Midland division had a long association with the town, garaging vehicles there until 1987. The main trunk route 280 to Oxford was operated until July 1995, this scene taken just before that on 11 May. A 'brand refresh' took place in late 1994 with Cityline red vehicles running city and interurban routes. The driver even wears the red tie and epaulettes and has use of the new Wayfarer ticket machine. Ford of Althorne acquired the bus in 2003. (Author's collection)

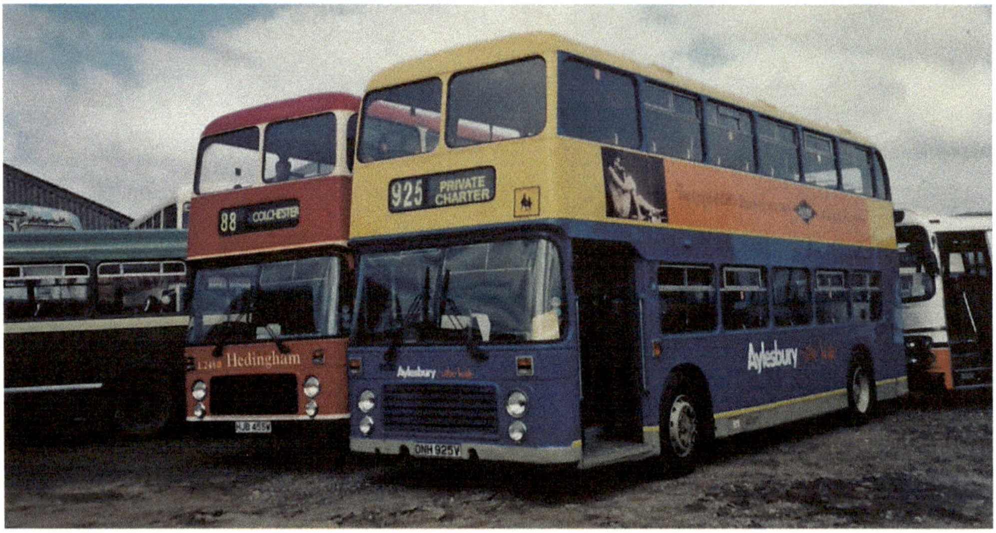

The Aylesbury allocation of Luton & District also included thirteen long-term Bristol VRs with ECW bodywork. These were well cared for and a pair remained in the town up until 2000. The Shires blue and yellow livery had been applied to 5035 (ONH 925V), formerly 925, attending the Oxford Bus Museum's VR day on 22 March 1998. It is in the company of Hedingham Omnibuses' Bristol VR HJB 455W, ex-Wycombe Bus. 5035 was scrapped a year later, but for the other VR fame beckoned. Used by the BBC in 2008 for the *Doctor Who* story 'Planet of the Dead' along with the VR on page 9, the twenty-eight-year-old bus carried false plate W974 GHM during filming. This bus is now preserved.

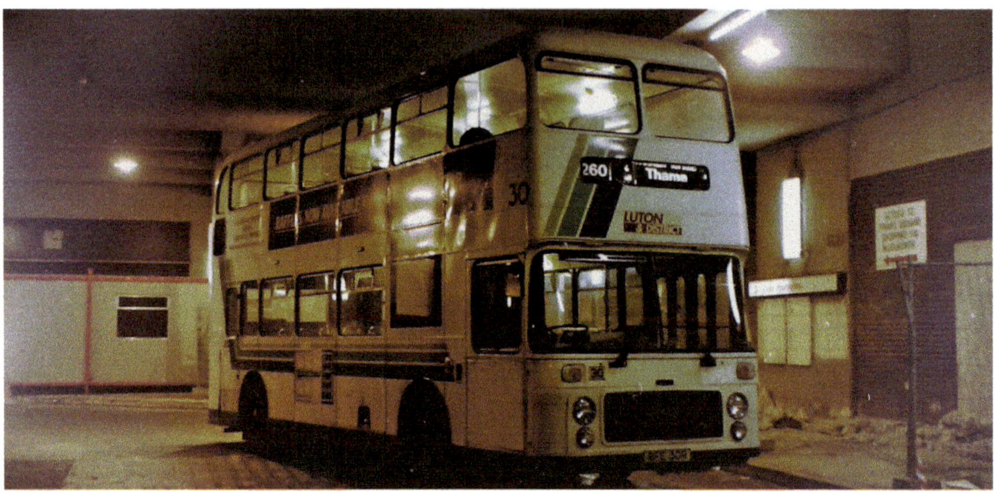

In 1992 Luton & District acquired ten Bristol VRs from Lincoln City Transport for Watford and Hemel Hempstead depots. Further examples hired from Lincoln were quite nomadic and by October 1992 ECW-bodied RFE 30R, numbered 230, was in use at Aylesbury following a spell at Dunstable. Work had just started on the bus station's first makeover and in this picture the gloom of the old facility can be appreciated. Working route 260 to Thame, via additional villages to the 280, the full height of these vehicles restricted their use. Commendably, correct blinds were used but the fitment of such a small destination screen on such a high-looking vehicle makes for an odd appearance. (Author's collection)

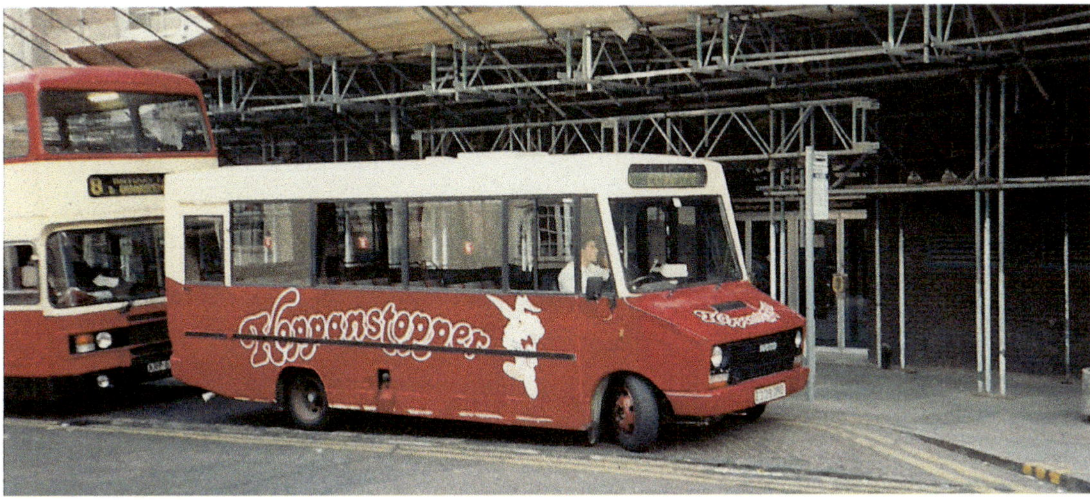

During the bus station refurbishment Walton Street and Great Western Street were used as pick-up and set-down points. Luton & District launched the 'Hoppanstopper' brand in November 1987 for minibus services and in March 1988 nineteen Dormobile-bodied Iveco 49.10s were delivered, eight of which were allocated to Aylesbury. By April 1993, when this view was taken in Walton Street, 61 (E339 DRO) had received a more standardised livery from the original white and blue scheme which featured the Chiltern Hills. The Hoppanstopper rabbit had, however, been reapplied.

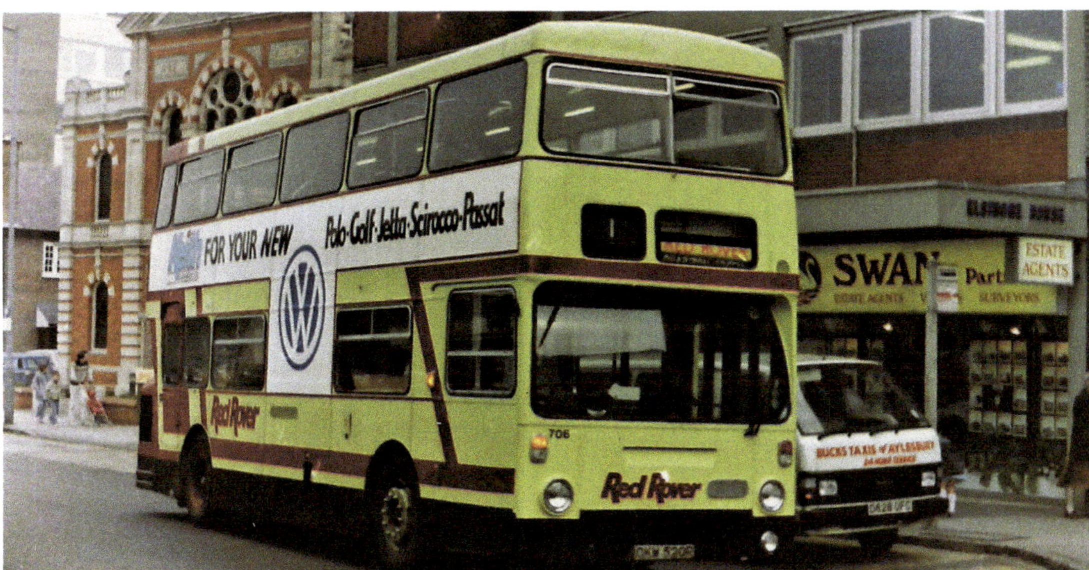

The name Red Rover had been associated with Aylesbury since 1927, the company building up a network of local services. In 1955 the company was taken over by Keith's Garages and subsequently acquired by Luton & District in January 1988 with a number of vehicles retaining Red Rover's livery. Some of L&D's own fleet also had Red Rover fleet names applied. Eight Daimler Fleetlines with MCW bodywork were acquired, three originating with South Yorkshire PTE and the rest with London Transport. Of the former group, 706 (OKW 520R) is about to turn into Buckingham Street depot still advertising Keith's Garages. (Author's collection)

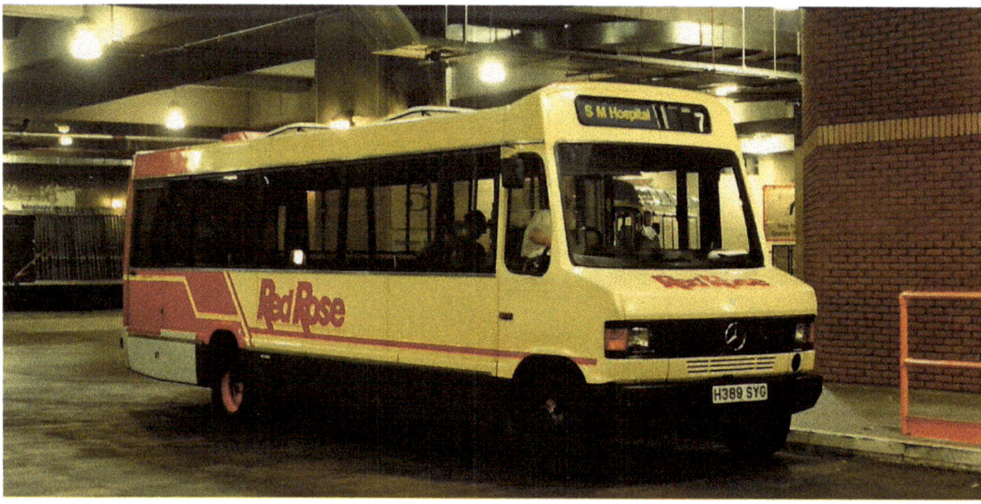

Eventually the Red Rover name was dropped but there were several other local operators using 'red' in their fleet names, Red Rose being one such company. Formed in the early 1990s, many interesting vehicles have been used over the years, which included H389 SYG, a Mercedes-Benz 811D with rare Optare StarRider E bodywork. The twenty-six-seater was acquired when a year old from Optare, which had used it as a demonstrator. This model kept the more typical Mercedes front end (compared to the more stylish example on page 21) and only a handful were built. This is Bay 4 in the brighter, refurbished bus station in summer 1994 after the traffic flow had been changed to anticlockwise. (Author's collection)

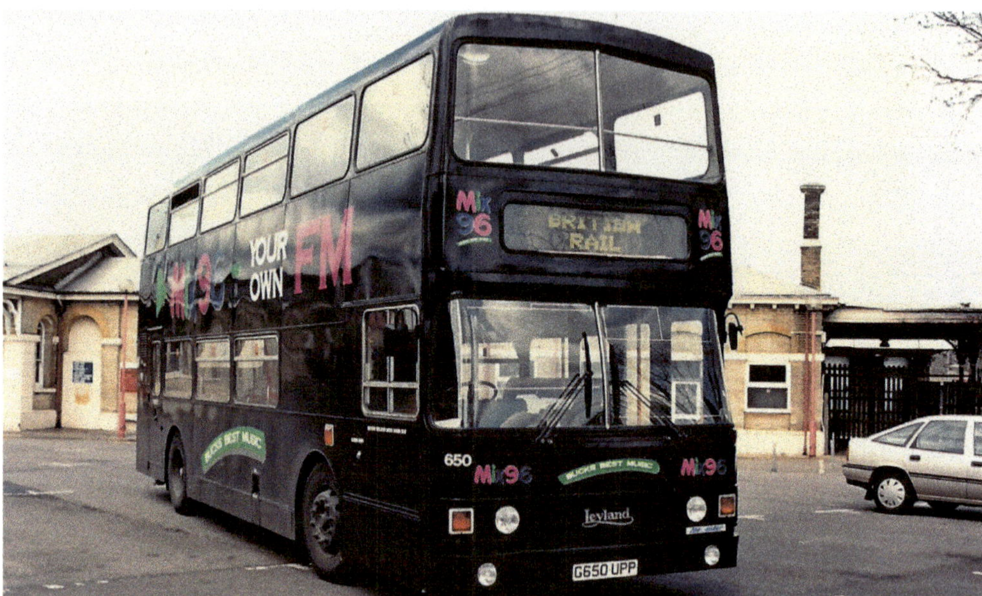

December 1989 saw the arrival at Aylesbury of six Leyland Olympians with Alexander RL bodywork. The batch clocked up twenty years' service here and was used on all manner of work. In 1994 650 (G650 UPP), later numbered 5100, received this striking overall black livery for local radio station Mix 96. Working a rail replacement duty at Princes Risborough, the destination was still correct, although privatisation was imminent. (Author's collection)

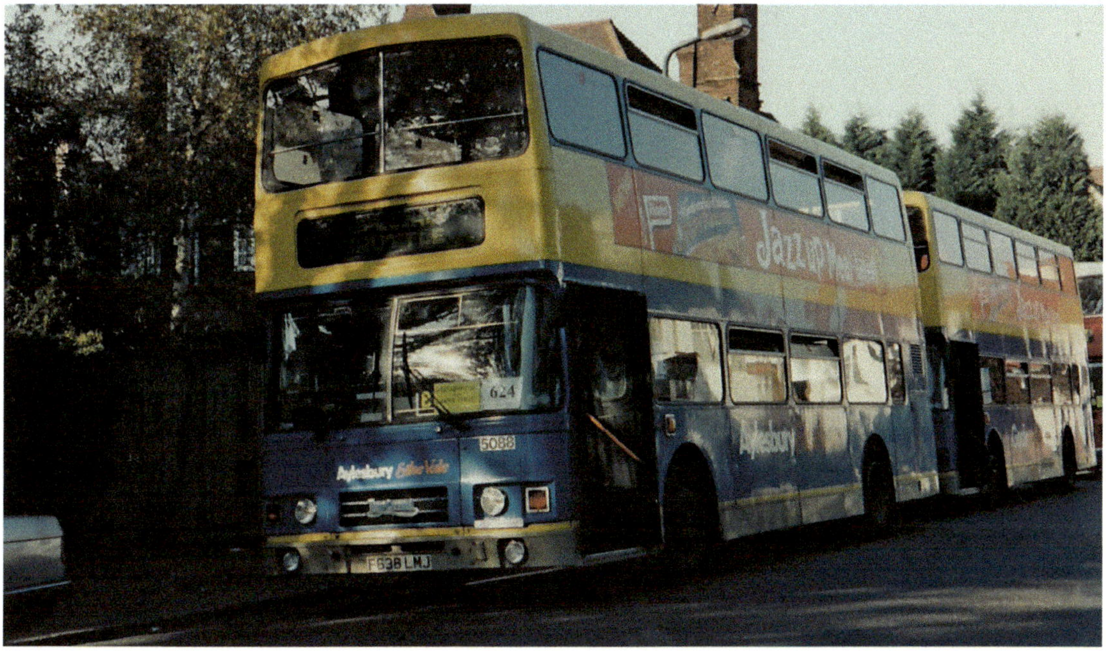

New at Luton depot in 1988 Leyland Olympian 638 (F638 LMJ) had become 5088 and had transferred to Aylesbury by the time of this 19 October 1997 view. Rail replacement service on behalf of the Jubilee Line was being undertaken, with both this vehicle and a similar example from Hemel Hempstead laying over at Coverdale Road, Kilburn.

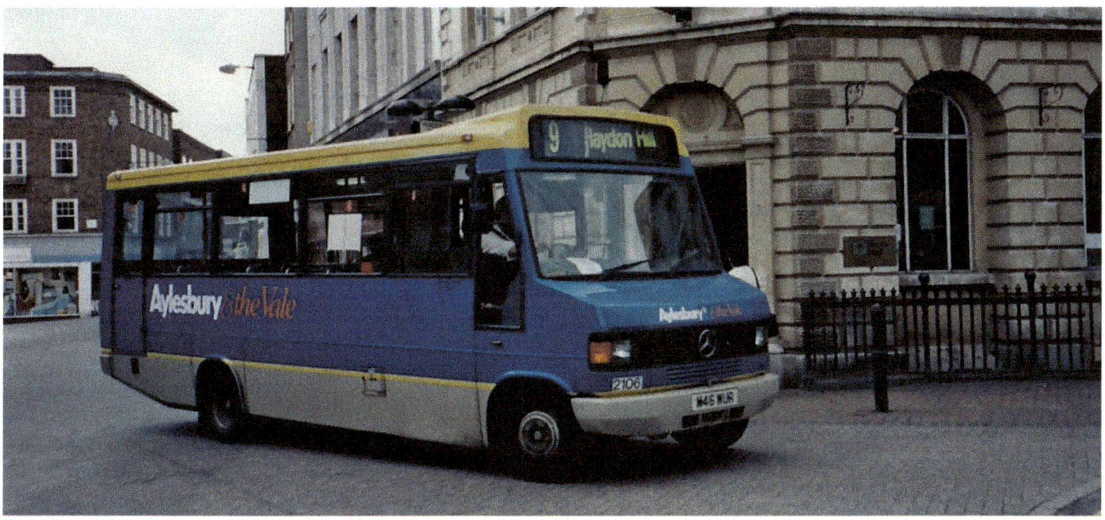

Following privatisation Luton & District operated a large number of minibuses of varying types at all depots. By the mid-1990s replacements for earlier examples were needed and more standard types appeared. One of eight delivered in July 1995, and the first to wear the Shires blue and yellow livery from new, 2106 (M46 WUR) was originally numbered 184. Aylesbury received half of this batch of manual gearbox Mercedes-Benz 709Ds with Plaxton Beaver bodywork. Turning from Market Square to Kingsbury Square on 29 June 1998 the bus works cross-town route 9, which was interworked with route 8.

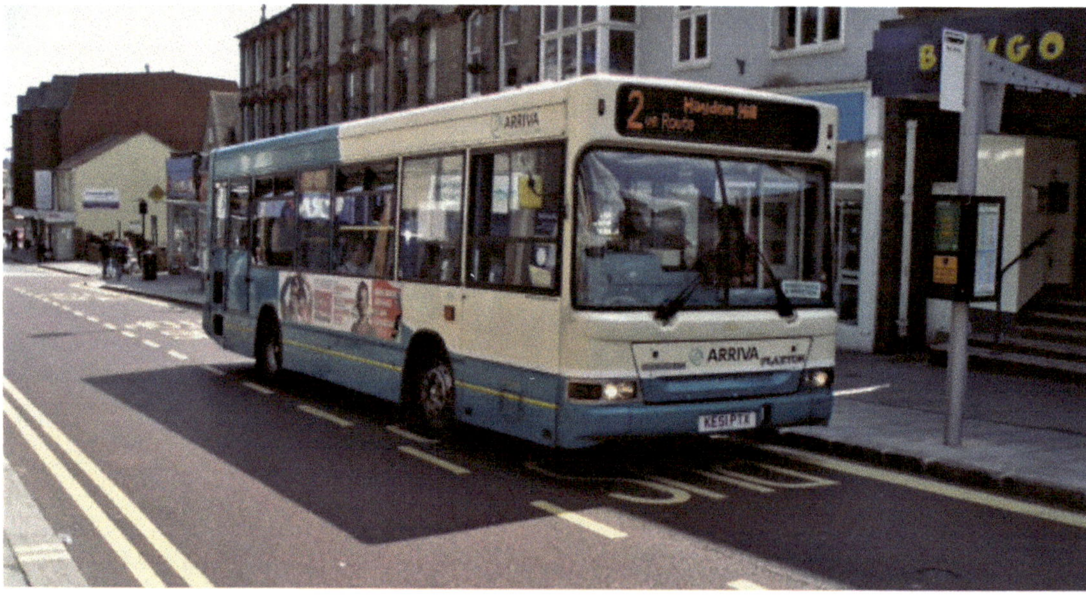

In turn Aylesbury's minibuses would be replaced with low-floor vehicles. The smart lines of the Plaxton Mini-Pointer sit on a Dennis Dart SLF chassis, with 3509 (KE51 PTX) forming part of a larger batch delivered when Arriva the Shires was combined with Essex. Market Square had been fully pedestrianised and the town centre had seen substantial regeneration by the time this 7 May 2008 view was taken. Buses radiated around the town centre area and this one loads on High Street for Haydon Hill.

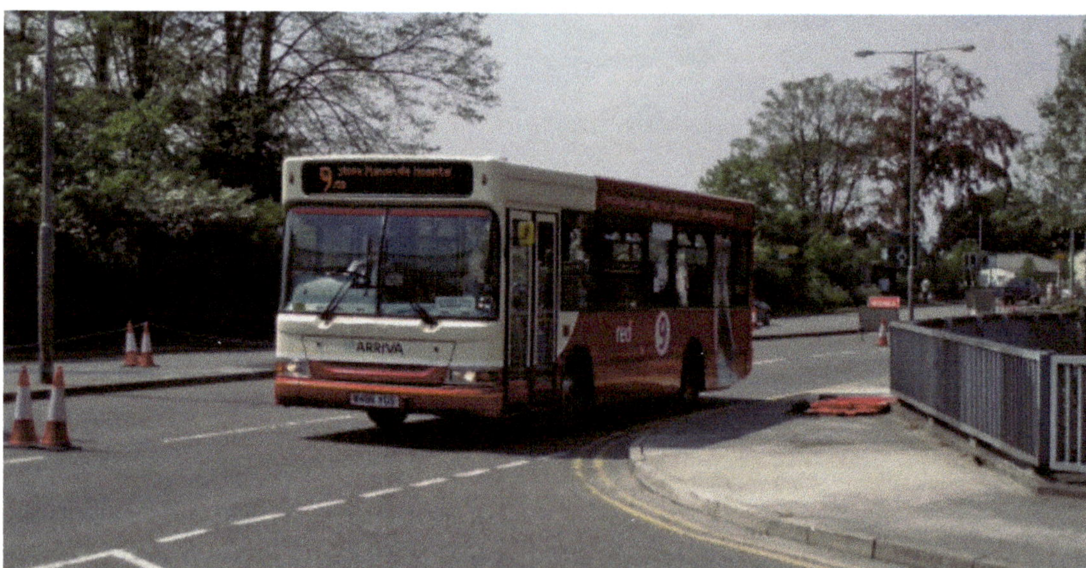

More commonly associated with its London operations, Arriva also had vehicles painted in a red version of its corporate livery at Aylesbury and High Wycombe. As part of Buckinghamshire County Council's 'Rainbow routes' scheme route 9 was clearly red and applied to Mini-Pointer Dennis Dart SLF 3486 (W486 YGS) at Friarage Road bound for Stoke Mandeville Hospital. This area now benefits from a direct bus lane to the railway station and improved pedestrian access.

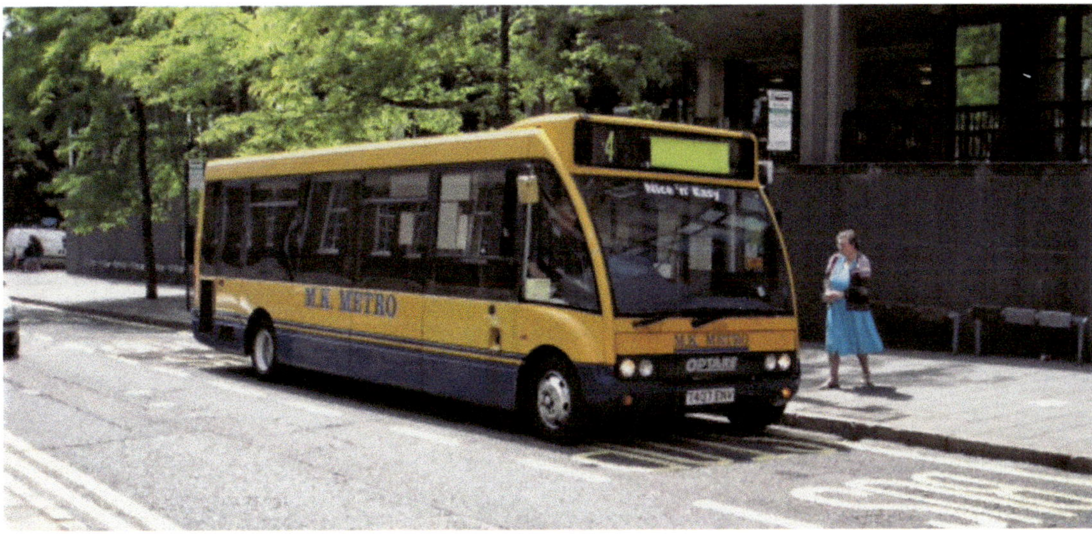

Friars Square bus station was refurbished for a second time in 2008 with buses once again moved out onto temporary stops in Walton Street and Great Western Street. Arriva the Shires acquired the operations of MK Metro in February 2006 and, after a short while, vehicle transfers occurred. These saw Aylesbury receive MK Metro-liveried Optare Solo T407 ENV, new as 7 and now Arriva 2420. It is loading on Walton Street on 11 June 2008 outside the County Hall building, a fifteen-storey brutalist structure that can be seen from many miles around. This bus would transfer through Arriva to Guildford and traffic now flows along this street in the opposite direction.

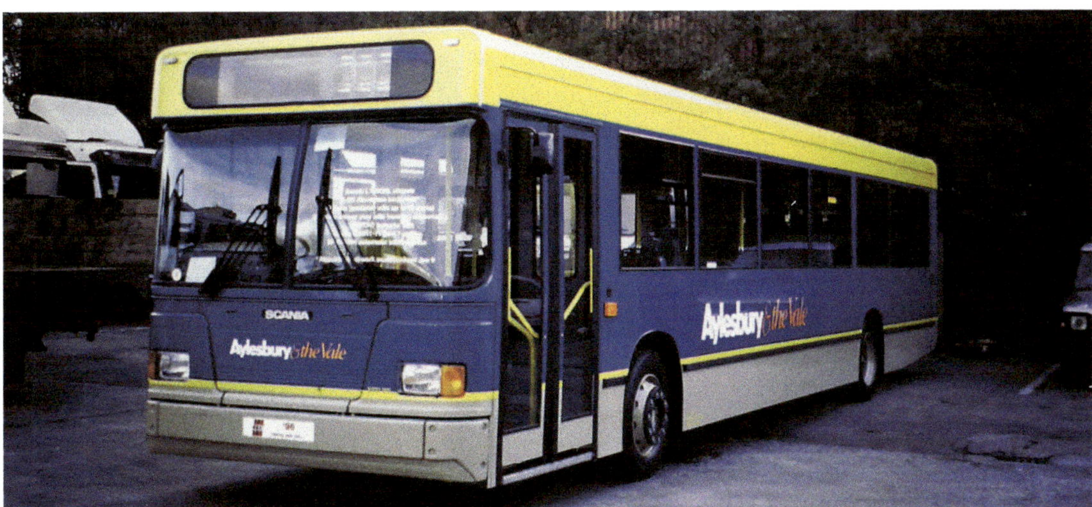

Luton & District Transport, trading as the Shires, received twenty-seven East Lancs European-bodied Scania L113CRLs in late 1996. Aylesbury was allocated four, numbered 713–716 (N713–6 EUR), which were the first new single-deckers delivered in this livery, one of the batch having attended a trade show on behalf of East Lancs prior to delivery. British Bus Group favoured this chassis and body combination and their other constituent fleets received similar vehicles. This was the dawn of the low-floor era and the change would soon be made to that type of vehicle. (Author's collection)

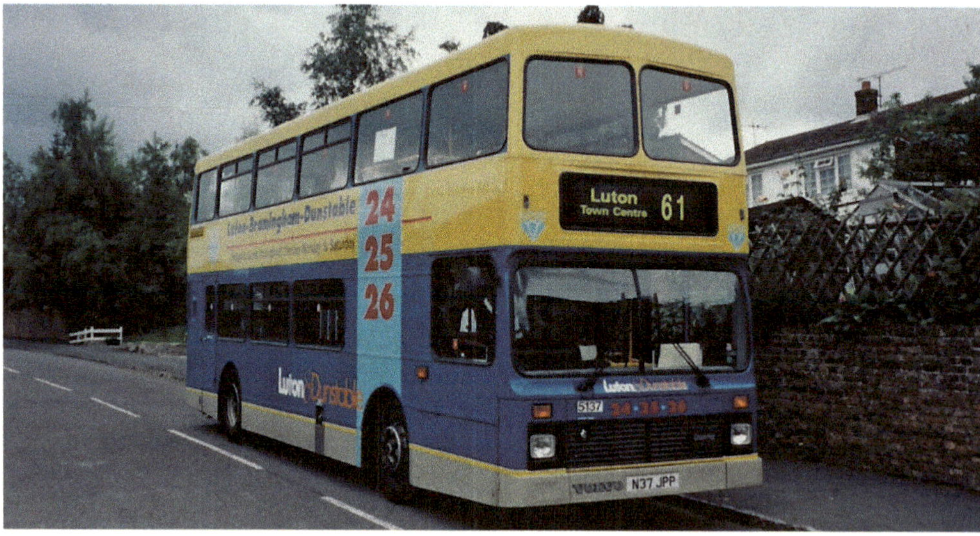

Replacements for LDT the Shires' large fleet of ageing double-deckers began to arrive in the mid-1990s. Delivered to Luton in May and June 1996 were ten Volvo Olympians with Northern Counties Palatine bodies. Also new in yellow and blue, many of the batch had 'Sapphire' branding as applied to 5137 (N37 JPP), previously ON037. However, on 29 June 1998 it had strayed onto route 61 at the village of Edlesborough. Jointly worked between Aylesbury and Luton depots, the route had a total journey time of an hour and a half. Crossing three counties (Bucks, Herts and Beds) and the Chiltern Hills, some picturesque locations were features of the 61.

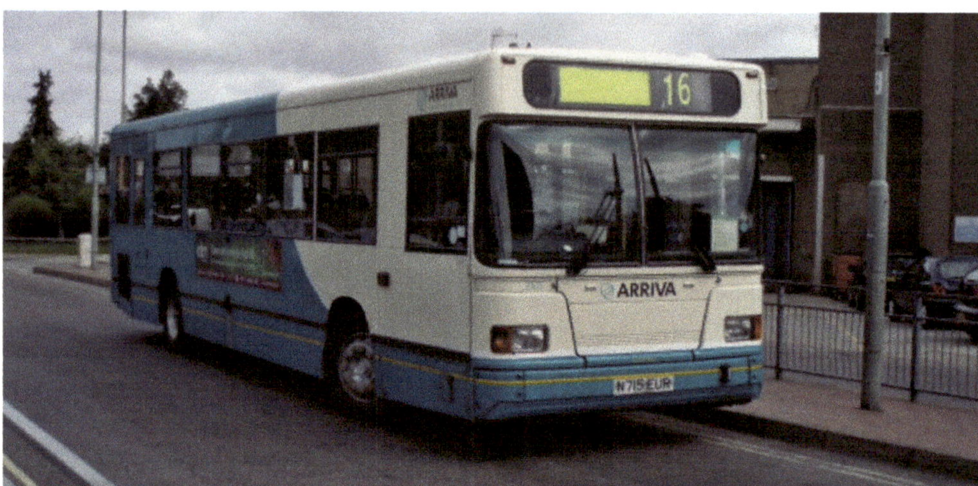

Now in Arriva corporate colours 3165 (N715 EUR), formerly 715, has headed west of its home town and across another county boundary, this time with Oxfordshire, to Bicester's Bure Place bus station. This basic facility, which had views of a car park and Tesco delivery bay, has since been completely redeveloped. Route 16 worked several variations on different days of the week and served one of Bicester's two railway stations. LDT had specified roller blinds on new vehicles, citing electronic equipment as unreliable. Regrettably, this view on 11 June 2008 doesn't show us a screen too helpful either.

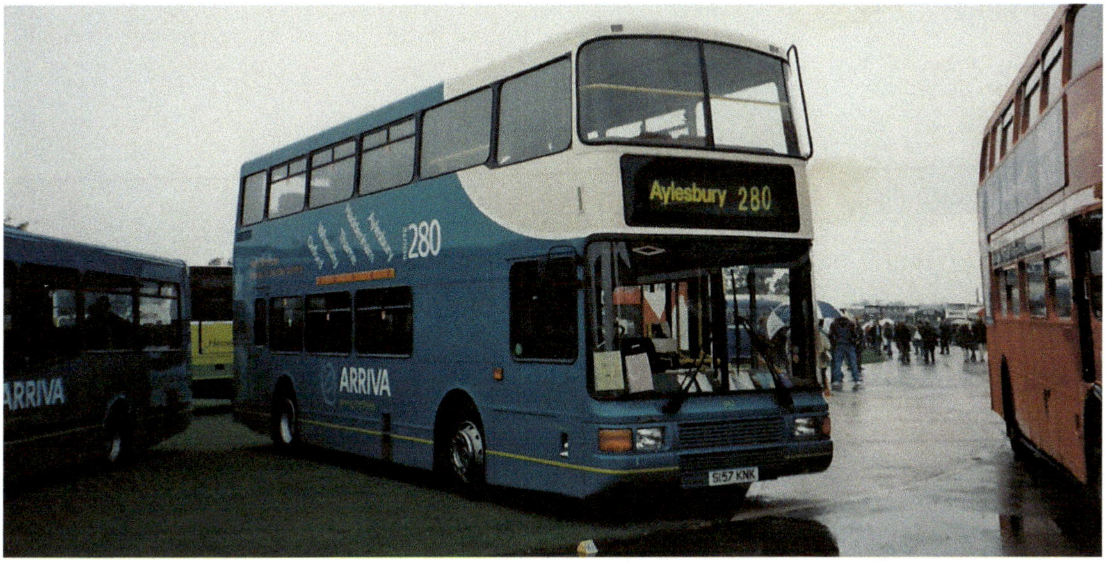

The first new vehicles to be delivered in Arriva corporate livery were fifteen handsome Northern Counties Palatine 2-bodied Volvo Olympians in September 1998. They were split between Watford and Aylesbury, which received six branded for service 280. Sixty-eight coach seats were fitted, which were well-suited for their use on this route, as well as proving quite comfortable on a trip to Showbus at Duxford where 5157 (S157 KNK) is seen on 27 September 1998. Interestingly the 280 was never renumbered under any change of network or scheme, and still runs as such today as a reminder of the series once used by City of Oxford in this area.

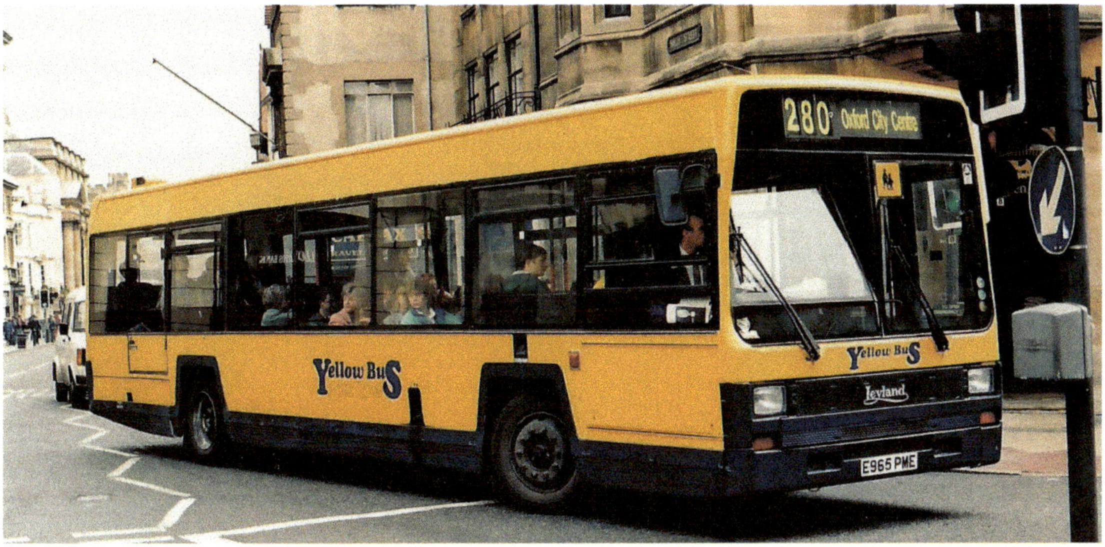

In November 1994 Motts Travel acquired two Leyland Lynxes from Atlas Bus of Acton, which had used them on LRT work, mainly route 112. Becoming 965/966 (E965/6 PME), both would pass to LDT the Shires the following July. This early 1995 view shows 965 at Carfax in Oxford turning onto St Aldates, terminus of the 280 at the time. Three operators worked the route, LDT the Shires only from Aylesbury to Thame, although this was soon to change. Motts also had workings on the 230 meandering around more intermediate villages. (Author's collection)

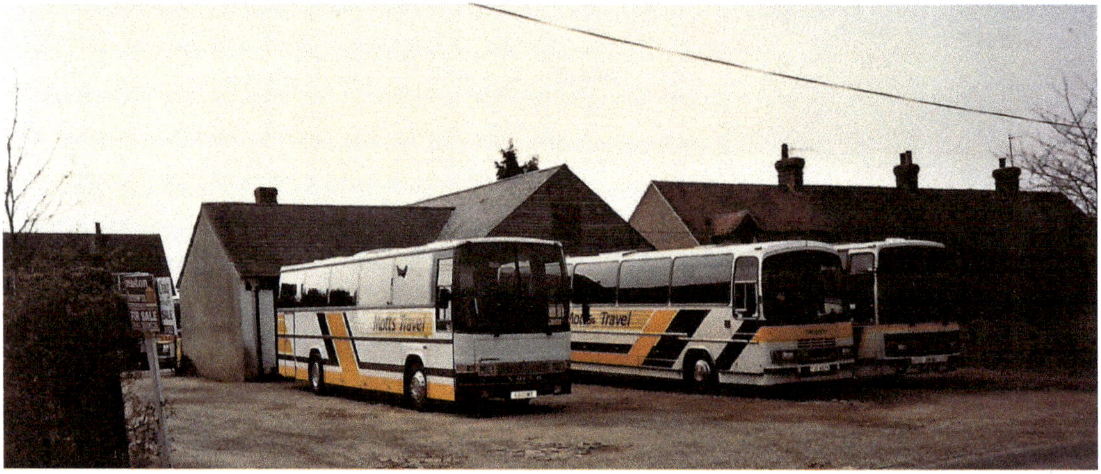

Motts Travel today operates from a purpose-built facility at Stocklake in Aylesbury. Head office prior to this was at Stoke Mandeville village, with a number of outstations also in use. One such example was at Risborough Road, Kingsey, near Haddenham. Four vehicles are seen at this facility in early 1992. Long-standing 6601 MT (ONV 649Y) was a Jonckheere Jubilee-bodied Volvo B10M new to Tellings. Sandwiched is YJO 957X (later XBW 473, 5812 MT) with similar chassis but with Plaxton Supreme bodywork, which was new to Motts. On the right is JBW 68Y (6957 MT, RDW 27Y) also a B10M and with Plaxton Paramount 3500 body new to BEBB, Llantwit Fadre. A styling comparison can be made between the two Plaxton vehicles, which were built at much the same time. Just visible behind the garage is SUR 283R, which we saw in photo 131. This site has now been rebuilt as a residential dwelling.

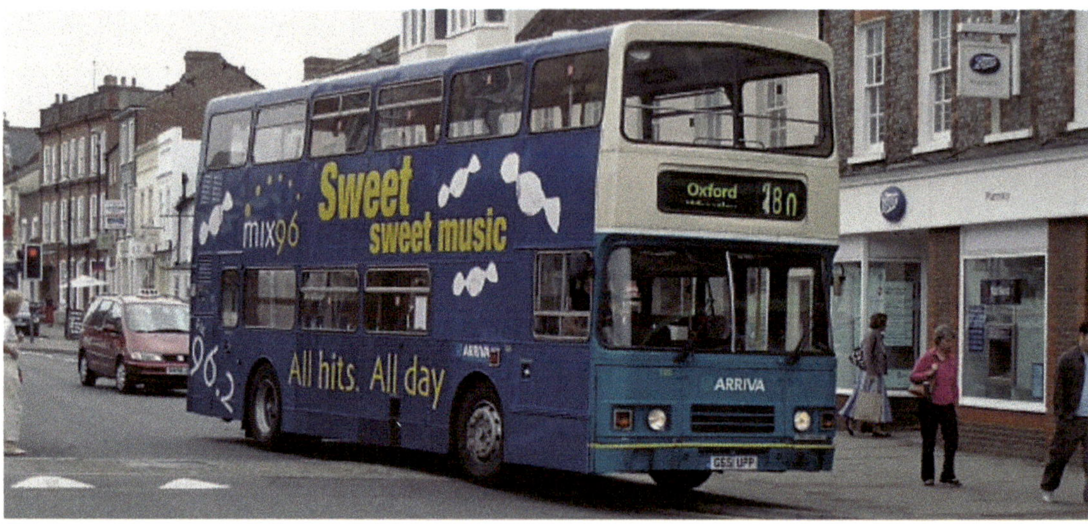

On the route between Aylesbury and Oxford is the market town of Thame. Long-standing Aylesbury-based Leyland Olympian 5101 (G651 UPP), formerly 651, of Arriva the Shires pulls onto the main bus stop opposite the Town Hall on 2 June 2008. Members of the batch would have worked over this route many times, enjoying the extension to Oxford gained from July 1995. The dot matrix destination equipment fitted from new has been replaced with roller blinds, and Mix 96.2 was still on air but with a different vehicle and colour scheme carrying their overall advert.

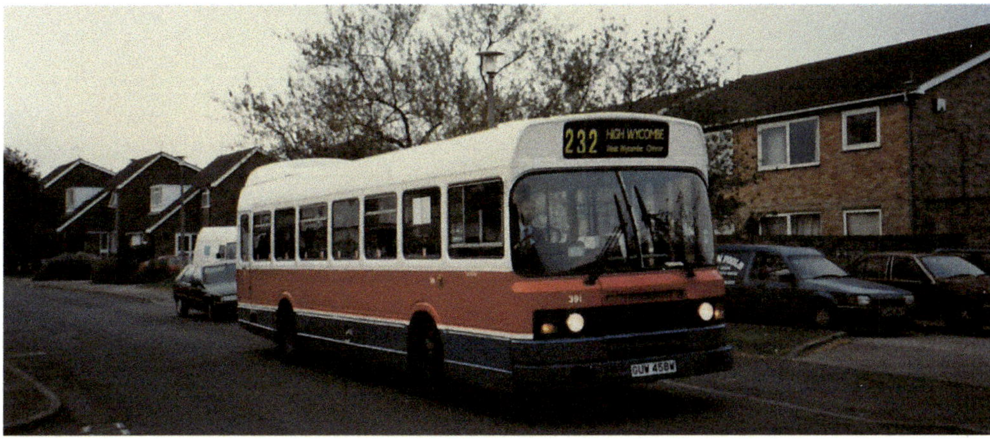

Wycombe Bus Co. and predecessors ran hourly between Thame and High Wycombe, with routes 331 and 332 having several variants all operating via Chinnor. The tender for the town service in Thame had been won by a number of operators over the years, Wycombe Bus gaining it in the late 1990s and tagging it onto the end of the route. The 2xx number series is again in evidence and was used by City of Oxford for its journeys on the route, which ended in 1995. Wycombe kept the number 232 for two round trips and Leyland National 2 391 (GUW 458W), formerly Centrewest LS458, operates along Cromwell Avenue, Thame, on 11 April 1997. With Oxford Bus-inspired detailed blinds it had departed Wycombe at 06.35 and was due to leave here at 07.25. Buses on the Thame routes were usually interworked with those to Great Missenden.

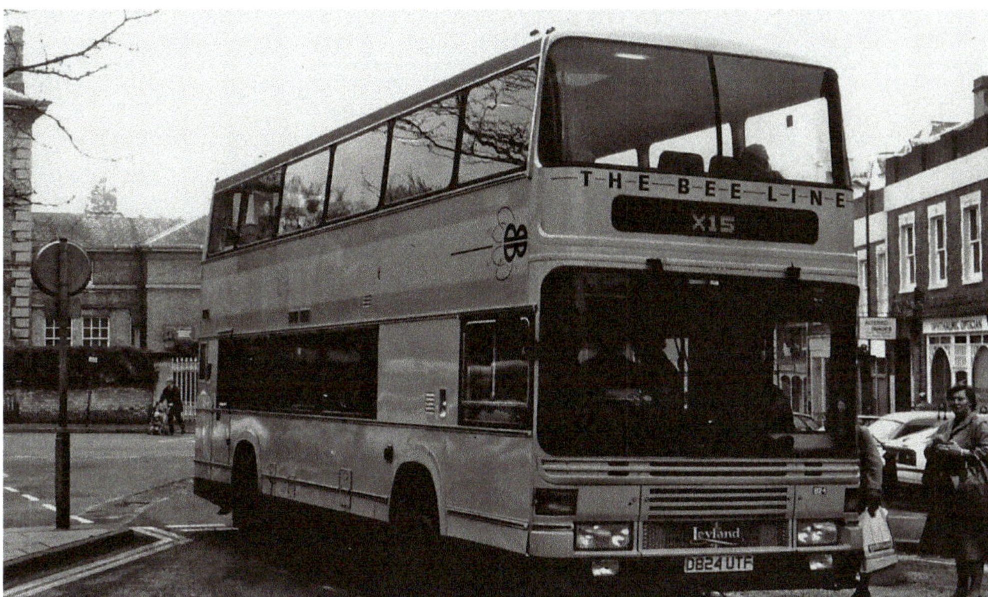

Travelling north from Aylesbury on the X15 once more, we enter Bedfordshire to serve Leighton Buzzard. Loading on the High Street on the 10.42 departure to Milton Keynes, the driver sets the Almex ticket machine for the next fare. Showing the original lines of the ECW coach bodywork Leyland Olympian 824 (D824 UTF) hadn't long arrived at High Wycombe depot from Bracknell in this winter 1989/90 view. Luckily, one of this unusual trio is now preserved. (Brian Botley/ author's collection)

Milton Keynes and North Buckinghamshire

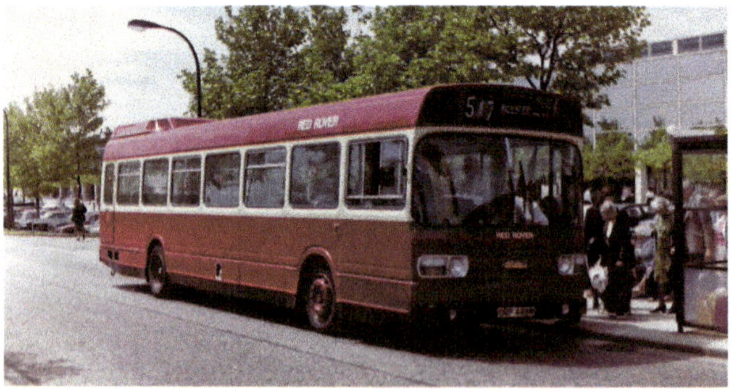

In January 1988 Red Rover was taken over by Luton & District and the majority of the twenty-three vehicles acquired were sold on relatively quickly. Buses from their own fleet replaced them including newly repainted Leyland National 468 (ORP 468M) with Red Rover fleet names. In the summer of 1988 it was loading at stop G3 on Midsummer Boulevard on the 13.58 517 service to Aylesbury via Bicester and a whole host of villages in between. This route operated Tuesdays only and Aylesbury wouldn't be reached until 16.15. Today the shopping opportunities of Bicester draw in crowds equally as big as those of Milton Keynes. (Author's collection)

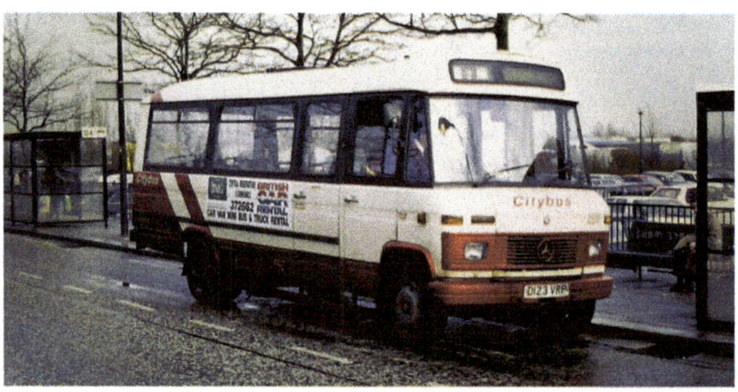

In October 1986 ninety-two Mercedes-Benz 608D minibuses replaced all but a handful of Milton Keynes Citybus' conventional vehicles overnight, on a new city network named 'Street Shuttle'. Under Cambus Holdings (CHL GROUP) ownership the liveries used were brighter and more pleasing than that of the initial white scheme. In the red and cream Citybus variant is 23 (D123 VRP), one of the first forty-five to carry Robin Hood bodies, the remainder having Alexander AM bodywork of similar appearance. Awaiting custom at stop E4 on Midsummer Boulevard in 1995, the background today is completely different, comprising the theatre district and Xscape leisure complex. (Author's collection)

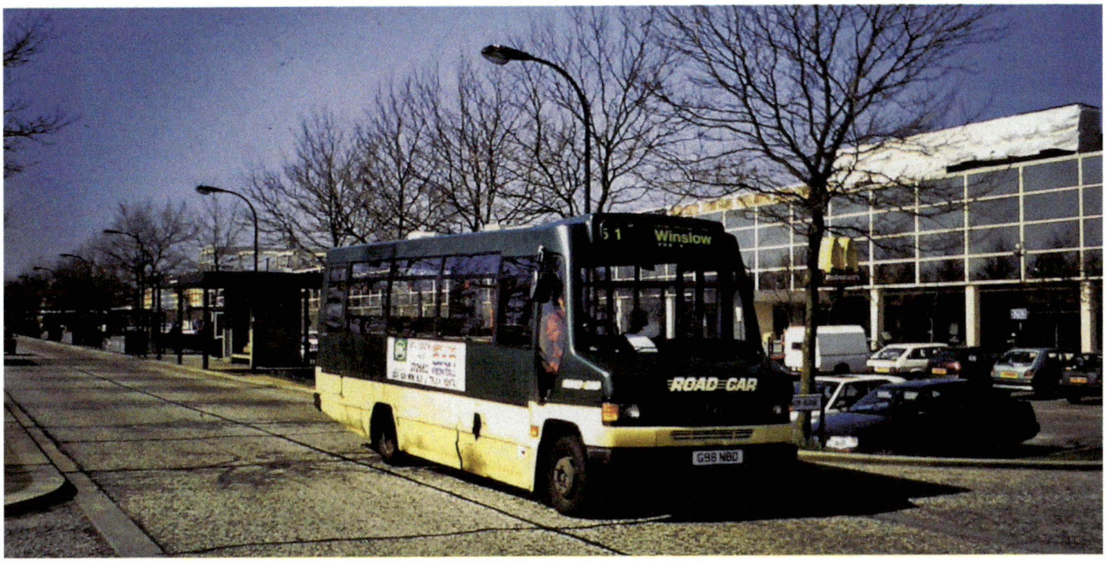

There is a 'state-side' feel to this 1995 Midsummer Boulevard view, with grid roads and golden arches, but Mercedes-Benz 709D 98 (G98 NBD) is heading for Winslow, Bucks, and not Arizona! The 'Road Car' identity was a low-cost unit set up for contracts and tenders such as the 51, which served a number of villages en route. Eight of these Dormobile Routemaker twenty-nine seaters joined the fleet in 1989/90. The view behind the bus is now occupied by Midsummer Place and an extension to the main shopping centre. (Author's collection)

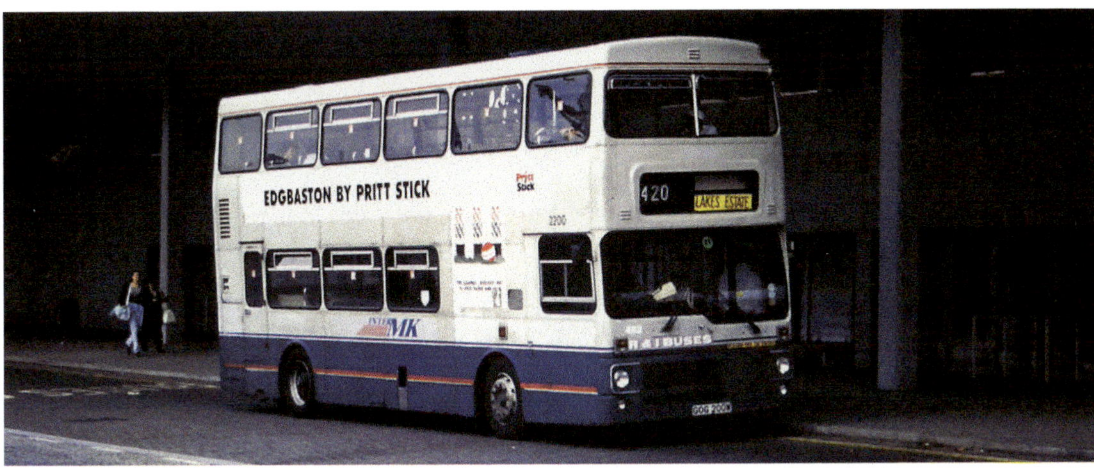

Many operators ran in Milton Keynes on tendered work but few competed directly with Citybus on commercial routes. An exception was R&I Buses of Acton, North London, who set up 'Inter MK' in March 1992, their route numbers originating with United Counties. With five routes eventually being operated extra capacity was hired from West Midlands Travel in the shape of Leyland Nationals and MCW Metrobuses. WMPTE 2200 (GOG 200W) numbered 482 is seen waiting at the Central bus station through bays on the main north-south 420 service on 4 September 1993. The AES Datafare ticket machine is visible and the bus carries a Birmingham-themed side advert. R&I ended operations in Milton Keynes on 15 January 1994 and the bus returned to service with West Midlands, eventually being scrapped in March 1998. (Author's collection)

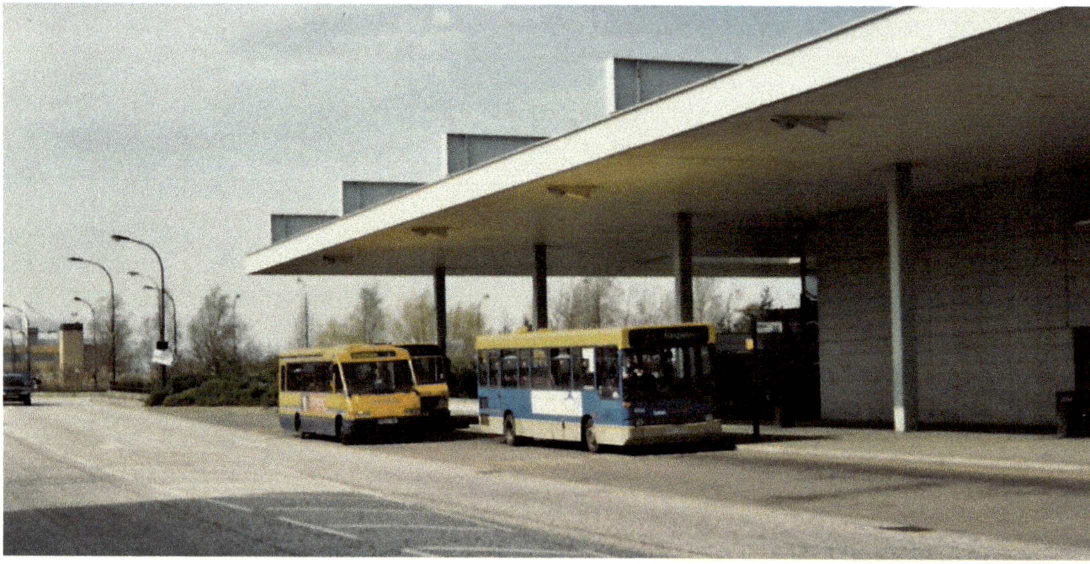

Central bus station opened in May 1983, a facility that would be the envy of most towns. Never utilised to its intended capacity, by the late 1990s only a handful of passenger services called there. Thereafter it was used as a crew change point and parking area. Seen on the through bays on 19 April 2000 were an ex-Buffalo Travel Dennis Dart and two Mercedes-Benz minibuses of MK Metro. These are an Optare StarRider, one of several acquired from East London and, tucked in alongside, a Plaxton Beaver new to MK Metro. The hockey stadium to the left of the view has since been rebuilt to become Network Rail's national operations centre.

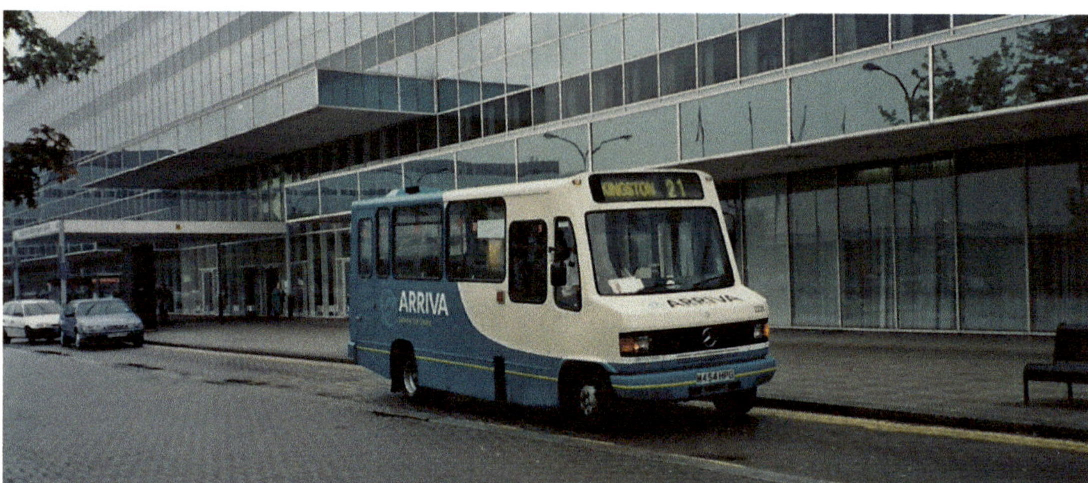

Arriva is now the principal operator in the 'new city'. More of its routes ran to and from Milton Keynes than within it when this 15 September 1999 scene was taken. Evening and Sunday tendered routes were operated along with all-day city route 21, which was run jointly with MK Metro to Kingston local centre via the Open University. Also at this time only two stops existed directly outside the railway station and, at the officially named bay 31, we see 2226 (M454 HPG), an Alexander AM-bodied Mercedes-Benz 709D. This was new to Guildford & West Surrey as 454 in January 1994. Numerous retail outlets have now replaced the glass office fronts and, in a logical move, many more bus stops are now located along this side of the street.

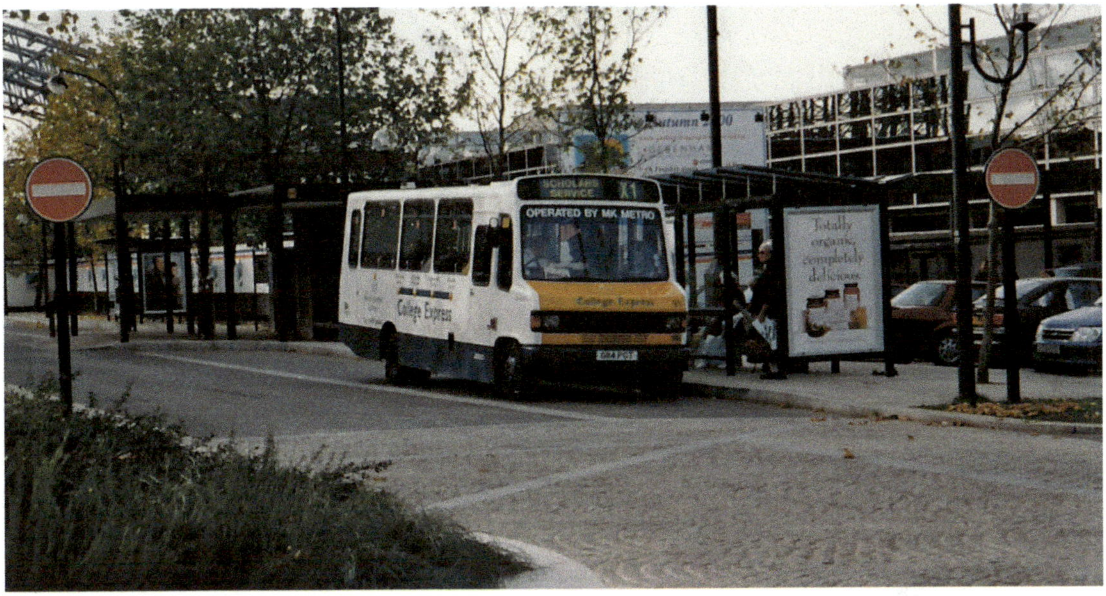

MK Metro acquired former Wycombe Bus Co. Alexander AM-bodied Mercedes Benz 811D 714 (G114 PGT) is new to London General and now numbered 95. Operating the X1 Milton Keynes College Express to Leadenhall Campus, for which it carried a special livery, it would eventually be replaced by a Dennis Dart to provide a greater capacity. In this 9 November 1999 view, on the left the new Midsummer Place shopping centre is under construction, which would permanently block Midsummer Boulevard as a through route.

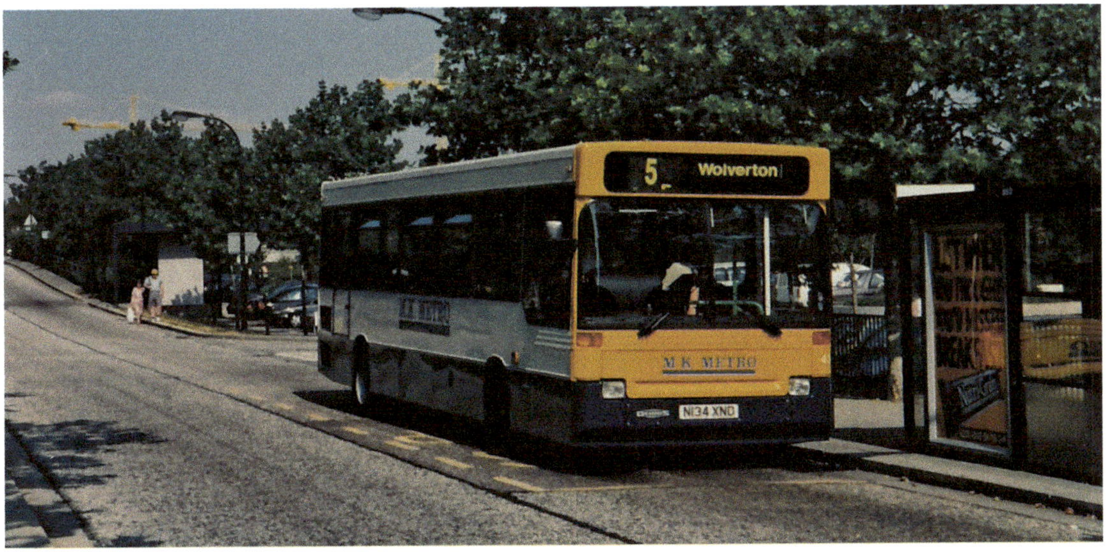

The premier route operated by MK Metro was the 5. This ran from Bletchley Lakes estate through the city centre to either Wolverton or Stony Stratford on the fast grid roads in similar fashion to those initially developed. The Dennis Dart proving its worth as a cost-effective minibus replacement, Plaxton Pointer-bodied 434 (N134 XND) was one of a trio acquired from Stewarts of Dukinfield in 1997. Seen on 7 August 1997, the newly acquired 434 is loading on Midsummer Boulevard stop H4 beside The Point cinema.

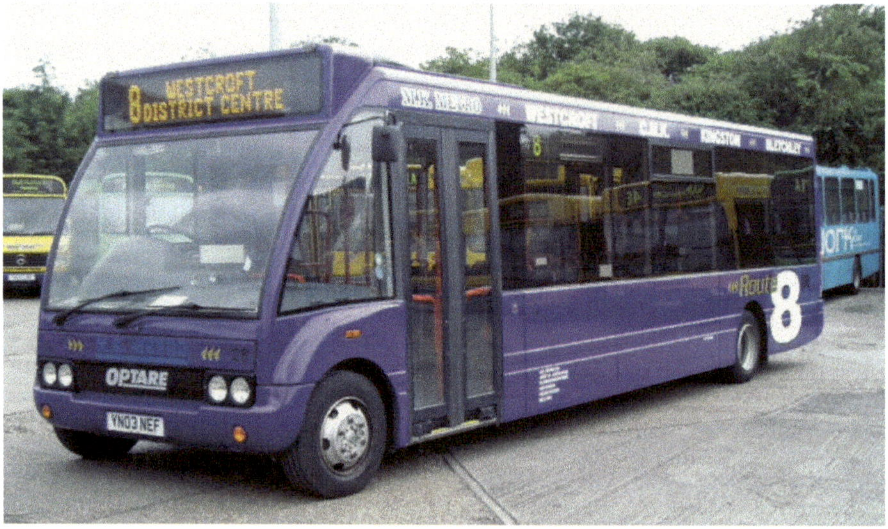

Julian Peddle's preferred livery colour of yellow was adopted by MK Metro. However, shortly before sale to Arriva two other strong colour schemes were introduced along with route branding. The low-floor vehicle of choice in Milton Keynes was the versatile Optare Solo. Twenty-four were bought new and seven others acquired second hand, which included a seat belt-fitted pair in April 2005 from Weavaway, Newbury. Both were painted purple and branded for route 8 as demonstrated by 28 (YN03 NEF) manoeuvring around the main Bleak Hall depot on Chesney Wold on 29 May 2005. This bus became Arriva the Shires 2445.

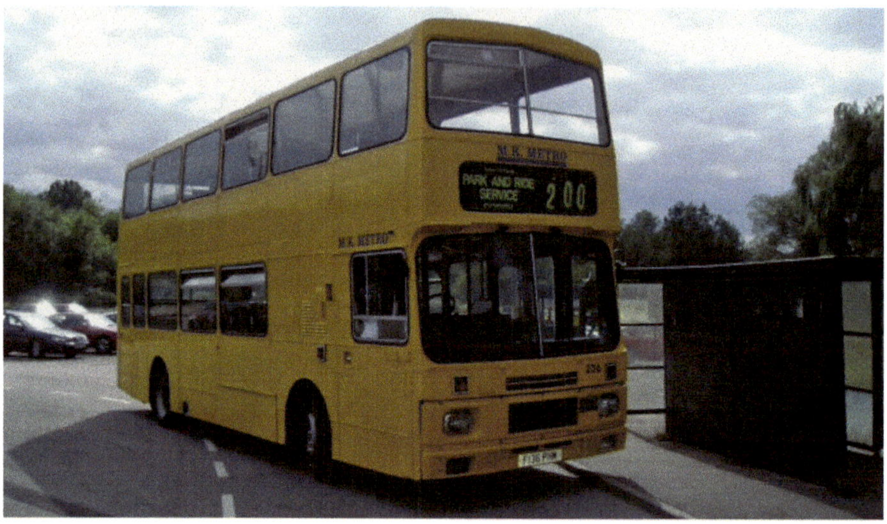

Few double-deckers have operated from Milton Keynes since deregulation, although there was a Bristol VR revival by Citybus in the early 1990s. MK Metro never ran more than a handful at a time and when this view on 6 August 2005 was taken three of these ex-Grey Green Alexander RV-bodied Volvo Citybuses were in use along with an Optare Spectra. P&R facilities were established at Milton Keynes Coachway by M1 junction 14, and a permanent route began in 2000 having only been seasonal until then. Now with single door, 236 (F136 PHM) awaits custom at Coachway car park, the site of a now much-improved facility. The bus shelter had been relocated from Elder Gate by the bus station.

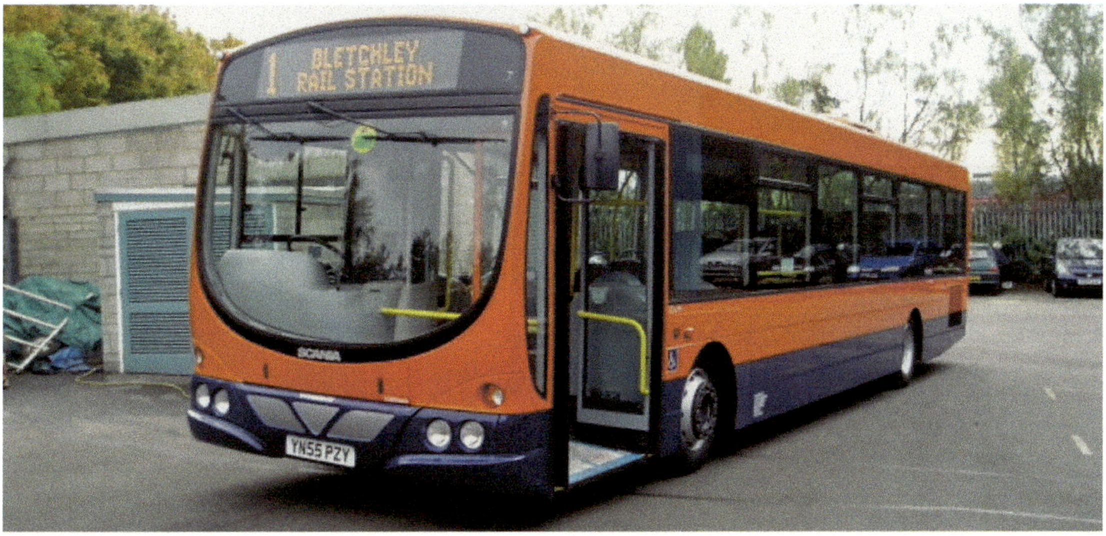

Full-size heavyweight single-deckers were also relatively few in number at MK Metro. Major investment in 2005/06 saw eight Wright Solar-bodied Scania L94UBs arrive in orange, the second of the bold colours, for quality route 5. Two 55-plates arrived on 18 October 2005, with the remaining six being 06-plates and delivered under Arriva ownership. What would become 81 (YN55 PZY) stands at Bleak Hall 'van centre', a facility at the Leadenhall end of Chesney Wold. This was used by the tendered Community Transport fleet and had an inspection pit for MoT use. With Arriva they slotted neatly after the nineteen similar vehicles Luton had received and eventually repainted in corporate livery. This example became 3621 and was still in use with the Group at Telford in 2019.

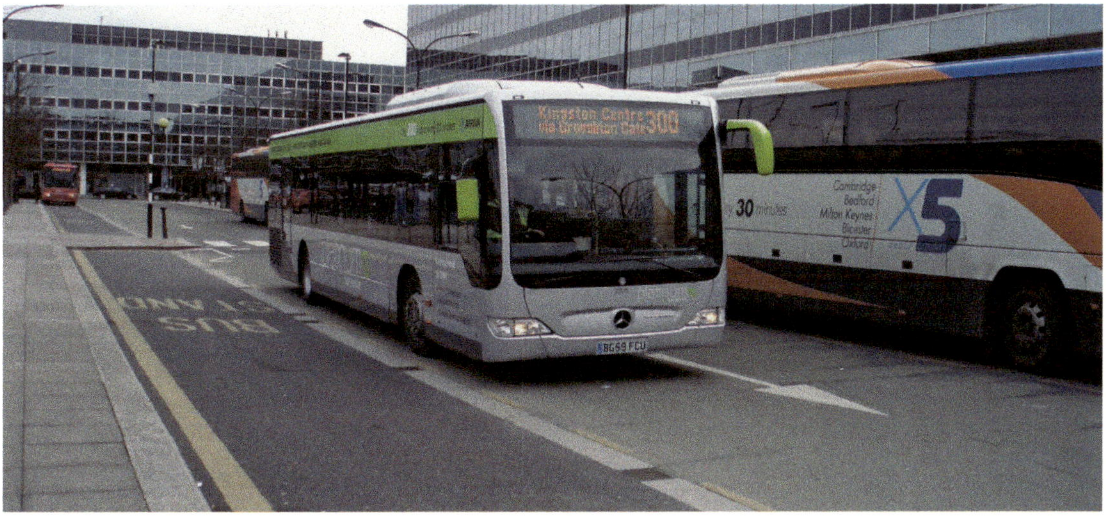

Mercedes-Benz three-pointed-star badges once again graced new vehicles in the new city in 2010. Somewhat different from the 1986 deliveries, these five smart Citaros were for use on Platinum route 300 and included 3925 (BG59 FCU) at Milton Keynes Central station on 8 March 2010. The route served new housing and industrial areas to the east of the city and later served Woburn Sands. The whole batch was replaced with standard-liveried Alexander Dennis E300s and the Platinum vehicles transferred to High Wycombe and Aylesbury for the new 'Arriva Max' brand.

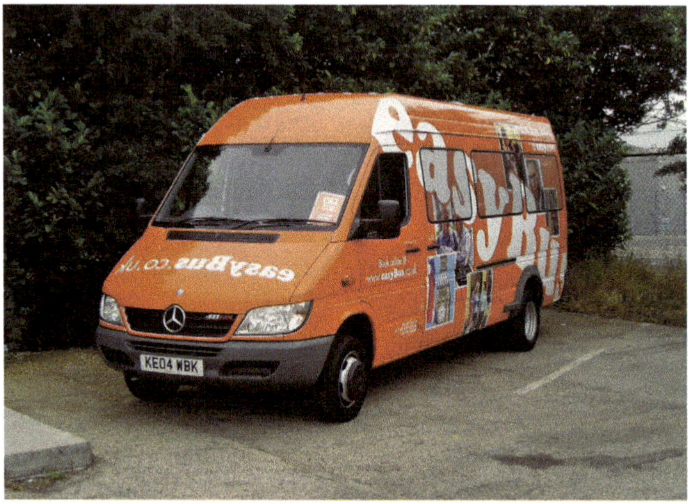

EasyJet entrepreneur Sir Stelios Haji-loannou founded Easy Group in 1998 and has run all manner of businesses from the airline to pizza delivery, and even cinemas. In August 2004 MK Metro was chosen to run 'Easy Bus' from Milton Keynes to London, initially terminating at Hendon Underground station. Using Mercedes-Benz 411CDI sixteen-seaters the route, numbered EB2, picked up outside The Point cinema in Milton Keynes (at that time operated by Easy Group) and bookings were made via the internet. A separate rota of drivers operated the route, which soon changed its London terminal to Baker Street. 304 (KE04 WBK) lays over at MK Metro's Bleak Hall depot on 25 May 2005, one of the twenty such vehicles used on this, and the Luton Airport service, which was run by Lutonian. The operation lasted only about twelve months.

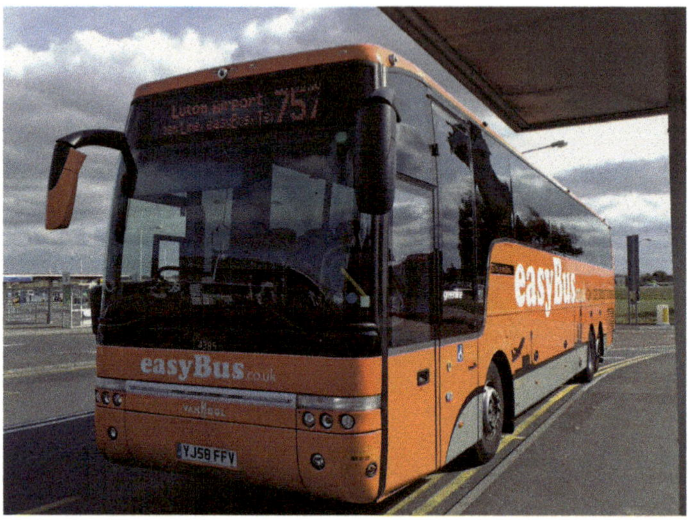

A number of operators worked in partnership with Arriva the Shires to allow ticket acceptance on their established Green Line 757 route from Luton Airport to London Victoria. After initially running their own route from the airport Easy Group would become one of these operators. The Easy Bus name and group's distinctive orange colour scheme was applied to Van Hool Acron 4385 (YJ58 FFV) of Arriva, one of a batch of sixteen vehicles employed on the 757. A wheelchair lift was also fitted and the coach is seen at Luton Airport on 11 September 2009. The front fleet name vinyl is no longer reversed for reflective effect. (Raymond Bedford)

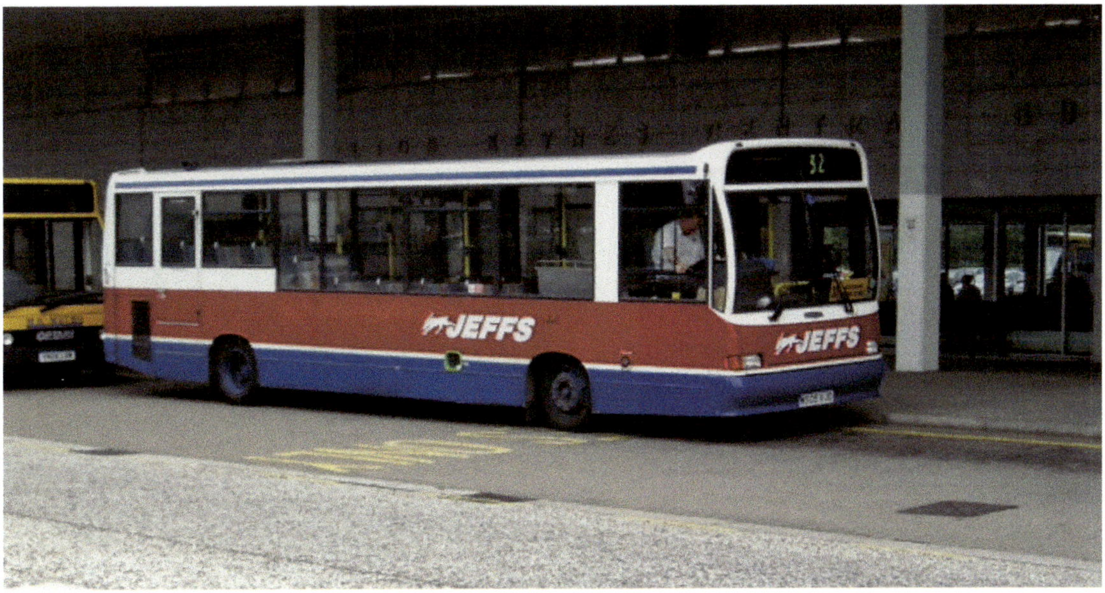

For many years the service between Oxford and Milton Keynes, via Bicester and Buckingham, was numbered 32 and operated by Paynes of Buckingham, part of the Jeffs Coaches group. Seen at Milton Keynes Central bus station on 24 August 2004 was dual-door Marshall-bodied Dennis Dart M505 VJO, which Jeffs had purchased from the Oxford Bus Company. The 32 was subsequently cut back to start at Buckingham, and after the tender for the route was lost in 2007 M505 VJO was sold on for further service in South Wales. Jeffs ceased trading in 2015.

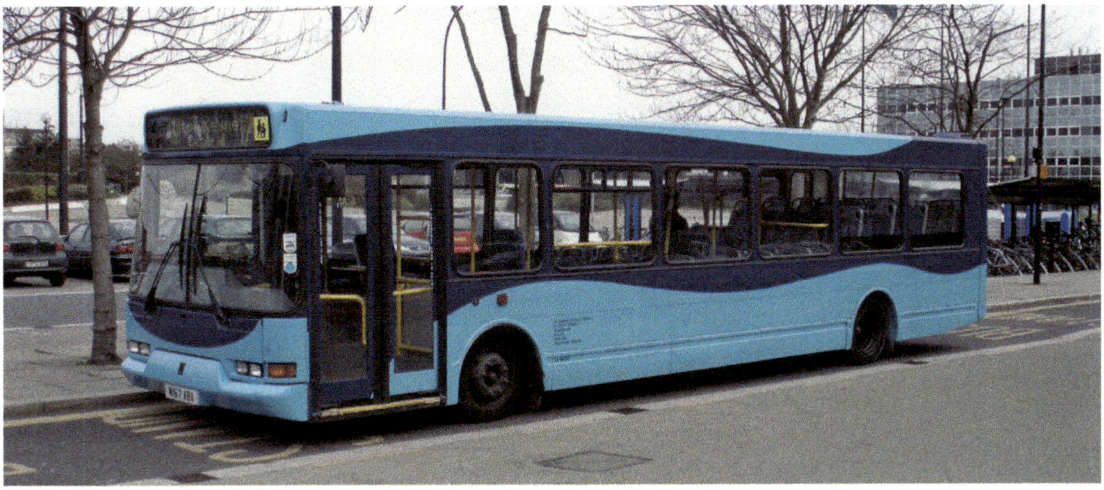

Since deregulation operators from Aylesbury have played a part in the tendered work on offer at Milton Keynes, Vale Travel being one such company. In earlier years vehicles used by many companies ran in as-acquired condition but today a smarter scene exists with uniform liveries. However, sometimes needs must and East Lancs Spryte-bodied Dennis Dart SLF W167 ABA, new to Bluebird of Middleton where it was numbered 5 and registered W5 BLU, is still carrying their livery. Having worked briefly for Compass Bus, Durrington, in October and November 2008, it moved north to Aylesbury and on 8 March 2010 is seen laying over at Milton Keynes Central bus stand working infrequent service 17 to Cranfield.

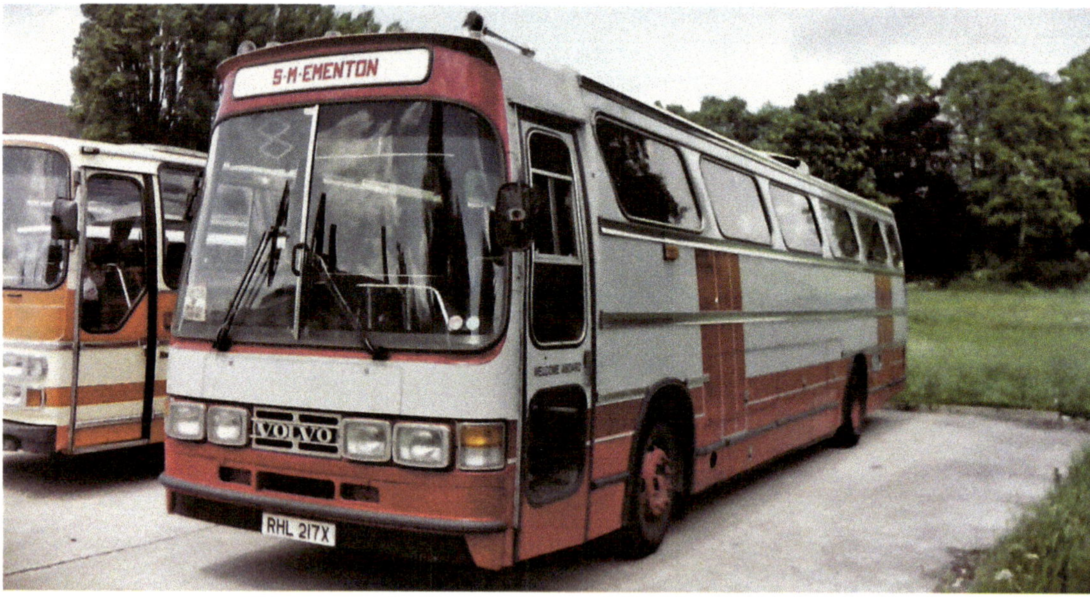

Just across the northern county boundary lies the Bedfordshire village of Cranfield, best known for its university, business park and aerodrome. It was also home to coach operator S. M. Ementon, who ran a fleet of interesting vehicles over the years. This Duple Dominant Goldliner-bodied Volvo B10M had been new to Target Travel, Cramlington, in 1982 as OCN 424X, subsequently re-registered RHL 217X. The 'parallelogram' windows were common on coaches built for the Scottish Bus Group and give an American coach-style appearance. (Author's collection)

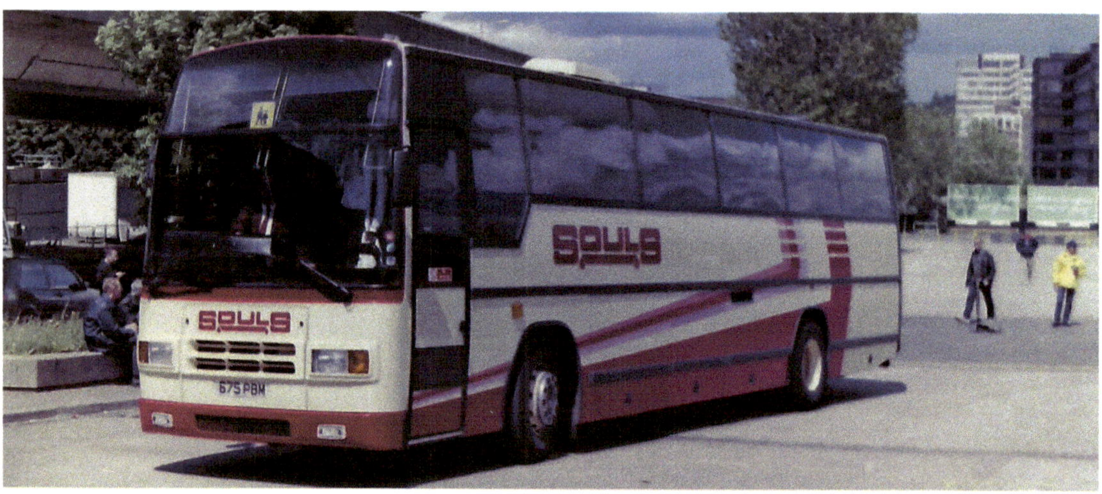

Also north of MK is the historic Buckinghamshire town of Olney, where the Soul family ran a number of businesses. The stance of the driver suggests a manual gearbox, then commonplace, although today the automatic box reigns supreme. Equally common were trips to Wembley Stadium or Arena for all manner of occasions. Seen at this location is Plaxton Paramount 3500-bodied Volvo B10M 675 PBM. Numbered 26, it was previously registered F443 DUG being acquired in 1996 from Classic Tours, Paignton, but new to Wallace Arnold in 1989. (Colin Lloyd/author's collection)

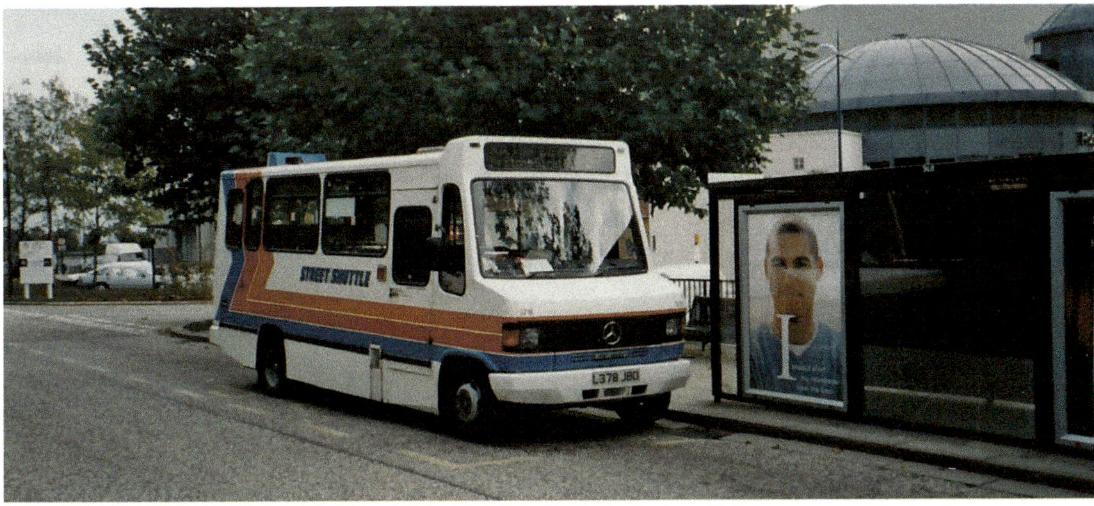

In north Buckinghamshire we once again catch up with vehicles of the Stagecoach Group, which runs into the county from depots in Northamptonshire and Bedford. The Street Shuttle name was conceived by United Counties around the time of deregulation and used by them and Milton Keynes Citybus. Representing the standard Stagecoach minibus of the time 378 (L378 JBD), later 40378, is an Alexander AM-bodied Mercedes Benz 709D with manual gearbox. Standing at Midsummer Boulevard stop B4 by the now completed theatre district on 20 October 1999, at this time there were five routes to Northampton, all with variations at different times or on different days of the week. The service pattern today is much more straightforward and customer-friendly.

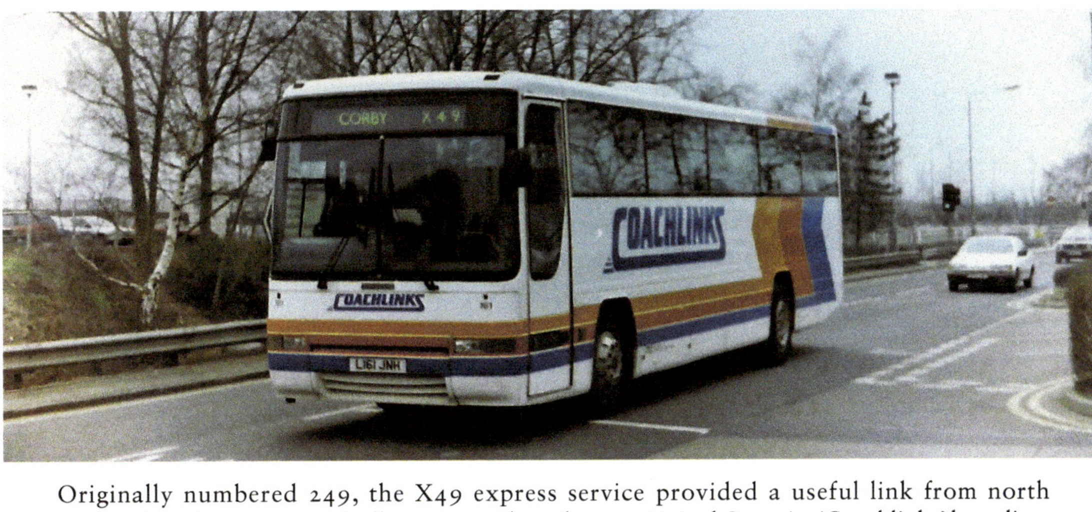

Originally numbered 249, the X49 express service provided a useful link from north Buckinghamshire towns and villages to London. Showing United Counties 'Coachlinks' branding, 161 (L161 JNH) was one of thirteen early production Plaxton Premiere Interurban-bodied Volvo B10Ms. This Plaxton product was a no-frills Premiere that Stagecoach used across its UK companies. At the time five return journeys ran on Mondays to Saturdays, with four on Sundays, from Corby to London Marylebone, calling at Milton Keynes Coachway then using the M1 to Brent Cross. In 1995 the coach is seen by Brent Cross bus station served by some of the journeys. The route eventually ended in April 2004 and the coach became 52161 in the Bedford depot school bus fleet. (Colin Lloyd/author's collection)

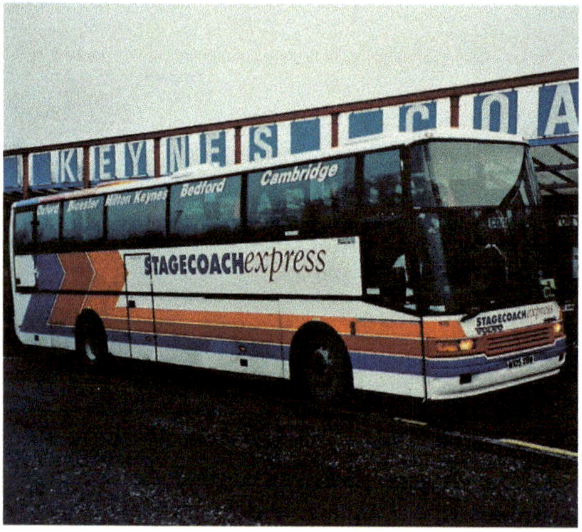

September 1995 saw the introduction of Stagecoach Express X5 between Cambridge and Oxford. Former Wallace Arnold Volvo B10Ms were initially used but were replaced in 1999 by ex-Oxford Tube coaches. 105 (M105 XBW), a Volvo B10M with Berkhof Excellence bodywork, was previously Thames Transit number 25 and the only one painted for use on the X5, others acquired being used on the associated Virgin Trains contract. It is loading at the old Milton Keynes Coachway for its former home city on 27 December 1999. The other former Oxford Tubes carried Jonckheere bodywork.

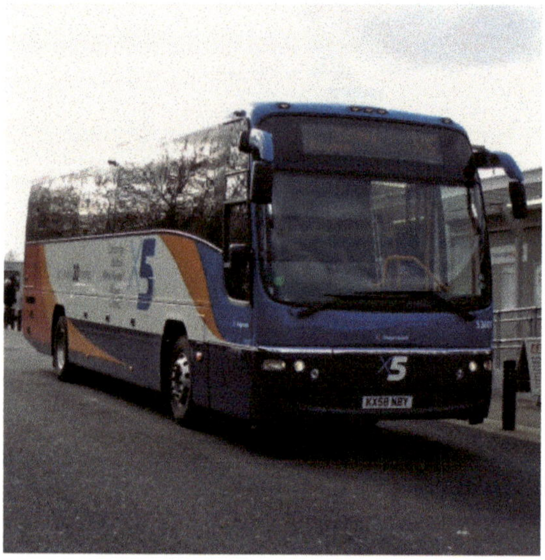

April 1989 saw the introduction of Milton Keynes Coachway, a facility some 100 metres from M1 junction 14 and built to encourage more coaches to stop at Milton Keynes. The Central bus station was a 6-mile round trip from this motorway junction, or twenty-six roundabouts in Milton Keynes language! Twenty years later a much-improved facility was under construction and a temporary site was in use on Silbury Boulevard, by Campbell Park. The X5 had proven a great success and in 2008 a fleet of seventeen brand new vehicles was launched. These were forty-nine-seat Plaxton Panther-bodied Volvo B9Rs and drivers on the route received smart new uniforms. 53607 (KX58 NBY) loads at the temporary Coachway on 14 March 2009.

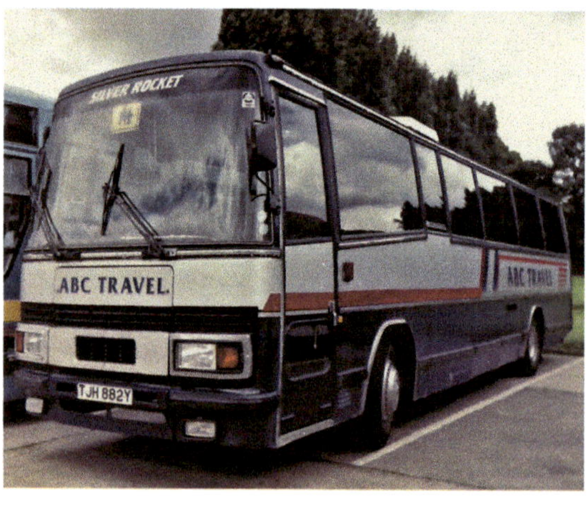

ABC Travel was a taxi and bus operator based in Moulsoe on the north Buckinghamshire border, with an office at the old Milton Keynes Coachway. School and contract work was undertaken as well as the original service between the Coachway and city centre, which used a National Express-liveried minibus. *Silver Rocket* TJH 882Y was a Bedford YNT with Plaxton Paramount 3200 body new to Reliance of Newbury in 1983. (Author's collection)

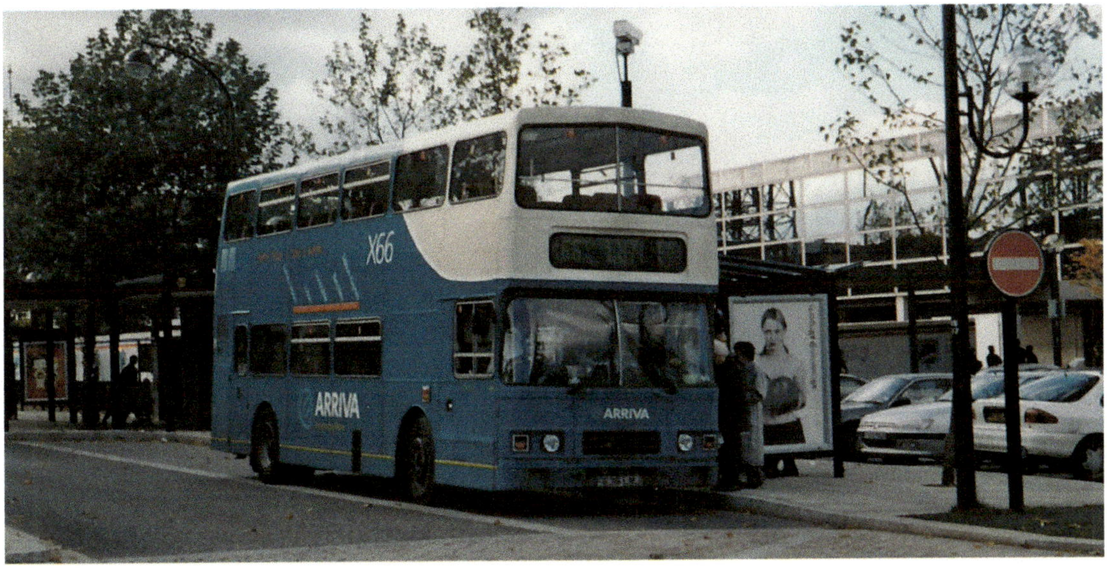

Many 'X' routes served Milton Keynes from all directions; an hourly service from Luton was the X66, which ran along A5 Watling Street for much of its journey, and also serving Bletchley. At one time the route was a hot bed of competition with Buffalo Travel and Stagecoach United Counties also operating along it. Arriva the Shires Leyland Olympian 5086 (F636 LMJ), new as Luton & District 636, was one of three of the type to have coach seats. It is loading in Midsummer Boulevard for its home town on 27 October 1999. Today buses take a route via the Luton and Dunstable guided busway.

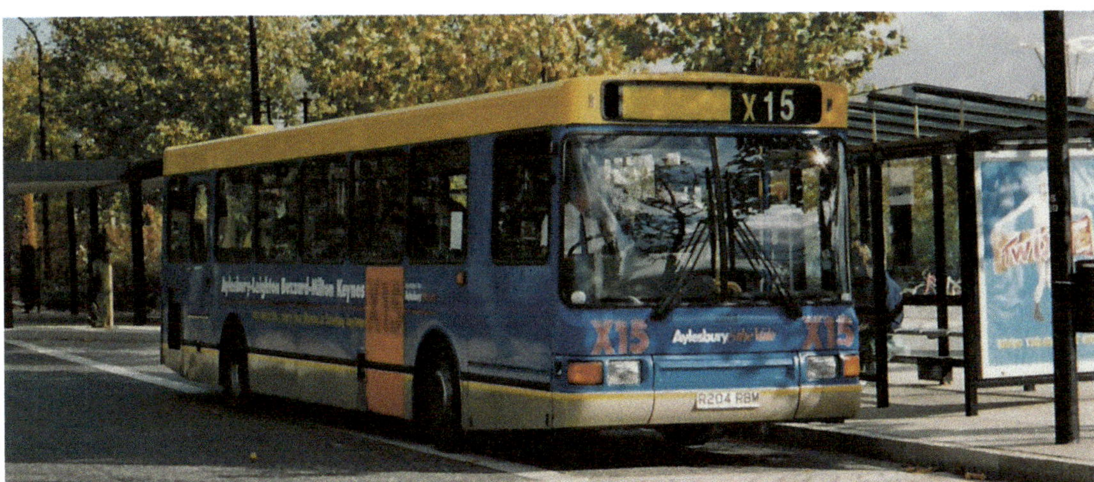

Once more we join the X15 service, which had become another hourly 'X' route serving Milton Keynes from Aylesbury, a shadow of its original self. The last buses delivered to LDT the Shires pre-Arriva, in yellow and blue livery, were also the last step-entrance single-deckers received. These were Scania L113CRLs with Northern Counties Paladin bodywork. Setting down on Midsummer Boulevard by The Point on 27 October 1999 is 3204 (R204 RBM), which is branded for the route. Despite being an Aylesbury vehicle, no blinds were shown. Perhaps the driver may return to Reading? If not, we can catch three Arriva buses to get back there, although our Buzzabout has now simply become a Daysaver.

Bibliography

Books

Holmes, P., *British Bus Systems: Number 3 – Thames Valley* (Transport Publishing Company)
Parfitt, A., *Luton and District: A Profile 1988/89*
Watts, J. W., *Ramblings From My Old Armchair*
South East Bus Handbook (Capital Transport/British Bus Publishing, various editions)
LOTS fleet books London Bus and Tram (various editions)

Websites

Oxford and Chilterns Bus Page
MA Penn bus site
Rob's Bus Zone
Courtney Coaches
Hodges of Sandhurst
Red Rose